GOTHAM
YANKEE

GOTHAM YANKEE

A Biography of William Cullen Bryant

BY

Harry Houston Peckham

NEW YORK / RUSSELL & RUSSELL

to

E. B. P.

PREFACE

THERE ARE, I believe, four especially good reasons for a new biography of William Cullen Bryant. In the first place, Bryant is a figure and a man of prime importance. In the second place, no biography of Bryant has appeared for more than forty years—no detailed biography for more than sixty. In the third place, tradition has grievously misrepresented Bryant the man, depicting him as a frigid and uninteresting personality, if not as a puritanical prig. In the fourth place, there is an abundance of documentary material on Bryant.

Despite the fact that John Macy and a few other authorities on American literature have denied Bryant a place in the ranks of major authors, three facts remain incontrovertible: (1) Bryant stands head and shoulders above any American poet who preceded him, and he probably equals any nineteenth-century American poet with the exceptions of Poe and Whitman; (2) Bryant was one of the foremost journalists in the heyday of great personal journalism; (3) Bryant was long a leading citizen of our chief city and of our country.

Only three biographies of Bryant have heretofore appeared: those by Parke Godwin (1883), John Bigelow (1890), and William Aspenwall Bradley (1905) respectively. And of these three works, Godwin's alone is more concerned with the man's life and his journalistic activities than with his poetry. For the rest we have Allan Nevins's fascinating, sound, and illuminating chronicle *The Evening Post* (1922). But Professor Nevins, of course, is interested mainly in Bryant as an editor; he finds little reason for discussing Bryant's verse, and still less reason for narrating Bryant's early life. There is, then, no modern biography of William Cullen Bryant.

As for the old biographers, they have inadvertently painted the man Bryant in colors much too drab, and these drab portraits have been all too readily accepted by tradition; few literary historians have taken the trouble to do any much-needed retouching.

As one recent authority has truly stated, William Cullen Bryant has come to be thought of as a perpetual octogenarian, an oldster who never knew what it was to be young or romantic—or frivolous. In this connection, the only Bryant portrait photograph that has ever gained wide circulation is one taken very late in the poet-editor's long life. And Bryant's official biographer, Parke Godwin, has done very little to counteract the rather forbidding effect of that patriarchal, bewhiskered portrait. Out of a mistaken sense of filial piety toward his eminent father-in-law, Godwin has deliberately refrained from commenting frankly or freely about Bryant's most interesting, most humanly revealing letters. As for Godwin's successors, Bigelow and Bradley, they have accepted the traditional portrait with scarcely any reservations whatsoever.

We need, then, a new appraisal of Bryant; and, fortunately, we do not lack material with which to make such appraisal. Godwin has published more than three hundred letters covering almost seventy years of the poet's life. It is largely from these letters —and from literary, social, and political histories—that I have drawn data with which to essay a biographical narrative from a fresh point of view. My bibliography indicates that my indebtedness is great. It does not, however, tell the whole story of my obligations. Of the many individuals who have kindly assisted me in my work, I feel that I should make especial mention of Mr. Stephen T. Riley, Assistant Librarian, Massachusetts Historical Society, and Mr. Donald A. Shelley, Curator of Paintings and Sculpture, New York Historical Society. Indebtedness is also due the Ohio University Research Committee and the Ohio University Fund, Inc., without whose approval and aid I could not have published this book.

Gotham Yankee is not a "fictionized" biography. It eschews fictitious characters and settings and datings; it undertakes to record accurately all of the important events of Bryant's life and to interpret soundly and honestly the salient aspects of Bryant's work; it seeks at all times to present a true rather than an imaginary William Cullen Bryant.

André Maurois, in his *Aspects of Biography*, says that the biographer has no right to invent conversations and incidents— a preachment which is ethically and scientifically sound, but which (fortunately, I think) M. Maurois has not always practiced in his own admirable creative work. In my story of the life of Bryant, as the reader will readily perceive, I have introduced a few bits of dialogue and a few meditations for which, obviously, I could produce no documentary evidence. For such dialogues and such mind-readings I offer no apology. Instead, I offer the plea that, to the best of my knowledge and belief, I have introduced nothing not calculated to paint an authentic portrait.

H. H. P.

Ohio University
Athens, Ohio
January, 1949

CONTENTS

ILLUSTRATIONS

GOTHAM
YANKEE

BRYANT AS A YOUNG MAN

CHAPTER I

A Delicate Child and Slender

1

IT WAS early November, 1794. President Washington, in the red-brick city of Philadelphia, sat brooding over the many cares of state: the recent Whiskey Rebellion in the wilds of western Pennsylvania; the scarcely less recent efforts of the impudent Citizen Edmund Charles Genêt to ally our decent young republic with the frenzied, murderous, anarchistic Jacobins of France; the conversations of Mr. John Jay with His Majesty's supercilious ministers in London; the scurrilous pen-lashings inflicted by the whole pack of anti-Federalists, headed by that rascal Philip Freneau; the pomposity of the egotistical Vice-President, John Adams; the too-democratic, too Francophile tendencies of the lately retired Secretary of State, Tom Jefferson; the brilliant but sometimes frustrated efforts of Alex Hamilton to place the nation on a sound financial footing; the temperamental Pierre Charles L'Enfant's unfinished plans for the new capital on the Potomac. No wonder the aging general often sighed wearily; no wonder he often "wished to God" that he and Lady Martha were well out of perturbed Philadelphia, back amid the broad acres and warbling Negroes and mild autumn sunshine and vari-colored foliage of tranquil Mount Vernon.

Meanwhile, up in the Hoosac region of Massachusetts, one of

President Washington's most ardent supporters was having his cares too. If His Excellency could have known, he would doubtless have sympathized in his austere, rather frigid way. But how could a Virginia patrician know of Peter Bryant, an obscure young Yankee village doctor, even though Dr. Peter did go occasionally to Boston to sit as a Federalist in the state legislature?

Late in the afternoon of November 3, 1794, Dr. Peter Bryant might have been returning on horseback to his home in the village of Cummington. Perhaps he was coming from up Plainfield way, for many of his patients dwelt to the north of Cummington. Big and sturdy and twenty-seven, jauntily Bostonian in attire from tricorn hat to buckled breeches to buckled shoes, Dr. Bryant might have looked more like a gay young city blade than like a struggling, ill-paid country physician and chirurgeon. But this afternoon his face must have worn an expression of great anxiety.

It was not so much that a raw north-east wind was blowing, that thick clouds were lowering, and that the gorgeous red and orange foliage of only a week ago had almost entirely disappeared. It was not even that he had had a hard day, what with bloodletting and tooth-pulling and the administering of calomel to unwilling mouths; for Dr. Bryant was accustomed to hard days. No, it was neither the weather nor a trying afternoon that caused his young face to wrinkle with unwonted care.

Ordinarily, perhaps, Dr. Peter might have looked forward to a quiet evening at home. True, an importunate knock at the door might summon him to a late call miles away, but on many and many an evening he could relax at the fireside with his hobbies.

Tonight, however, there would be no rereading of Mr. Pope's *Homer* or Dr. Goldsmith's *Deserted Village*. There would be no minuets played on the fiddle or the viol that Dr. Peter had shaped with his own dexterous hands. Tonight there would be a portentous event—let it be hoped, a blessed one—right in the doctor's own home; for the hour of Sarah Snell Bryant's second confinement was almost at hand. Now Sally, like her husband, was tall and buxom; even that very morning, a Monday, she had done the family washing and churned the family butter. Still, one could never tell about an accouchement. Many an infant, as Dr. Bryant knew from years of practice, was delivered stillborn; and many another infant survived but a few hours or a few days. Moreover, should the child live, there was always the problem of another

[2]

mouth to feed, another body to clothe—a problem which might be as vexing in a small, incipient family like the Bryants' as in the large family possessed by almost every middle-aged couple of that prolific day.

In all of Dr. Peter's solemn thoughts, however, there would be no trace of resentment, no dispostion to kick against the pricks. Back of Peter, on both sides of the house, lay four generations of Puritan ancestors. Stephen and Ichabod and Philip Bryant had all of them doubtless been possessed of "a simple-minded and austere piety";[1] and the same must have been true of Peter's maternal forbears, the Howards. And although Peter himself had acquired somewhat more liberal views—what intelligent man of the late eighteenth century had not been influenced more or less by deism?—Peter could hardly have doubted the justice and inerrancy of God Almighty. At this very moment, perhaps, the young doctor was paraphrasing the words of the patient Job: "The Lord giveth; the Lord taketh away. Blessed be the name of the Lord." Or perhaps he was thinking fondly of the few happy married years that he had already passed with "sweet Sally Snell"; of the joy that they had had in their winsome first-born child, Austin; of the fact that Sarah's parents, like his own, had migrated to Cummington from the old town of Bridgewater, in Plymouth County, a scant twenty miles inland from Plymouth and the Cape Cod Bay.

2

The event in the Bryant household on that evening of November 3, 1794, proved to be indeed a blessed one. At seven o'clock Sarah was safely delivered of another man-child, and so well did she stand the ordeal that two days later she was sitting up all day and making a coat for little Austin. And a few days thereafter she and Peter doubtless took the babe to the Congregational meeting-house, where he was christened William Cullen (after an illustrious Scottish professor of medicine).

The baby did not thrive quite so well as the mother. In fact, it was soon apparent that he had not inherited the sturdy physique of his parents. Undersized, subject to more than his share of colic, and constantly threatened with the pulmonary trouble so common in the New England climate, he gave his parents many and many an anxious moment. Perhaps their greatest worry of all

[3]

was the fact that this sickly, diminutive boy had an abnormally large head—a head that appeared almost a deformity. To correct this abnormality, Dr. Bryant prescribed a strange treatment: during the summer of William Cullen's fourth year the child was taken repeatedly to a spring near the house and there immersed, often in water so chilly as to evoke shrieks from the luckless little patient. What effect these treatments may have had upon the large head we are not told; but at any rate the tiny, delicate body grew a little larger, a little tougher. Indeed, William Cullen was destined to become one of the longest-lived of the whole tribe of Bryant.

3

Constant contact with the out-of-doors tended to strengthen the lad further. Of course Peter and Sarah did not want the youngster hanging around the house except when the weather was severe or when he was conning his lessons. Consequently, most of his early recollections were of fields and woods; of the appetizing smell of boiling maple sap on a sunny, windy March afternoon; of the tender green of April foliage, sprinkled by intermittent showers; of the colors and aromas of orchards in May; of swimming in humid midsummer; of the tang and drip of cider-presses in early autumn; of brown chestnuts and cream-colored hickory nuts when the frosts came; of skates and sleds, snow-balls and snow forts, in the long, white New England winters.

Of Cullen's early indoors life, most of his recollections were associated with meals and studies and bedtime and religion. Especially, for several reasons, did he remember the religious activities of the household. For one thing, he was compelled to memorize the Westminster Catechism, a task for which he had no aptitude and in which he found little interest; perhaps the utter lack of concrete imagery in the Catechism rather than its severe religiosity was what irked him. For another thing, although Dr. Peter was not a rigid Calvinist, there were other important influences in the Bryant household—influences as strongly and as strictly Calvinistic as any that Jonathan Edwards or Solomon Stoddard ever brought into Hampshire County. As far back as William Cullen Bryant could remember, his maternal grandfather, Ebenezer Snell, dwelt under the Bryant roof. And old Ebenezer, although a layman—a farmer and a justice of the peace—was a model of

Puritan piety and orthodoxy, an upstanding pillar in the Congregational meeting-house. It was Ebenezer who insisted upon holding family prayers regularly, both morning and evening. And it was Ebenezer who constantly implored an angry God to be merciful to His unworthy but truly penitent servants. In this connection, how vividly little Cullen recollected his grandfather's favorite petition: "Let not our feet stumble on the dark mountains of eternal death." One's feet, then, were in constant danger of stumbling; and those towering Hoosac hills, so imposingly visible from the west windows of the Bryant cottage, were evermore to be associated with death, Death, DEATH!

With man's mortality ever in mind, little Cullen and his brother were constantly admonished to walk in the straight and narrow way. Perhaps such way would not lead to salvation, for in John Calvin's universe none but the Elect could be saved, and no one but God Almighty knew who the Elect were. Certainly, however, a dissolute life or a careless life would lead to everlasting damnation. And so, day after day, Cullen and Austin were warned to give heed to their conduct.

It does not appear, however, that many of these warnings were uttered by the mildly indulgent, mildly skeptical, mildly worldly Dr. Peter. Not that Peter was by any means a libertine; except for such little frivolities as his fiddle and his pagan poetry, Peter Bryant was a model of rectitude, even for Puritan Cummington. But Peter was no sermonizer; he was a doctor of physic rather than of theology. No, the sermons came mostly from old Ebenezer —and from Ebenezer's piously reared daughter Sarah. In this connection, speaking in his old age of his mother, Cullen wrote: "She discouraged all bad habits in her household, such as drinking, tobacco chewing and smoking, and idleness and profanity." [2]

By no means all of Cullen's thoughts, however, dwelt upon saintly living and saintly dying. As we have already observed, he had a normal, animal appetite for the out-of-doors; and if he was too delicate to indulge quite freely in the games of more lusty boys, he was at any rate very active in body as well as in mind. Inspired by the reading of Pope's *Iliad*—apparently the first work of imaginative literature that he ever knew—Cullen, with his brother Austin, whittled out wooden swords and shields; and, unseen in the barn, the two spent many a thrilling hour enacting the combats of Hector and Achilles and Agamemnon.

[5]

Quite as fascinating to Cullen were the reminiscences of his father, who—strangely for a rural physician—had been a rover beyond the Atlantic and beyond the Equator for one almost unbelievable year. When Cullen had been but a babe in arms, his usually cautious, generally home-loving father had been struck by a sudden rash impulse: namely, to engage himself as ship's surgeon on a Yankee merchant vessel. Probably this impulse had been inspired by one Dr. Laprilete, a French West Indian refugee physician who had imparted to Peter most of his medical knowledge (and, perhaps, some of his liberal philosophy and theology). At any rate, Peter had left his family, secure in the knowledge that they would be well cared for by Grandfather and Grandmother Snell, and had sailed upon a voyage that was to take him as far as the East Indies—a voyage that was to be memorable for shipwreck, for capture by a crew of French privateers, and for months of detention amid the palm trees and the rice fields and the dusky naked heathen of the island of Mauritius.

Between Homer's *Iliad* and Peter's wonder-year wander-year, then, young William Cullen Bryant thought often of the indubitable fascinations of this world rather than of the possible horrors of the world to come. Even his prayers, indeed, took on a distinctly mundane tenor. For while Grandfather Snell prayed audibly about the mountains of eternal death, young William Cullen often prayed silently that he "might receive the gift of poetic genius and write verses that might endure." [3]

CHAPTER II

Shade and Dust and Cobwebs

1

ONE NIGHT when Cullen
was in his fourteenth year
a family conference appears to have been held in the Bryant cottage. In a two-family New England household, such as that of the Bryants and the Snells, momentous decisions were to be reached in the democratic New England way; that is, by miniature "town meetings" in which every adult would offer his counsel. Before the conference would get under way, family prayers would have been said and the children would have retired for the night. There were, by the way, five Bryant children now: Austin, Cullen, John, Arthur, and little Sarah. The family conference undoubtedly had to do with Cullen, for Cullen was the problem child of the family. It was not that Cullen was a bad boy; under the watchful eyes of the circumspect Sarah and the sedate Snell Grandparents no Bryant child had opportunity to be wayward. But Cullen, now grown almost to a man's stature, was at the same time the most gifted and the most delicate of the Bryant boys. Clearly, Cullen would never make an efficient farmer. Why, at haying he moved so languidly that his heels were always getting in the way of Grandfather Snell's rake. On the other hand, this slender, anemic fourteen-year-old boy was already an established poet. Had he not written "The Embargo," a brilliant satire on

the blundering President Jefferson? And had not "The Embargo" been published in Boston and praised far and wide by the delighted Federalist press, including the *Monthly Anthology*? [1] Obviously, Cullen was the one Bryant boy who must have a higher education.

The family conference that night must have presented an arresting picture. In one corner of the living-room, we may imagine, sat Grandmother Snell nodding drowsily over some knitting that was by no means expedited by the feeble light of the tallow candle. In the opposite corner, perhaps, sat Sarah energetically plying a spinning-wheel which she seldom had time to touch until after family prayers. And before the cheerfully blazing pine logs in the great fireplace sat the two men, Ebenezer Snell and Peter Bryant. It seems to have been a quiet evening for Dr. Peter, but of course Peter never knew when a knock at the front door might summon him out into the night. We fancy that tonight old Ebenezer Snell, pious though he was, sat puffing thoughtfully at his long church-warden pipe; and we fancy that when Ebenezer had filled and lit his pipe, Peter had rather hesitantly followed suit. Sarah, as we have observed, did not approve of tobacco, and, consequently, we may well believe that in the Bryant domicile no pipes were smoked in the children's presence. But now that the children were in bed, the fragrant weed could be enjoyed without the danger of setting a bad example to the young ones.

"Ay," grunted Ebenezer drily between puffs, "the boy must have an education. And to get it he must go hence." His three listeners doubtless nodded approval. Or, at any rate, the nods of Peter and Sally would be nods of approval. As for Grandmother Snell, she had probably been nodding on general principles ever since prayers had been concluded.

Cullen, it was agreed, must go away somewhere for further schooling. Neighbor Briggs, who kept the Cummington school, was good enough, both as preceptor and as wielder of the birch; but Briggs's instruction did not go much beyond the three *R's,* and Cullen's active young mind was already several leaps beyond anything that Briggs had ever taught him or ever could teach him. Now it was high time that Cullen was learning Latin and Greek, if not in some Berkshire or Hampshire academy, then under some inexpensive private tutelage. And ultimately, if it should be at all possible, Cullen was to go to college.

[8]

To Grandfather and Grandmother and Sarah, as to most New Englanders of that day, the word *college* would suggest training for the Christian ministry. And to Sarah, at least, that would be indeed a happy suggestion; for nothing, we may well believe, would have given her greater joy than to see one of her sons become a preacher of the Gospel. But Peter, whose enthusiasm for the theology of John Calvin was by no means ardent, was not at all sure about that. As he saw the matter, a course at college might or might not make a boy a parson. New England colleges, he would admit, had been founded mainly for the purpose of instructing young men in divinity. Not all collegians, however, became parsons. Had not all of the Adams boys—John and John Quincy and their cousin Sam—gone through Harvard College, and had not all of them become men of affairs? Then what about that other eminent son of Harvard, the brilliant and eloquent and statesmanlike Fisher Ames, four times returned triumphantly to the Congress in Washington to uphold the noble cause of Federalism? So far as that was concerned, could not even a medical man aspire to collegiate culture? Most medical men did not. But was that not due to the silly English-American custom of classing physicians and chirurgeons with barbers and shoemakers and tailors? Why, on the continent of Europe—especially in France and Holland—physic had long been regarded as a learned profession. Coming much nearer home, Peter could remind his Sally and his Snell-in-laws that he himself had once qualified for Harvard—and that only lack of funds had prevented him from pursuing his baccalaureate degree. As for Cullen and college—well, they would cross that bridge when they came to it. Perhaps Cullen had neither the eloquence nor the affability to make a good preacher and pastor. Certainly, however, the lad did not lack either for brains or for talent. At the very least, he must have tolerable instruction in the classical languages and literatures. And Tom would be just the man to teach the young whelp.

Tom? Why, of course; by all means! If ever there was a Christian and a scholar, it was Tom; for Tom knew his Cicero and his Virgil, as well as his Calvin's *Institutes* and his Hopkins's *Doctrines*. And there would be no foolishness about Tom. If Tom would consent to take young Cullen in charge—and there was no reason to suppose that he would not—the boy would indeed be instructed in the way in which he should go. The boy would learn

[9]

not only Latin and ethics and divinity, but also such deportment as befitted a modest, orthodox young Christian—assuredly not the artificial manners of mincing young fops in Boston and Cambridge (where worldliness and Unitarianism were running rampant); but, rather, such truly Christian graces as Dr. Timothy Dwight inculcated upon the young gentlemen at Yale. So it was agreed that the very next morning a letter should be dispatched to Tom—in other words, to the Reverend Thomas Snell, Sarah Bryant's brother, who lived at North Brookfield, in Worcester County.

2

Tom Snell's reply was both prompt and favorable. He would deem it a privilege as well as a pleasure to provide bed and board and tuition to Sally's boy. And so a few weeks later, William Cullen Bryant, accompanied by Dr. Peter, was taking the longest journey of his young life: forty-five miles eastward, as the crow flies. They must have gone by stage-coach, for the Snell-Bryants apparently possessed no chaise, and the doctor's horse was hardly adequate to carry Peter and Cullen and Cullen's luggage. At any rate, they certainly passed through Northampton, the thriving Hampshire county seat, where Cullen was probably getting his first glimpse of what appeared to him truly metropolitan life— the kind of life that he was to know so much more extensively and intensively in many years to come.

Tom Snell proved to be a highly efficient teacher. Within eight months his young pupil was reading Cicero's orations and Virgil's *Aeneid* with the greatest of ease, and for the latter work he was forming such a genuine love that presently he was trying his hand at a metrical translation of the tempest scene in Book I.[2]

And Uncle Tom was quite as particular of young Cullen's morals as of his Latin. One evening when the boy should, perhaps, have been conning declensions and conjugations he was rummaging through the closet of his room. There, hidden in what Uncle Tom had supposed to be the safest of places, lay a dusty copy of Mrs. Ann Radcliffe's *Romance of the Forest*. It did not long escape the eager eyes or the eager fingers of Cullen. Its very title, of course, intrigued him. Never before, we may well believe, had he had a Gothic romance in his hands. Quickly he fell to reading it—with an avidity that increased with every page. What

[10]

a handsome, dashing rogue was La Motte! What an incomparably lovely girl was the graceful, willowy Adeline! What an enchanting place was the ruined abbey in which they had sought refuge, and how annoyingly complicated it was that Mrs. La Motte should be there too! (Cullen earnestly hoped that the abbey would be a safe retreat—that La Motte's creditors and Adeline's persecutors would never find them now.) Before the lad had proceeded far, however, Uncle Tom had entered the room and stood peering disapprovingly over the young reader's shoulder. More in surprised sorrow than in anger, the older man commanded the youth to surrender the book immediately. Sternly, but not unkindly, Uncle Tom explained that the reading of novels is a pernicious habit—that all novels are factually untrue, and that most of them are ethically unsound as well. Uncle Tom doubtless regretted, at this juncture, that he had not burned *Romance of the Forest* instead of hiding it in the closet. Surely, however, we cannot blame Uncle Tom Snell for the fact that years later William Cullen Bryant took particular pains to obtain another copy of *Romance of the Forest* and read it from cover to cover.[3] Rather let us blame the perversity of human nature—a perversity at least as old as the Garden of Eden.

3

Cullen stayed for only one year at the home of Uncle Tom Snell. That year benefited him physically as well as mentally and spiritually. When he returned to Cummington in midsummer, 1809, he was so rugged and manly and mature that the family scarcely knew him for their little Cullen. At haying he wielded the rake as never before; no longer was the importunate Grandfather Snell at his heels. At table he ate with a gusto which half delighted, half embarrassed his fond but frugal elders. No longer was he subject to the headaches and stomach-aches that had plagued his childhood—a happy change in circumstance that he himself attributed to the fact that Uncle and Aunt Snell did not use pewter dishes. And in the evenings, especially when it was rainy, he pored over such solid books, both English and Latin, as he could find in his father's small but well-chosen library. Manifestly, Tom Snell and his worthy wife had done a good job of instructing and nurturing their young nephew.

For some reason, however, it was decided that the lad should

[11]

not return to North Brookfield in the autumn. Perhaps the Reverend Thomas Snell was not qualified to instruct Cullen in the two subjects that the boy now needed most to learn: Greek and algebra. Perhaps North Brookfield was a little too remote to please either Cullen or the remainder of the family; surely during the year just past the youth must often have grown homesick, and just as surely the remainder of the household must often have pined for his presence. Spartan as rural New England folk were in the early nineteenth century—more Spartan, in all probability, than we restive, migratory moderns can ever quite realize—their sense of family solidarity, their love for the associations of hearth and home, was perhaps their predominant quality.

At any rate, it was soon arranged that during the winter of 1809-10 young Cullen should have a new tutor: the Reverend Moses Hallock, of Plainfield. Now, since the township of Plainfield adjoins that of Cummington, the journey could be made with impunity on foot; and, moreover, Cullen could spend his few holidays and most of his week-ends under the home roof.

The months with Parson Hallock passed quickly and profitably. Before Christmas young Cullen had read the Greek New Testament from St. Matthew to Revelation, and—what seemed more satisfying to the poetic boy—he was reading the original Homer with a delight such as he had never quite found even in Virgil. Like Johnny Keats at Enfield, his American contemporary Cullen Bryant at Plainfield must indeed have traveled in realms of gold during that winter of 1809-10. If Chapman could speak out loud and bold as compared with the mincing, artificial, colorless Augustan Pope, how much louder and bolder and more thrilling must have been the sonorous words of the magical Homer himself! Yes, under the tutelage of the pious and learned Moses Hallock, Cullen had his eyes opened to new and glorious horizons. And in the following spring, under the same able tutelage, he found algebra not too irksome.

The upshot of it all was that Peter decided to send Cullen to college. Harvard and Yale, of course, were out of the question; but, fortunately, by this time there was a new college—a college not too remote or too elegant for the slender purse of Dr. Peter Bryant. The college that Peter had in mind was Williams. Located in the village of Williamstown, a scant twenty-five miles from Cummington, this college was by far the most accessible of all. It was, moreover, a place where simple living was taught and practiced, for neither its situation nor its clientele were calculated to appeal to wealthy metropolitans; its few-score students were, almost without exception, the sons of farmers and villagers from the counties of Berkshire and Hampshire. It was, in short, just the kind of college that the Snells (even more than Peter) would approve of.

Peter lost no time in applying for Cullen's matriculation at Williams College. And, since Cullen had already fully demonstrated his proficiency in the four freshman branches—English, Latin, Greek, and French—it was arranged that he should take an examination to determine his qualification for sophomore standing. His Latin and Greek, as we have already observed, he had learned from Parsons Snell and Hallock respectively; his French he had apparently learned from his father. In the early years of the nineteenth century, by the way, sixteen was not an unusually tender age for an American boy to become a college sophomore. A few years before Bryant entered Williams, Fenimore Cooper had been a Yale freshman at fourteen; and a few years after, Waldo Emerson was to be a Harvard freshman at the same age. A few years later still, fifteen-year-old Henry Wadsworth Longfellow would enter Bowdoin College—with sophomore standing.

4

Consequently, on a sunny September afternoon in 1810, William Cullen Bryant entered Williamstown in company with his father. It was a most memorable occasion. Although Williamstown was not nearly so far from home as North Brookfield had been, it somehow appeared much newer and stranger to Cullen. Why, scarcely more than a township's width to the west and to the north—and clearly visible from such eminences as Sheep Hill— lay the "foreign" lands of York State and Vermont respectively. Never before, of course, had Cullen set eyes upon any acres save those of Massachusetts.

And during those first twenty-four hours at Williamstown there were other, equally memorable experiences. There was his first night ever to be spent at a tavern. There were his wistful glances back toward Cummington—glances which always and inevitably met the towering form of Greylock Mountain. There was the stately white Congregational meeting-house, with its tall steeple, its big clock, and its four slender portico pillars, where Cullen would attend chapel each week-day and each Lord's Day during the months to come. There was ivy-clad West College, already venerable despite the fact that it was scarcely twenty years old, where Cullen would receive the first group instruction that he had known since district-school days. There was the "new building," East College, a plain brick structure on the opposite side of the college green. And, stretching from College to College, there was the avenue of Lombardy poplars, which, as Cullen Bryant recalled fifty years later, formed at that time "the sole embellishment" [4] of the college grounds.

Most memorable of all, perhaps, on that first day, was his meeting and conversing with the president of the college, the Reverend Dr. Ebenezer Fitch, "a square-built man, of a dark complexion, and black, arched eyebrows." [5] If Cullen was timid upon being ushered into the presence of this learned man his timidity quickly melted away, for Dr. Fitch was the soul of courtesy and sympathetic fatherliness.

5

Cullen had little difficulty in passing the examination that admitted him to the sophomore class. Consequently, he was at once exempted from further intensive study of the languages and assigned the more "advanced" subjects of geography, rhetoric, and logic,[6] together with a few more difficult algebraic problems than Parson Hallock had taught him. At that time the Williams College faculty consisted of the president, a professor, and two young tutors; and since Cullen was only a sophomore, not an upperclassman, he had neither the president nor the professor for his instructor. The tutor who taught all sophomore subjects appears to have made little impression upon him, for in his memoirs of his college days he does not even mention the young preceptor's name. Much more vividly did he recollect the professor, Chester Dewey, the "most popular" of the quartet of Williams instructors, and apparently a more magnetic person that President Fitch. Dewey, at that time, was a prepossessing youth in his late twenties, only ten or eleven years Cullen's senior. A tolerable Greek and Latin scholar, and a more than tolerable mathematician, he was positively brilliant in the natural sciences, especially botany, for which he had an almost poetic passion. Years later William

Cullen Bryant recalled that Dewey's chapel talks were always interesting, whereas President Fitch's were frequently dull—almost as dull as the long sermons that the reverend gentleman preached in the white- pillared meeting-house on Lord's Days.

6

Just what Cullen Bryant's non-intellectual diversions at Williams may have been we do not know. Of course we are certain that he entered no formal athletic activities, for intercollegiate baseball and football lay many years in the future. Equally certain are we that he indulged in little rowdyism, for we are assured upon the best of authority that "he associated with the more orderly and studious scholars." [7] The old Williams College list of fines for misdemeanors—one penny for absence from class, three pennies for lateness to prayers, two shillings for employing a barber or a hairdresser on the Sabbath, and three shillings for drunkenness [8]—were never posted for the benefit of youths such as William Cullen Bryant. Indeed, from what we know of Bryant's life in general, one fancies that at Williamstown, as elsewhere in the country, his favorite outdoor diversion was roaming the woods and the fields, perhaps occasionally botanizing with the enthusiastic young Professor Dewey.

7

Of Cullen Bryant's intellectual pleasures at college we know considerably more. We know, for instance, that he made a metrical translation of Anacreon's ode on Spring—a translation so good that a practical joker had no difficulty in palming it off upon some of Bryant's fellow students as the work of the distinguished Irish poet Thomas Moore.[9]

We know also that like nearly all other college students of his day he took an active part in a literary society. In the early years of the nineteenth century the college literary society had somewhat the same function that the Greek letter fraternity was to have increasingly after the founding of Kappa Alpha at Union College, in Schenectady, New York, in 1825. When Bryant was a student at Williams, the only Greek letter fraternity was Phi Beta Kappa, and it had chapters in but four colleges: William and Mary, Harvard, Yale, and Dartmouth. Consequently, in Bryant's

college days the social life of the college, as well as the extracur-
ricular activities, centered in the literary societies.

At Williams in Bryant's time there were two rival societies, the
Philologian and the Philotechnian. Each of these societies met on
one evening a week, at which time a program of debates, orations,
and declamations would be held, and the programs were so or-
dered that every member of the society would participate at least
once during a term. Criticism of the programs was largely in the
hands of the students themselves, but the tutors appear to have
acted in a regular advisory capacity. Bryant, at the solicitation of
his roommate, John Avery, joined the Philotechnian society.

It was at a session of Philotechnian that young Bryant once
made a bit of an ass of himself. It seems that he had chosen to
declaim a passage from Washington Irving's *Knickerbocker's History,* one of the current best sellers of the day. So far, so good! But
Irving's humor proved altogether too much for the young de-
claimei. Hardly had he got well under way when he was so con-
vulsed with laughter that he simply could not continue the recital.
Truly the pompous, obese Wouter Van Twiller, five feet six
inches in height, six feet five inches in circumference, and looking
for all the world like a beer-barrel on skids, was sufficiently ludi-
crous to throw even a solemn lad like Cullen Bryant into hys-
terics of risibility. The other students shrieked with laughter too,
not at Irving's drollery—for the abortive declamation was well-
nigh inarticulate—but at the contortions and giggling of sixteen-
year-old Cullen. As for the overwhelmed young performer, he
quickly did the inevitable: sheepishly took his seat amid the boisterous mirth of everyone except the nettled tutor-adviser.

8

Bryant made only one other memorable appearance upon a
Philotechnian program, and that was chiefly significant because at
it he read an original poem which paints a decidedly unlovely
picture of his Alma Mater. Here is the stanza that has been pre-
served:

> *Why should I sing these reverent domes,*
> *Where Science rests in grave repose?*
> *Ah me! their terrors and their glooms*
> *Only the wretched inmate knows,*
> *Where through the horror-breathing hall*

The pale-faced moping students crawl
Like spectral monuments of woe;
Or drooping, seek the unwholesome cell,
Where shade and dust and cobwebs dwell,
Dark, dirty, dank and low.

Rigorous indeed was student life at early nineteenth-century Williams College. Even in the dead of winter the boys must be out of bed by half past five, for the devotional services which ushered in the college day began promptly at six o'clock. And between bed and chapel there were the chores attendant upon dressing and ablution. A noxious whale-oil lamp must be lighted; a smoky wood fire must be started in a rusty, ill-drawing potbellied stove; and while the room was in the process of thawing, the half-clad student must run, pitcher in hand, to the college well to pump enough water for his frigid morning "wash." Then came chapel, usually in an unheated meeting-house, where one of the two professors or one of the two tutors made a tedious reading of Scripture and a still more tedious extempore prayer.[11] After chapel there was a frugal breakfast, usually of bread, milk, and cheese. And then followed a day of class recitations which, for the most part, must have been as drab and uninviting as the musty, stuffy rooms in which they were held.

All of these forbidding details, however, could hardly have been in the mind of young Cullen Bryant when he wrote those caustic verses for the Philotechnian Society; for it must be remembered that if the Williams students led a Spartan life at college in 1810 and 1811, most of them led an equally Spartan life at home. Of a certainty, no son of Peter Bryant—and, more particularly, no grandson of Ebenezer Snell—had the slightest opportunity to lead a Sybaritic existence. As a matter of fact, we are by no means certain that Cullen ever found Williams especially irksome. Was there ever a generation of college students who did not take occasional delight in grumbling—grumbling about noisome and uncomfortable dormitories, meager and rancid commons, dry and profitless convocations, dull and overexacting instructors?

9

One day, however, there occurred a colloquy which shows that young Bryant was, if not exactly dissatisfied with Williams, at least unsatisfied. Like Dr. Peter, Cullen clearly realized that there were colleges more distinguished and presumably more attractive than the rustic little college at Williamstown.

Seated in the evenings in his room, across the study table from his roommate, John Avery, Cullen would sometimes fall to talking and day-dreaming when he should, perhaps, have been memorizing Aristotle's rules of rhetoric or the Eleatic system of logic.

On this particular occasion, however, it was young Avery who started the idle chatter. Avery, it seemed, had had great news from home that day—news to the effect that he would not have to endure another year of Williams College. No, for his father had promised to send him to Yale the next autumn.

A dreamy youth—more esthetic, more mystical, less Puritanical than most of the Williams boys—Avery had often envisioned greener intellectual pastures and more fragrant and varicolored intellectual gardens than grew within the austere precincts of Williams. Already resolved to become a rector in the Episcopal church, John Avery had yearned for a more urbane atmosphere than that at Williamstown. And now his father had written, giving him the coveted permission to withdraw from Williams and matriculate at Yale.

What could Cullen Bryant say of such news? He could only mumble that the news was glorious—that is, for Avery—and he might add, more wistfully than hopefully, that he too might find it possible to transfer to Yale.

Oh, if Bryant could! agreed the eager Avery. Honestly, declared Avery, his one regret at leaving Williams was the thought of leaving Bryant. The matter of college roommates was a gamble, a lottery. And what Avery would get at Yale, to share his bed and study-table, the dear Lord only knew. Avery *might* catch a Tartar —or a milksop. One never could tell. But Avery was sure that the one good thing that old Fitch had ever done for him was to quarter him with W. C. Bryant. John Avery, in his own not-too-humble opinion, had picked very few plums at Williams, and most of them had been as sour as swill. But when he drew Bryant for roommate and bedfellow—well, sir, he had drawn a prize indeed.

No greater prize, protested young Bryant feelingly, than he himself had drawn. And who knew? Bryant and Avery might be roommates at Yale the next year. Certainly Bryant was no more enthusiastic about Williams than Avery was. And as for Yale— well, that had always been Bryant's idea of a college that *was* a

[18]

college. Yes, Bryant too might decide to go to Yale the following year. Stranger, more surprising things had been known to happen—happened, indeed, every day.

There was, however, more assurance in Cullen's voice than in his mind. He knew very well that Dr. Peter, from the first, would have preferred Yale for him. But equally well did he know that even this year at Williams had been a severe drain upon the slender family purse. Country doctors charged their patients a mere pittance—and, even so, they managed to collect but a fraction of what they charged.

To the sanguine John Avery, already secure in his own plans, the matter of Cullen's accompanying him to Yale began to appear as good as settled. Conjuring up a score of contrasts between Yale and Williams—all of them favorable to the larger and more famous college—he babbled on and on with a care-free, imaginative boy's fervor. No more breakfasts of skimmed milk and stale cheese and moldy bread! At Yale they would have hot porridge every morning—with cream. And no more tedious chapel talks and rambling prayers droned through the proboscis of that weather-beaten windbag Fitch! Whenever old Fitch started preaching his worm-eaten chestnut about the day of small things, Avery began to squirm. And when Fitch started telling the Almighty about everything from Jericho to Blackinton Center, Avery could have screamed. Instead, he merely covered a yawn with his hand.

And then John Avery started dilating on some more of the joys of Yale. At Yale the students would not be country bumpkins. They would be men of the world: New Yorkers, Philadelphians, Southern gentlemen, some of whom had been to Europe. And the New Haven girls! Plenty of style and aplomb and wit as well as beauty there! Now Bryant would bear Avery out in the assertion that not within a radius of ten miles about Williamstown was there a girl worth looking at.

Of course Cullen laughed heartily at all of these pleasantries, especially at the quip about the girls. Up to and including his Williams days, his contacts with young women had been negligible, almost non-existent. Not necessarily, however, had young women been always remote from his thoughts. John Avery's glowing assertion about the belles of New Haven sounded reasonable enough to him. For why, in all conscience, should not a great center of culture and commerce have pretty girls by the hundred? As for John's disparaging remark about the maidens around Williamstown—well, that, too, seemed perilously near the truth. Now that Cullen came to think of it, he realized that not once since his arrival in Williamstown had he laid eyes on a feminine face or figure that would cause his heart to flutter even mildly. Even Cummington, in fact, had one damsel who far outshone any that he had seen at Williamstown. That would be pretty Betsey Gurney, whom Cullen had admired from afar for a couple of years.[12] But Betsey had plenty of other admirers—a few of whom, less bashful than Cullen Bryant, monopolized her society.

Cullen, however, even in these moments of idle chatter, was not disposed to discuss girls or any of the other frivolous things that his roommate had mentioned. To his serious young mind, Yale College suggested more substantial opportunities than mere contact with worldly-wise fellow students and clever New Haven belles. What sort of professors and tutors would there be at Yale? Frankly, would any of them be superior to Chester Dewey, who even John Avery must admit would have been a credit to a far larger, more famous college than Williams? Neither Cullen nor John knew much about the Yale faculty; but Cullen, at least, could finally recall three eminent names; Timothy Dwight, Jeremiah Day, and Benjamin Silliman.

Starting with Dwight, the Yale President, Cullen honestly wondered whether he and John would find old Timothy Dwight any more attractive or impressive than old Ebenezer Fitch. Certainly, some harsh things had been said about Dwight; so dictatorial and intolerant was he reputed to be that he was known far and wide as "old Pope Dwight." On second thought, however, Cullen opined that President Dwight must be a truly remarkable man. Had not Yale thriven under his leadership? And was he not the author of such great poems as *The Conquest of Canaan* and *Greenfield Hill?*

As for Day and Silliman, both of them were scientists of nation-wide repute, the former an expert in the higher mathematics, the latter a prime authority on both chemistry and geology. The versatile Professor Day, in addition to being thoroughly informed about equations, angles, and arcs, was also a learned doctor of divinity, known throughout the realm of orthodox New England Congregationalism as an eloquent preacher and a profound theologian. The brilliant Professor Silliman, whose lectures were said to be as captivating as they were scholarly, had spent more than a year abroad, studying under some of the foremost scientists of Europe.

Yes, clearly, Yale was a far greater seat of learning than poor little Williams. That very night, after Cullen had studied his logic, he would take quill in hand and communicate his new ideas to his father. He was sure that there could be no harm in that. And maybe—stranger things—

As he reiterated his decision to John Avery, his voice trailed off into a faint, inarticulate mumble. If wishes were horses, than not only might beggars gallop to the devil, but also might the worthy poor ride to the City of Sweetness and Light and receive the municipal keys. Cullen Bryant, child of nature though he was, did not dwell in spirit perpetually amid meadows, groves, and streams. At this period in his life, Northampton was quite the largest town he had ever seen—and that only fleetingly—but Northampton was by no means the largest town that he had any desire to see. Much as he doubtless loved the scenery around Williamstown—Birch Brook and Hemlock Brook and Green River, Sheep Hill and Stone Hill and towering Greylock—the realms of gold in which his spirit traveled were by no means all of them far from the intensive human scene. To him the crowd was not all madding; its strife, not all ignoble. Rurality he craved (in his bucolic moments); rusticity he despised at all times. Never at this stage of his life—never at *any* stage of his life—had he the slightest desire to pass his days as a village Hampden or a mute inglorious Milton.

10

Cullen's long letter to his father seemed to bear richer fruit than the youth had dared to hope. Ay, wrote Dr. Peter in response, Cullen might apply to Dr. Fitch for an honorable dismissal from Williams, and, such dismissal granted, might apply for entrance to Yale the following autumn. Thanks to favorable weather, spring plantings about Cummington had been earlier this spring than usual, and, in consequence, there was every promise of an uncommonly bountiful harvest. That, in turn, should mean that in the months to come, several accounts of long standing might be stricken from Dr. Peter Bryant's ledger. Now so far as actual instruction was concerned, Dr. Peter was by no means sure that Cullen would learn any more at Yale than at Williams. But the reputation of a college could not be ignored; certainly a diploma from Yale would be a far better passport into the world of affairs than a diploma from Williams. Then, too, Dr. Peter was not unmindful of the social value—yes, even the intellectual value —of cosmopolitan contacts.

The seventeen-year-old's cup of happiness was full to running over. No doubt there ensued another colloquy between him and young Avery—a joyful colloquy punctuated by even more ardent mutual congratulations than before.

11

That summer of 1811 was a happy one at Cummington. By day, when Cullen was not working in the fields, he would roam the wooded hillsides, studying flowers and trees and birds and wild life, reciting Greek poetry sonorously, and often romping with his brothers Arthur and John. And at night, after the late midsummer sunsets, he would sit in his bedroom enthusiastically studying the history and philosophy and ethics and difficult Greek that would prepare him for advanced standing at Yale. Of the happiness of those summer days, Arthur Bryant remembered especially with what verve Cullen would declaim certain choruses of Sophocles; and John Bryant remembered especially being "tossed about," always playfully and good-naturedly, by his big, spirited collegian brother.[13]

12

But even before the bloom of summer had faded, Cullen Bryant's joy and enthusiasm were to come to an abrupt end. One August evening when pastures were brown with drought and purple with ironweed, and when grain fields were reduced to stubble, Cullen sat with his father upon the doorstep of the Bryant cottage, Dr. Peter puffing meditatively upon his favorite church-warden pipe. For a long time only the sounds of late summer—the chirp of crickets and the sporadic call of wood birds— broke the silence. Evidently the doctor, if not his son, had something uncommonly serious upon his mind.

Finally Dr. Peter opened conversation—timidly, haltingly,

more in the manner of a shy adolescent than in that of a respected physician and middle-aged *pater familias*. The fact was that the doctor had uncommonly bad news for his son—news so bad that the youth was too startled, too stunned, to utter a word in reply. The sum and substance of the matter was that Cullen would be unable to enter Yale—unable even to return to Williams. Times, it appeared, were grown uncommonly hard. In spite of fairish crops, the patients were not paying up those days, nor could they pay. The blame, of course, lay with the accursed administration in Washington. Jim Madison was worse than even Tom Jefferson had been. Nought cared Madison or those other bigwigs down on the Potomac for thrifty Yankee folk; they were all for those lazy, prodigal Virginia planters and the ne'er-do-well adventurers of the Ohio country. And, mark Peter Bryant's words! Before another twelvemonth rolled around, Mr. Madison would be playing cat's paw to that scoundrelly tyrant Bonaparte. Ay, he would have us in another war with Mother England, and all the shipping trade of Boston and Salem and the other ports would be ruined.

And so William Cullen Bryant was never to go to Yale—and never to go back to Williams either. His college days, which were only a little more than begun, lay all in the past.

Was Bryant's failure to get to Yale a calamity? Or was it a blessing in disguise? Vernon Parrington is sure that it was the latter; for, as that distinguished authority insists in his *Main Currents in American Thought*, "the narrow classicism and ungenerous dogmatisms" of Yale could have done Bryant little good.[14] There is a great deal of merit in Professor Parrington's contention. Although Yale outstripped Harvard in the natural sciences, she was no match for her older sister in the humanities. It was the liberal Unitarianism of Cambridge, not the orthodox Congregationalism of New Haven, that was to inspire most of the notable literature of our nineteenth-century American Renaissance. No Emerson or Thoreau, no Holmes or Lowell, no Prescott or Motley or Parkman came out of the halls of Yale. No Longfellow was at hand to instruct and inspire the young men who entered those halls. No, with one conspicuous exception, Yale could boast no literary stars of the first or even the second magnitude; she must content herself instead with such feebly glowing luminaries as James Abraham Hillhouse, James Gates Percival, and Nathaniel Parker Willis. Of our major nineteenth-century authors, James Fenimore Cooper was the only one ever to matriculate at Yale. And Calvinistic Yale seems to have played little part in the molding of the Episcopalian Cooper. Did she not, indeed, banish him in disgrace before he had completed his junior year? We cannot, then, repine that William Cullen Bryant did not get to Yale; rather, we must suspect that he was fortunate to have escaped it—and that what was Bryant's good fortune was the good fortune of American literature as well.

CHAPTER III

To Him Who in the Love —

1

CULLEN FULLY compre-
hended the aspersions that
his father had cast upon the Democratic Republicans in Washington. In the environment in which he had been born and
suckled and reared he had never had occasion to learn that there
could be such a thing as respectability outside the party of Washington and Hamilton and John Adams. In Massachusetts, of
course, all gentlemen were Federalists; and, therefore, none but
the riffraff were left to be Democrats. "Jacobins, sansculottes, and
miscreants" were what old Judge Theodore Sedgwick, an esteemed contemporary of Grandfather Snell, had tartly called
them.[1]

Not for a moment, then, could young Cullen Bryant doubt
that times in that late summer of 1811 were grown hard; that the
rabble-rousing Jim Madison was largely responsible for the de-
plorable situation; and that with Madison in the Executive Mansion for nearly two years more, times bade fair to decline from
hard to ruinous. Young Bryant's convictions on the subject went
much deeper than his father's recent words—much deeper, indeed,
than the mere circumstances of his whole environment. As we
have previously observed, this erstwhile Williams College sophomore—an adolescent barely bewhiskered enough to ply his grand-
sire's Sheffield razor once a fortnight—was already taken seriously

[25]

as a poet. And the poem that had given him his reputation was a scathing satire upon Jefferson and Jeffersonianism.

One day in the spring of 1807, when Cullen was still a pupil in Mr. Briggs's district school, he had overheard Dr. Peter and another prominent citizen of Cummington discussing and denouncing the Embargo Act, by which President Jefferson and his too-docile Congress had banned all foreign trade for a period of two years. In this action the motive of the administration had been laudable enough: to prevent further friction between the United States and the belligerents in the Franco-British war. Already Napoleon's Berlin Decree, the British Orders in Council, and the Chesapeake affair had rendered America's nautical trade both difficult and dangerous, and Mr. Jefferson was but trying to spare his young nation from what he conceived to be further unnecessary tribulations. But to dyed-in-the-wool Federalists of the Cummington stamp the Embargo Act was a craven and a disastrous move. Why should proud young Columbia, gem of the ocean and sovereign of lands so broad that they reached clear across the Mississippi to the Mexican and the Oregon countries, bend a knee to European tyrants, especially to that ruthless, unprincipled dictator Bonaparte? And why should honest merchants and sailors of Boston and Salem, of Falmouth Neck (Portland) and Providence and New Haven and the other thriving Yankee ports, be deprived of a decent livelihood?

Cullen, being a stripling of twelve years, had taken no part in this conversation; but, child though he was, he had pondered most earnestly upon it. In fact, before many days he had begun shaping his deliberations into couplet verses similar to Mr. Alexander Pope's.

2

The result had been a satiric poem of more than two hundred lines, "The Embargo," in which the young versifier had extolled Commerce and Agriculture as twin blessings of mankind; had execrated the vile miscreant who would strangle these blessings; had vented his scorn upon the stupid, tattered rabble who had put this miscreant and his evil associates into power; and had even called upon the servile, immoral, tyrant-loving Jefferson to resign the presidential chair. It was a pompous, artificial poem—even more pompous and artificial than the neo-classical satiric pieces that had served as its models. A few lines will suffice to reveal its general tone and temper.

> Oh, let not prating History proclaim
> The foul disgrace, the scandal to our name!
> Write not the deed, my hand! Oh may it lie,
> Plung'd deep and mantled in obscurity!
> Forbid it Heaven! that while true Honor reigns,
> And ancient Valour glows within our veins;
> (Our standard Justice, and our shield our God),
> We e'er should tremble at a despot's nod! [2]

But when Dr. Peter had found these verses one day upon Cullen's table, he had read them with surprised and delighted enthusiasm. Here was true Federalist sentiment, brilliantly expressed. No wonder the good doctor had thrilled with paternal pride. Clichés and banalities there might be in those verses; but, what with smooth pentameters, easy and correct couplet rhymes, and apt tropes and epigrams, the poem as a whole was an amazingly able performance for a child of barely thirteen.

Of course the piece must be published. After a few minor revisions, suggested by father and executed by son, the poem had been taken to Boston, where in 1808 it had been printed in a pamphlet entitled *The Embargo; or Sketches of the Times, A Satire; by a Youth of Thirteen*. And as soon as the pamphlet had come from the press, the youthful author's proud father had lost no time in circulating it among his Federalist friends and legislative colleagues.

At least one prominent Boston literary periodical, the *Monthly Anthology*, had thought well enough of "The Embargo" to accord it a handsome review.

> If this poem [declared the reviewer] be really written by a youth of thirteen, it must be acknowledged an extraordinary performance. We have never met with a boy at that age, who had attained to such command of language and to so much poetic phraseology. Though the poem is unequal, and there are some flat and prosaick passages, yet is there no small portion of fire and some excellent lines. . . .
>
> . . . .
>
> If the young bard has met with no assistance in the composition of this poem, he certainly bids fair, should he continue to cultivate his talent, to gain a respectable station on the Parnassian mount, and to reflect credit on the literature of his country.[3]

Prompted by the attention given "The Embargo," Dr. Peter had decided to have the poem reprinted, this time with several other of the young bard's efforts which had appeared in the Northampton paper, the *Hampshire Gazette*. The result had been *The Embargo, or Sketches of the Times; a Satire; Second Edition, corrected and enlarged; together with The Spanish Revolution, and other Poems.* "By William Cullen Bryant. Boston. Printed for the author, by E. G. House, No. 35 Court Street; 1809." No longer was the precocious author's name to be kept a mystery. Indeed, in a mildly truculent "advertisement" prefixed to the verses, all readers (and critics) are assured that "Mr." Bryant is a native of Cummington, in the county of Hampshire, and that "many of the inhabitants" of the aforesaid Cummington can vouch for the fact that William Cullen Bryant was born no longer ago than November, 1794.[4]

"The Spanish Revolution" group had consisted of the title poem and half a dozen shorter pieces, including a metrical translation of Horace, Twenty-second Carmen, Book I. All of these shorter pieces had been done in heroic quatrains; "The Spanish Revolution," in some sixty-odd heroic couplets.

"The Spanish Revolution" is, by the way, a better poem than "The Embargo": less puerile, less banal, less biased. Taking for its theme the Spanish revolt against Napoleon in 1808, the beginning of the Peninsular War, it shows a striking awareness of European affairs, of the menace of Bonapartism, and of the determination of a spirited people to resist the tyranny of a rapacious invader. Moreover, despite the fact that its phrasing is generally as stiff and trite, its heroic couplets generally as mechanical and monotonous, its personifications generally as colorless and tedious as might be expected, it contains a few surprisingly good images. Here are a dozen characteristic lines:

> And now the peasantry, awaked to rage,
> With Gallic armies 'mid the streets engage;
> How dire the din! what horrible alarms,
> Of shrieks and shouts, and ever-clanging arms!
> Keen sabres glare, deep-throated cannons roar,
> And whizzing balls, in leaden volleys pour;
> Whilst clouds of dust amid the blue immense,
> Hang o'er the scene, in ominous suspense;
> Confusion o'er the deathful fray presides,
> Insatiate Death the storm of ruin guides;

[28]

And wild-eyed Horror screaming o'er the fight,
Invokes the curtains of chaotic night.
Such lines, although they may possess neither originality nor distinction, have at least the merit of briskness and animation.

It is, then, no wonder that John Avery, Cullen's roommate at Williams, had called young Cullen "an eminent poet," and that Cullen had casually, unabashedly accepted the compliment as a matter of course.

3

But as the summer of 1811 waned into autumn, William Cullen Bryant found little satisfaction in recalling past triumphs. Far less delightful thoughts crowded his mind—thoughts of a glorious Yale College that had *almost* become his alma mater; thoughts of Williams days that glowed much more brightly in retrospect than they had glowed in actuality. Indeed, when the bitterly disappointed young Bryant thought about his life at all, it seemed to him—ridiculous idea for a seventeen-year-old—that all of his best and happiest days lay in the irrevocable past. What could the future offer for a lad who had no bent for husbandry or physic, no funds for the further pursuit of the liberal arts?

When clear, crisp October days arrived, Cullen spent more and more of his too-ample leisure time tramping through luxuriant Cummington woods—almost always alone. Back in happy July, when bright college days at New Haven had appeared to live just beyond the southern horizon, the woodland romps with his brothers had been all very well; but now he seldom wished for companionship other than his own somber thoughts. His own somber thoughts—and the "mild and healing sympathy" of Nature!

One October morning, perhaps, when sunshine and a cloudless sky accentuated the red and gold of maple and beech boughs, and the marshy places gleamed with the pale blue of fringed gentians, Cullen was taking one of those solitary woodland rambles. It may be that on the night before, he had been a somewhat reluctant participant in a husking bee or an apple-paring, a "sociable" in which there had been much idle chatter of teen-aged boys and girls, much gossip among youthful matrons, and—despite the presence of the minister and the deacon—more than a little sampling of cider and grog on the part of some of the men. Such levity, for which Cullen Bryant had no stomach at that time, only set him to thinking of the vanity of human delights and human wishes.

How transitory was even the longest of human lives, and how much more transitory were all of the merriments, all of the day-dreams, of youth! In only a few more twelvemonths, blooming little Miss Seventeen, who had been the life of the "sociable," would be a faded, haggard wife and mother, and the most vivaciously gossipy young matron would be a feeble, wrinkled granny in a chimney corner. By mid-century the vast majority of that jolly company of last night would be reposing in the graveyard. Identical would be the fate of mighty conquerors like Bonaparte, brilliant parliamentarians like Mr. Charles James Fox, wise statesmen like Mr. John Adams, scintillating wits like Mr. Brinsley Sheridan, dazzlingly beautiful women like Madame Recamier. Why, then, gather rosebuds, when their color and their aroma and their charm could be enjoyed but fleetingly at best? Countless times upon times, since the beginning of the flight of years, the grim story had been told and retold. Yesterday's crowded mart had become today's wilderness or continuous woodland—as witness Babylon and Nineveh and Carthage! Wherever men trod the globe they could be assured that they and all their living fellows were but a handful in comparison to the multitudes slumbering eternally in its bosom.

As Cullen strolled along, some lines from "The Grave," a poem by a Scottish Presbyterian divine, the Reverend Robert Blair, kept repeating themselves in his mind:

> *Eternal King! whose potent arm sustains*
> *The keys of hell and death.— The Grave—dread thing!*
> *Men shiver when thou'rt named. Nature, appall'd,*
> *Shakes off her wonted firmness.— Ah! how dark*
> *Thy long-extended realms, and rueful wastes!*
> *Where naught but silence reigns, and night, dark night,*
> *Dark as was chaos, ere the infant sun*
> *Was roll'd together, or had tried his beams*
> *Athwart the gloom profound.—*

Morbid thought for a moderately healthy boy of seventeen? Doubtless! But it must be remembered that Cullen Bryant, throughout his short life, had heard a great deal of pious Calvinistic talk about the grim reaper. As far back as he could remember, had he not heard Grandfather Snell, at family prayers, implore the Almighty for deliverance from stumbling on the dark mountains of eternal death? And many of Dr. Peter's ministrations, casually or emotionally recounted at board or fireside, had been at death beds. Moreover, much of the verse that had changed and romanticized poetic standards in the eighteenth century had been of the "Graveyard School." Consequently, if on a bright, blue October morning following an evening of mild jollity the disillusioned young Bryant pondered overmuch upon human transitoriness, he had not a little inspiration for his pensiveness.

"Man that is born of woman is of few days, and full of trouble," says the author of the book of Job. And how many, many times had Cullen Bryant heard those doleful words repeated at family prayers and in the Cummington meeting-house!

But the trees of the Cummington woods! Many of the large ones, as was shown by the annual rings, had been seen by generations of redmen before Stephen Bryant, Cullen's first American ancestor, had come to Plymouth colony in the early years of the reign of Charles I. And many of those trees, if spared the woodman's axe, might be seen by Cullen's great-great-grandchildren. Even older than the trees—older by countless thousands of years— were the rock-ribbed Hoosac foothills, the majestic Westfield River, and the complaining brooks that fed it.

The transitoriness of man; the permanence of the inanimate! That was young Bryant's theme on this gorgeous October morning, and the more he meditated upon it, the more he found his meditations shaping themselves into heroic lines far more eloquent and exalted than the lines of "The Embargo" or "The Spanish Revolution." In fact, when he returned home toward noon, he rushed breathlessly into the house, mounted the stairs to his room two steps at a time, seized quill and ink-pot and foolscap, and began penning some of the noblest lines that he was ever to write in a lifetime of four score and four years.

"Thanatopsis"—for that was what he called his new poem— diverged in one important respect from "The Grave" of Robert Blair. The Scottish minister had ended his poem with words of orthodox consolation anent the resurrection and the eternal heavenly bliss of the elect. The Yankee son of Peter Bryant wrote nothing here to show a Christian faith in immortality. The one certainty expressed by him at this time was that in "a few short days" each mortal man would "go to mix forever with the elements." Years later Bryant was to add to the poem a sort of postscript (lines 66-81) in which he admonished the reader to lead so exemplary a life that he might approach the grave "with unfaltering trust." In the "Thanatopsis" of 1811, however, there are probably no sentiments to which Ben Franklin or Tom Paine or any other eighteenth-century deist would have taken exception.

In this connection, we cannot be certain as to precisely how much deism young Cullen Bryant may have got from his father. Deistically inclined as Dr. Peter Bryant undoubtedly was, he does not appear to have aired his liberal theological views very freely at home. Deference to the more orthodox beliefs of Sarah and his Snell-in-laws seems to have prevented him from venturing further than an occasional cautious hint as to the superiority of natural religion to revealed religion. At Williamstown, however, Cullen certainly heard deism expounded in a favorable light—not, we may assume, by the Calvinistic President Fitch, but probably by young Professor Chester Dewey (outside the classroom), and still more probably by some fellow student such as John Avery. Just as certainly, during his brief Williamstown sojourn, he came into contact with deistic books, perhaps even with Tom Paine's *Age of Reason*.

4

Cullen completed the draft of "Thanatopsis" (present text, lines 17-66), sanded and folded the manuscript, and laid it away in his desk, where it would be hidden from the inspection of vulgar or captious eyes. For the time being, he could not bear to have it seen even by the sympathetic, understanding Dr. Peter. He may have felt that upon further meditation he might wish to revise certain lines. In any event, he appears to have had the wise conviction that before showing the poem to anyone he would do well to let it "cool off" for a while.

Some time later—nobody knows precisely when—Cullen surreptitiously transferred "Thanatopsis" to his father's desk, where it would be sure to be found sooner or later. Thither "Thanatopsis" came to light in the summer of 1817—under unusual circumstances.

In June, 1817, Dr. Peter Bryant, while on a visit to Boston, had come upon an old Hampshire County friend, one Willard

Phillips. Phillips, though a lawyer by profession, had a lively interest in literature and was at that time engaged with Richard Henry Dana and other members of the Anthology Club in editing a new literary periodical known as the *North American Review*. Recalling that Peter Bryant (or perhaps a son of Peter's) was literarily inclined, Phillips had importuned the doctor to contribute something to the *Review*, "either prose or poetry." Thereupon Dr. Peter had promptly conveyed Phillips's wishes to Cullen —by letter to the town of Great Barrington, where, as we shall see a little later, Cullen was practicing law at the time. In his letter the good doctor had apparently told a small white lie, by implication if not in so many words; for he seems to have given Cullen to understand that Phillips had particularly stipulated that the contribution should be from Cullen's pen. Why so ingenuous a man as Peter Bryant should not have been perfectly frank, both with Phillips and with Cullen, is a little puzzling. Perhaps he had feared that the extreme youth of the author of "Thanatopsis" would prove an insuperable barrier: either that Cullen would refuse to contribute, or that Phillips would refuse to accept the work of a teen-aged boy. (For, so far as the good doctor knew, Cullen had written nothing since his brief college days.) At any rate, Cullen had not been co-operative. For one reason or another, he had been dilatory in replying to his father's letter, whereupon Dr. Peter had taken it upon himself to supply the wants of Willard Phillips.

Perhaps the good doctor wept for pride and joy when he discovered and read the manuscript of "Thanatopsis." Anyhow, tradition insists that he hastily carried it to "a lady"—a neighbor lady, *not* the matter-of-fact Sarah or the still more matter-of-fact Grandmother Snell—and, with tears streaming down his cheeks, exclaimed: "Oh! read that; it is Cullen's." [5]

Dr. Bryant soon returned to Boston, this time in his capacity as state senator from Hampshire County. Not yet having heard from Cullen, he decided to turn "Thanatopsis" over to Willard Phillips without further ado.

When Phillips read it he was both delighted and surprised— delighted at the depth and beauty and dignity of the poem; surprised that the *North American Review* should receive an original contribution so thoroughly excellent. As for Phillips's colleagues in the Anthology Club, they shook their heads in skepticism; they simply could not believe "Thanatopsis" to be an original American poem. Richard Henry Dana, in fact, declared that Phillips had been imposed upon; for, he insisted, "No one on this side of the Atlantic is capable of writing such verses." [6]

Phillips, however, stood his grounds. He explained that Dr. Peter Bryant, who had submitted the poem to him, was an old and intimate friend of his, highly respected as man, as physician, and as legislator. Such a man would be incapable of committing or conniving at a fraud. And so, apparently, the other members of the Anthology Club were mollified. At any rate, "Thanatopsis" made its appearance in the September, 1817, issue of the *North American Review*. As was the custom at that time, the poem was printed anonymously. Incidentally, Phillips supposed it to be the work of Dr. Peter, not Cullen. Probably if he had been told that the author was a lad of barely seventeen, he would have been as skeptical as Dana or the others.

5

"Thanatopsis" as every school-boy (and school-girl) knows, is the work upon which Bryant's poetical reputation has rested for a century and a quarter; yet to imply that it created a widespread sensation in its day would be to misrepresent the facts. In the first place, the *North American Review* of 1817 was a periodical of small circulation, even for a country of well under ten million inhabitants; by 1826 the *Review's* circulation had barely exceeded the three-thousand mark.[7] In the second place, even the literate few who read the *North American* had had little opportunity to acquire a taste for current poetry of any real depth or body, or for imagery, phrasing, or unrhymed heroics so excellent as those of "Thanatopsis." Although the banalities and artificialities of the school of Pope had passed well out of fashion, American poetry readers in 1817 had not yet had their ears attuned to first-rate romantic verse. Scott and Byron, at that time the most influential poets in the old country, were hardly better known or more widely enjoyed on this side of the Atlantic than such second-raters as Thomas Campbell, James Montgomery, Thomas Moore, and Henry Kirke White. As for Wordsworth and Coleridge, they were virtually undiscovered by the American reading public until years later. The difficulty was, as a leading authority on Bryant has pointed out, that the United States in the early years of the nineteenth century was "a country where poetry was regarded as a polite metrical exercise rather than as the highest human function." [8]

Fortunately, however, a few Americans such as Richard Henry Dana knew excellent poetry when they saw it, and, in consequence, Bryant's "Thanatopsis" gradually acquired a reputation almost as good as it deserved. In fact, by 1821 "Thanatopsis" was so far from being neglected that Bryant did not hesitate to give it a prominent place in his volume of *Poems,* this time in the amplified form in which we know the piece today.

Probably the most notable fact about the expanded "Thanatopsis" is the indubitable Wordsworthian touch in the introductory lines. In 1811 Bryant knew scarcely anything about "The Prelude," except that such a poem had been published a few years earlier. A decade later, thanks to familiarity with the greatest poet then living in England, Bryant could find Nature gliding "into his darker musings, with a mild and healing sympathy."

CHAPTER IV

To Drudge for the Dregs

1

ONE CRISP November eve-
ning in 1811, a few weeks
after Cullen had written the first draft of "Thanatopsis," another
family conference appears to have occurred in the cottage of Peter
Bryant. Evidently Dr. Peter had had a long, hard day—a day spent
mostly on horseback and at sick-beds. His physical exhaustion,
however, was not so great as his mental anxiety. At almost every
house he had visited, it appears, he had heard the same old story.
His patients would have liked to settle their accounts, either in
shillings or in produce; but times were harder than ever. That
imbecile Madison, down there in Washington, had out-Jeffer-
soned the rascal from Monticello, and the country was going to
the dogs with the speed of the Boston-Hartford mail-coach. Now
if only there were enough decent, intelligent folk in the country
to elect another Federalist president! Perhaps next November—
but next November was still a twelvemonth away, and March 4,
1813, was still more remote.

Obviously, it was high time for Cullen to start earning his
bread. Grown to man's stature, proficient in Latin and Greek,
and with a year of college to his credit, the lad was ripe to leave
family bed and board and make ready to become a productive
member of society.

But what calling should he choose? Proved talent, as well as the boy's obvious inclinations, would have answered "Literature," but in the United States of 1811 literature was not yet a profession. True, Mr. Washington Irving, only a couple of years before, had gained a host of readers and a resounding chorus of praise for his very clever *Knickerbocker's History of New York*. Irving, however, was a prose writer, not a poet; and, furthermore, it was commonly understood that he lived far more upon the family mercantile business than upon his pen. Then there was Philip Freneau, a versifier of indubitable gifts; but Freneau's livelihood came not from his verses, but from his editorship of a scurrilous sheet called the *National Gazette*. Besides, what self-respecting New England Federalist would wish to emulate a radical, Francophile, Jeffersonian knave whom the great and revered Father of his Country had dubbed "that rascal Freneau?"

As for Dr. Peter Bryant, he must long have cherished the thought that Cullen would follow in his footsteps—and in the footsteps of Peter's father, Dr. Philip Bryant, of Bridgewater, Plymouth County; and in the footsteps of Peter's maternal grandfather, Dr. Abiel Howard, of the same town and county as Philip Bryant. Indeed, Cullen had been christened after a celebrated Scottish physician and surgeon, Dr. William Cullen, of Edinburgh. But medicine in America, even in prosperous Federalist times, was not a lucrative profession. Few and far between were such luminaries as Benjamin Rush, of Philadelphia. No, the affectionate, indulgent Peter Bryant could not, in these dreary Jeffersonian Republican days, wish for his son such a life of hardship and scanty recompense as he himself had known.

By the process of elimination, the law seemed to be the one calling for young William Cullen Bryant to enter. Every community, large or small, had its chronic litigants as well as its chronic invalids—and lawyers, somehow, were much more adept at collecting fees than doctors were. Besides, the law was becoming more and more a stepping-stone to a distinguished political career, as witness such outstanding political figures as the Adamses and Timothy Pickering.

Would Cullen make a brilliant and persuasive lawyer and politician? Well, the lad was handsome enough, in a delicate way; and, even though he had never yet displayed any great eloquence, perhaps the orator's gift would come to him later. Naturally, a boy whose contacts had been entirely village and rural was a bit shy. Give him a few months in Boston (or even Northampton) society, and he might move court-room and legislative hall alike with his oratory. Of his intelligent interest in politics there could be no doubt. "The Embargo" had amply established that fact.

2

Study of the law meant, of course, apprenticeship in the office of some attorney, for in early nineteenth-century America virtually all lawyers learned their "trade" in that way. This country had never had Inns of Court, and the idea of legal instruction at college would have been considered as fantastic at Harvard or Yale or any other American institution of higher learning as at Oxford or Cambridge. True, Judge Tapping Reeve, of Litchfield, Connecticut, had long maintained what he called a law school— since 1784, to be exact—but Judge Reeve's "school" was little more than a big law office in a small town. Actually, there must have been a hundred experienced lawyers, in as many communities in Massachusetts, who could teach the law as well and as completely as Reeve or any of his assistants.

One such lawyer was Judge Samuel Howe, who lived down the road a scant six miles from the Bryant cottage, in the adjoining town of Worthington, and who, as a good Federalist, had long been on the most amicable terms with Dr. Peter Bryant. Accordingly, it was soon arranged that Cullen should be placed under the roof and the tutelage of Samuel Howe. And by December, 1811, we find the youth poring over the leather-bound tomes of Blackstone, Coke, and Littleton, and not altogether disliking his new task and new surroundings.

One favorable circumstance, so far as Cullen was concerned, was the fact that he was no longer marking time at home—no longer subjected to what he called the "peasant's toil" on the farm. Few though his leisure hours might be at Worthington, he still found it easier—for the first few weeks, at least—to think poetic thoughts while sitting in Judge Howe's office than while tramping a Cummington field behind a plough and a yoke of oxen.

A less favorable circumstance was the fact that Judge Howe did not permit him to read non-legal books in the office. Once as a temporary relief from the heavy abstractions of Blackstone, Cullen had tried *Lyrical Ballads*—under the Judge's very nose. And the Judge had not been at all pleased. Wordsworth and Coleridge, he had declared rather acidly, might be well enough in their place, but their place was most assuredly not in a law office. Of a certainty, neither the Ancient Mariner nor the Idiot Boy had any particularly urgent message for a young man who aspired to eminence at the bar.

Another fault that Cullen found with Worthington was that it was not New Haven or even Williamstown. Indeed, it was as small and dull and provincial as Cummington. As Cullen lamented in a letter to his friend John Avery, Worthington consisted chiefly of a blacksmith-shop and a cow-stable, and it offered no evening amusement more hilarious than rereading Mr. Irving's *Knickerbocker* in one's own room.[1]

3

As a matter of fact, the most exciting event of Cullen's Worthington sojourn occurred, ironically enough, not at Worthington but at the Bryant home in Cummington. It must have been on a December week-end in 1811, when Cullen had tramped the few miles home, as was his custom every Saturday evening, rain or snow or shine. It could hardly have been on Tuesday, December 24, or Wednesday, December 25; for Christmas in those days was no festive occasion among rural New Englanders. At any rate, Cullen became entangled in the first love affair of his young life.

It appears that a friend of Peter Bryant's, a "distinguished gentleman from Rhode Island"—even Godwin does not give the gentleman's name or further identity—came on a visit to Cummington. Accompanying the gentleman was a "beautiful and accomplished daughter," Evelina,[2] who was apparently of about the same age as Cullen. At first Cullen was frightened. Then he was smitten. Doubtless the young lady had far more style and polish than any girl he had ever met before. Very soon, in artificial, eighteenth-centuryish verses, our young poet was dilating upon the fair one's glossy hair, laughing eyes, rose-enameled cheeks, and snowy bosom.

Whether or not Cullen and the pretty Rhode Island girl had more than one meeting we cannot be sure. True, in one saccharine poem the young man recalled a lovers' twilight stroll beside a beech-shaded brook—a stroll in milder weather than a Cummington December would be likely to afford. This stroll, however, could easily have been a figment of the poet's imagination; for the shy, awkward, rustic young Bryant of those callow days must have been a far bolder lover in his dreams or on foolscap than in the actual presence of a fashionable young belle in a Regency gown and bonnet.

The rest of this love affair is much shrouded in mystery. For a time, it is said, an "earnest correspondence" was carried on—evidently much more earnest on Cullen's part than on the part of the young lady. And then the inevitable occurred. Perhaps the girl neglected to write. Perhaps she wrote, telling Cullen that she was not interested in him. At any rate, he was soon writing bitter verses, upbraiding the coquette for her faithlessness, and vowing that he would erase her image from his heart. His attempts at erasure, however, proved as unavailing as might be expected. Presently, therefore, the dejected youth was sighing—on foolscap again —for the peace and quiet of the grave.

4

Cullen's unhappy love affair with the beautiful but disdainful Evelina appears to have had serious repercussions. Evidently Peter and Sarah decided that the young man's well-being and peace of mind demanded a change of scene. No other reason has ever been given for his removal, early in 1814, to his Grandfather Bryant's home at Bridgewater, in southeastern Massachusetts, an ample hundred miles from the Cummington-Worthington district.

That the boy was glad to make the change there can be no doubt. At Bridgewater he would be far removed from the scene of his late disappointment—so far removed, indeed, that he could not possibly revisit the old scene for many months to come. At Bridgewater, moreover, he would be only twenty-odd miles from the Mecca of all New England, the great and renowned city of Boston, whose metropolitan wonders he had dreamed of all his life.

While living at his grandfather's he was to continue his legal studies in the office of Bridgewater's most prominent citizen, the Honorable William Baylies, a Massachusetts representative in Congress and a leading light in the Federalist party. Although Congressman Baylies probably had no more extensive legal knowledge than Judge Howe, he was certainly a more illustrious man.

And his appearance and bearing were quite as distinguished as his attainments. Indeed, when old-time politicians saw the Honorable Mr. Baylies walking or riding horseback along Pennsylvania Avenue in Washington, they declared him to be the living image of the great General Washington himself.

Contact with the prominent, cosmopolitan William Baylies seems to have increased Cullen's hankering for Boston. If the boy could only finish his legal studies in the New England metropolis, he would be *in medias res*, in the center of culture and industry, of art and letters and learning and fashion. Here in short order, he could rub off his confounded rusticity, and then such belles as Evelina would no longer look upon him as a bumpkin, no longer laugh up their puffed sleeves or behind their fans at his shyness and clumsiness. So strongly did the Boston idea grow upon him that he finally broached it in a letter to his father.

The reply he got was far from encouraging. The usually indulgent Peter, writing in one of his rare petulant moods, reminded Cullen that the young rascal had already cost him four hundred dollars; that there were other Bryant children to be considered; that Peter's present health was far from good; and that by no means all the glitter of Boston was solid gold. Let Cullen be thankful for the advantages of Bridegwater.[3]

5

Before Cullen had been in Bridgewater many months, someone there recalled the fact that he was an established poet, the boy prodigy who a few years earlier had created a mild sensation with "The Embargo." Thereupon he was invited to compose a Fourth of July ode, an invitation which he accepted without hesitation.

The year 1814, it would appear, was a peculiarly appropriate time for patriotic American verse; for we were in the thick of our second war with the Mother Country, and our forces, especially on the water, were winning their share of spectacular if practically unimportant victories. And young Cullen Bryant, it would seem, was exceptionally well qualified to write an impressive Fourth of July ode at such a time. Both poetic talent and a lively interest in current events should have made him so.

Bryant's "Ode," a declamatory poem in four-three *abcb* ballad measure, is as vigorous and ringing as might be expected. It finds, however, no cause for glorying in our War of 1812 or in any of its triumphs. In this connection, be it remembered that the War of 1812 was "Mr. Madison's war," not a Federalist affair. But more about that a little later. What, then, did our young poet find to sing about, if not the prowess of Perry on Lake Erie, of Decatur on the Atlantic, of Macdonough on Lake Champlain? He found events in Europe to be the all-inspiring theme. Let lovers of freedom everywhere (he declaimed) rejoice that the arch-tyrant had been overthrown and banished to the insignificant island of Elba. And let them thank the "Queen of Isles" for effecting his overthrow and banishment. Except for that brave act of Britannia's, America might be celebrating this Fourth of July, 1814, in hymning its own dirge instead of chanting its national holiday.

That the sentiments of young Bryant's ode were roundly applauded by the populace of Bridgewater there can be no doubt. Almost everybody in that hotbed of Federalism, from the Honorable William Baylies down to the humblest journeyman mechanic, had more enthusiasm for the island of his ancestors than for the party of Jefferson and Madison.

6

Preparation and delivery of the Fourth of July ode did not seriously interfere with Cullen's legal studies. Far removed from the painful memories recently associated with the Cummington-Worthington district, and genuinely stimulated by the comparative urbanity of a town and a region no longer "frontier," the boy read law and copied briefs with a fresh enthusiasm and retentiveness. The result was that by August he was ready for the preliminary bar examinations. And these he looked forward to with more gusto than apprehension; for taking the examinations necessitated a trip to the county seat, which happened to be that most ancient of all Massachusetts towns, Plymouth. This, in turn, meant a first view of the Rock and Cole's Hill and the Crowe house—and the ocean!

Cullen passed the bar examination as easily as, four years earlier, he had passed the Williams sophomore entrance examination. Writing jubilantly to Peter, he told of his new certificate, signed by Joshua Thomas and A. Holmes, Esq., and carefully blotted with snuff instead of sand. The one drawback—a gentle hint to Peter—was that the certificate had cost six dollars. And so, before reaching his twentieth birthday, William Cullen Bryant had passed his bar examinations; and before reaching his majority—at the August Term, 1815, to be exact—he would qualify as a full-fledged attorney.

7

Cullen's letters of this period show that social diversions, as well as legal studies and patriotic odes, helped him to forget the lovely but unreciprocating Evelina. They show also that he was far from being the puritanical prig that old-fashioned school histories of American literature have pictured him to be.

Writing to George Downes, a young man whose acquaintance he had made at Worthington, he laments that Bridgewater has no such comfortable loafing places as Mills's tavern or Taylor's grog-shop. He adds, however, that not for all the wealth of the Indies would he return to Worthington. As for the Bridgewater girls— well, naturally, they have more style and aplomb than the poor little rustic damsels of Cummington and Worthington. Moreover, they are pretty and vivacious and all manner of fun, especially since Cullen has learned to dance. Why, only the other night Cullen and five other youths and six girls had a most jolly ball, followed the next day by a sailing party on "a great pond" down Middleboro way. The morning had been unpromising, with thick dark clouds and "a devil of a mist," but by ten o'clock all was blue sky and sunshine. And at high noon, after two glorious hours on the pond, they had all sat down to a most delectable dinner topped off by fine grapes and peaches and "tolerable wine." As for the young ladies, they were "wonderfully alert and sociable," despite the fact that they had danced till three o'clock the night before.[4]

8

Cullen's Fourth of July poem showed that he was far from unmindful of wars and rumors of wars. By October, 1814, in fact, he was importuning Peter to allow him to seek a commission in the militia. Perhaps one of the vivacious young ladies at the ball and sailing party had rallied him about his civilian garb and suggested that he would look handsome in a uniform. Perhaps some of the other young men of Bridgewater had become military-minded. At any rate, we find him writing to Peter, begging for a chance to enter a military career.

[43]

Cullen would very much like, he explained in his letter, to defend his commonwealth and, at the same time, to procure a steady income, however small. Legal practice was all very well, but for years to come its financial returns would be meager and uncertain, especially in view of the fact that Peter could not afford to set Cullen up in a large town such as Boston. Moreover, there were social considerations; heaven knew that Cullen's training in the deportment of polite society had been painfully scant! What he needed, of course, was to have his "excess bashfulness and rusticity" rubbed off by that most excellent school of polished manners, a military life.

Cullen's October letter, like his Fourth of July ode, was as eloquent for what it omitted as for what it stated. Obviously, he was not at all desirous of entering the regular United States army and fighting the British; rather, he wanted to resist "the weakness and wickedness" of the administration in Washington and, if necessary, to throw off allegiance to the existing national government and help form an independent New England nation.[5]

Strange sentiments for a respectable, law-abiding young Yankee in the year 1814? Not at all. In this connection, let it be repeated that throughout New England "Mr. Madison's war" had been extremely unpopular from the very start. As war taxes mounted and merchant ships continued to lie idle in the docks of Boston and Salem and other ports, the Federalist Yankees grumbled more and more audibly that the stupid Madison was but the monkey to pull the chestnuts out of the fire for the tyrant Bonaparte. And while the merchants grumbled, some of the New England farmers did something more practical about the situation; they smuggled crops into Canada for the sustenance of the British forces. Even commonwealth officialdom rebelled against "Mr. Madison's War," New England governors refusing flatly to permit their militia men to co-operate with the armed forces of the republic. Before the year 1814 was out—only a few weeks after Cullen's letter—a Hartford Convention was to meet in secret session to consider ways and means of thwarting the Jeffersonians and their senseless, ruinous war. The "army," then, that Cullen Bryant wished to join would have had about the same status with the official Washington of 1814 as General de Gaulle's army had with the official Vichy of the recent world conflict.

Fate, however, frustrated Cullen's military aspirations; for

only a few weeks after he had written to his father he was seized
with an illness which sent him packing home to Cummington for
recuperation. Thanks to the humidity of the Cape Cod Bay region, the young man found himself once more beset by the pulmonary complaint which had bedeviled him in infancy and early
childhood. Never at Williamstown or at Worthington had he
coughed and snuffled as he was coughing and snuffling during
those bleak November days at Bridgewater. Under the skillful
ministrations of Dr. Peter and the comparative aridity of Berkshire County he rallied in due time. By the time he had fully recovered, however, the military crisis was over. On Christmas Eve,
1814, Great Britain and the United States had signed the Treaty
of Ghent, and eight weeks later the glad tidings reached Washington. No longer did New England feel obliged to raise an army
for the sake of resisting "the weakness and wickedness" of the
Madison administration. The "Era of Good Feeling," to be ushered in with President James Monroe, was now approaching.
Cockades and epaulets and swords became rarer and rarer sights.

Ironically enough, Cullen received his commission when the
fifing and drumming and marching were all over. On August 25,
1816, he was made an adjutant (lieutenant) in the Massachusetts
militia. The following February, after six months of complete
military inaction, he returned his sword and his commission to
Governor John Brooks in Boston.

9

By late autumn, 1815, young Bryant had completed his legal
studies, had been admitted to the bar, and was ready to hang out
his shingle somewhere. His fond dreams of Boston had completely
vanished—so far, at least, as the immediate future was concerned.
Even Bridgewater seemed much too large, much too fraught with
competition. As for the Cummington-Worthington district, the
experienced Samuel Howe could care amply for all of the litigation that might arise there. By the process of elimination, Bryant
turned to another Berkshire village with which he had become
familiar in boyhood; namely, Plainfield, where five years earlier
he had studied Greek and algebra under the tutelage of the Reverend Moses Hallock.

One mid-December afternoon Cullen set out afoot from Cummington, bound for Plainfield. That there would be an opening

for him in the latter village had already been ascertained; but now he must arrange for living and office quarters. That seven-mile walk brought back a throng of old memories; for back in 1810, just before his Williams College days, he had tramped the Plainfield road at least two-score or half a hundred times.

The afternoon was rarely sunny, rarely mild, for Berkshire in December. The hard, dry ground was snowless, and many traces of autumn yet remained. Brown oaks, green pines, and blue sky, beightened by the mellow sunshine, made almost an October richness of color. Not all the migratory birds had yet flown southward. It was indeed a kindly day—the sort of day that might well make one forget the near approach of the heavy-footed New England winter.

Cullen, however, was far from happy, far from enthusiastic. What though he was free and white and twenty-one? What though, at that very moment, he was literally going out into the world? The world appeared far more a maze of dreary uncertainties than a realm of roseate prospects. Gone were the dreams of Boston and poetic fame. Gone were the balls and picnics of Bridgewater. Gone were the days when he could call upon the indulgent Peter for relief from financial embarrassment. Gone, long gone, were the visions of a schooling such as the lucky John Avery had had at Yale. The time had come for Cullen to hoe his own row, and the row looked long and hard and stony.

The insignificance of Plainfield he remembered all too well. Surely a hamlet of a dozen houses, cross-roads and trading-post of a township made up of little, infertile mountain farms, offered scant prospects of opulence or even competence. The Boston boots and beaver hat, the coat and waistcoat and pantaloons made for him by the Bridgewater tailor, might have to serve him for an indefinite time; nay, he might even have to go back to the home-spun of pre-Bridgewater days. And if Worthington, with its black-smith-shop and cow-stable, had been dull, what would Plainfield be? Fortunate would Cullen be if he had even the solace of Mr. Irving's *Knickerbocker*. As for time and energy and inspiration to write poetry, all of that seemed to be a thing that he might as well forego and forget.

Looking beyond the immediate future, to fresh woods and pastures new, had he any valid reason to envision a rosy career? True, he had passed the bar examination with ease, and even now his breastpocket held generous "characters" from Judge Howe and Judge Baylies. With diligence he might promote himself to a larger town—say, Northampton or Bridgewater—and ultimately he might find himself in Boston, the city of his dreams. Then, too, there was possibly the State House in Boston or even the Capitol in Washington. To shine in legislative halls, however, required eloquence, and eloquence was not one of his marked characteristics. No, somehow he could not picture himself as a second William Baylies; he could not imagine himself strolling or cantering down Tremont Street or Pennsylvania Avenue and being pointed out as the Honorable William Cullen Bryant. Rather, he pictured himself growing old as a mediocrity in a profession for which he had never had more than a moderate enthusiasm; haply he would end his days as an undistinguished, impecunious country lawyer, down at the boot-heels and threadbare at the elbows.

While he was employed in these dismal cogitations, he suddenly noticed something that kindled his poetic imagination. Above the horizon, against the crimson sky of the waning December afternoon, flew a solitary bird winging its way southward to join its more prudent fellows. So remote was the creature that he could not identify it specifically, but from the manner of its flight he knew it to be some sort of waterfowl. Toward what warm, sunny shore of river or lake or ocean was it heading? At any rate its flight, in happy contrast to Cullen's faltering footsteps, was certain; and its destination, barring the bullet of some rapacious fowler, was no less certain. As surely as the dawn of another morrow, it would soon be screaming joyously among its fellows, soothed and cheered by the summery air of the Carolinas or Georgia or the Floridas.

Quickly the bird was gone, swallowed up in the abyss of the heavens. Its lesson, however, lingered on, an inspiration and an uplift to Cullen. Perhaps, after all, Sarah and Grandfather Snell were right about the wondrous ways of providence. In any event, here was further support for the argument from design which characterized Peter's more "natural," less "revealed" religion. If the good God marked and guided the certain flight of the solitary bird over hundreds of miles from zone to zone, surely He would lead aright the steps of an earnest young man upon the threshold of a useful and an honorable career.

Cullen's pace became livelier, his footsteps more buoyant. By

the time he reached the center of Plainfield he had another poem
—this time an eight-stanza lyric of melodious rhymed pentameters
and trimeters—quite ready for foolscap. This poem, "To a Waterfowl," was to find its way into print a little more than two years
later: in the March, 1818, issue of the *North American Review*.
And many years later Matthew Arnold was to agree with Hartley
Coleridge in pronouncing Bryant's "Waterfowl" lyric "the finest
short poem in the English language." [6]

"To a Waterfowl" was the second really distinguished Bryant
poem to be published. "Thanatopsis," as we have seen, first appeared in the September, 1817, *North American*. In this connection, we must be reminded that on that genial December afternoon when Cullen plodded so dejectedly toward Plainfield,
"Thanatopsis" was as yet unknown to the world. It still reposed
in the desk at Cummington.

10

Before Cullen had rounded out a year at Plainfield, opportunity knocked at his door and was cordially welcomed. Somehow
—perhaps through an advertisement in the Hampshire *Gazette,*
of Northampton, the chief county newspaper for both Hampshire
and Berkshire—it became known that one George H. Ives, of
Great Barrington, had built up a larger legal practice than he
could handle alone and was earnestly desirous of a partner. For
reasons that will soon be apparent, young Bryant lost no time in
closing a deal with Ives.

Bright and early on a clear October morning in 1816 he
packed his belongings in a knapsack, shouldered his meager but
precious luggage, and headed for Great Barrington, which lay
thirty-odd miles to the southwest of Plainfield. Doubtless, since
Cummington lay upon his route he paused there long enough to
greet and receive the blessings of his kinsfolk. Once more he
traveled afoot, for his brief Plainfield practice had been utterly
inadequate to provide him with a horse.

Long and tedious as was the walk to Great Barrington, Cullen
was much happier this morning than on that afternoon when he
had spied the waterfowl. With ten months of experience (which
looked much more agreeable in retrospect than it had looked in
prospect), and with the certainty that he was heading toward immediate and substantial advancement, he was more fully con-

vinced than ever that a kindly providence *was* guiding his steps aright. By the time he reached Stockbridge, three-quarters of the way to his destination, he may have been a bit weary and footsore, but spiritually he was more buoyant than ever. A few miles more and he would be at the tavern in Great Barrington, eating a hearty dinner that would be all the more delicious because of its belatedness. And tomorrow morning he would be ensconced in his new office chair, working beside Ives, whom all reports had pictured to be a capital fellow. As for Great Barrington, he was sure that he would love it. Almost as large as Bridgewater, it would be a welcome contrast indeed to rustic, insignificant Plainfield. As Cullen proceeded on his journey, he felt that heaven lay about him. Before him gleamed the gently flowing Housatonic River, whose meanderings his road would follow the rest of the way. Were ever the gold and crimson glory of the October woods, the green luxuriance of the Stockbridge meadows, and the gray silhouetted grandeur of the steep, craggy hills beyond the river more entrancing? Years later he recalled the beauty of that scene and the exultation of his spirits.[7] Our one regret must be that he did not recapture it in a poem.

11

On the whole, Great Barrington proved as interesting to young Bryant as Plainfield had proved dull. Located in the extreme southwest corner of the state, ten miles from the Connecticut border and only five from the New York border, Great Barrington was the most atypical Massachusetts town that Cullen had ever seen. Foreign names on shop windows and tombstones—Van Deusen, for instance—and the prevalence of gambrel roofs were reminders that here was one New England community of Dutch rather than Yankee origin. Here, indeed, was one spot in New England where a Stuyvesant or a Knickerbocker might have felt more at home than a Bradford or a Winthrop. Only the great elms bordering the streets were reminiscent of such towns as Northampton and Bridgewater.

As for the spirit of Great Barrington, it was markedly liberal and tolerant, both politically and religiously. Despite the fact that its qualified electors voted overwhelmingly Federalist at every election, Great Barrington did not forget—or wish to forget—that during Shays's Rebellion just thirty years earlier it had been a hotbed of disaffection. With regard to theological doctrine, these Great Barrington Dutch had long since departed from the Calvinistic tenets of their ancestors; most of them, for generations, had been easy-going, deistic Episcopalians who relished their dancing and their whist and their wine, and who made their religion not too uncomfortable for themselves or for their neighbors. Moreover, Great Barrington was, like Bridgewater, a sizeable town—a town so relatively populous that its citizenry had neither the time nor the inclination to pry offensively into each others' affairs. All in all, then, we may be sure that the son of Peter Bryant found Great Barrington decidedly preferable to Plainfield.

12

Cullen did well in Great Barrington, for he was both competent and diligent. Within a few months he was in a position to buy out his partner and become sole master of a practice worth more than a thousand dollars a year. Writing to his old Bridgewater preceptor, William Baylies, he could boast that despite the rivalry of the flourishing firm of Whiting & Hyde, he was "very well patronized." Moreover, he soon came to be recognized and honored as a leading citizen. On March 9, 1819, for instance, he was elected tithing man, his duties in his new office being to prevent unseemly conduct in church and to enforce proper observance of the Sabbath. A little later he was elected town clerk, a position that brought far more honor than remuneration, the stipend being five dollars a year. Later still, by order of the Governor of Massachusetts, he was appointed Justice of the Peace, in which capacity he performed the marriage ceremony at least twice.

13

Great as were young Bryant's competence and diligence in those days, his personality was perhaps his main asset. A handsome, refined, intelligent face, topped by wavy dark brown hair and flanked by curly brown side-whiskers; a well-set-up figure whose slenderness gave the impression of somewhat greater height than the young man actually possessed; and scrupulously neat dress, citified and a little dandified in cut, with a penchant for blue coats and varicolored (but never "loud") waistcoats—all of these made Cullen Bryant one of the most prepossessing and dapper young gentlemen in Great Barrington.

His native shyness having mellowed into an ingratiating modesty, he was a favorite at fashionable parties, where he danced gracefully, played whist with fair proficiency, flattered comely young ladies sufficiently (but not excessively), and partook (always moderately) of port or sherry or whatever wine happened to be served.

He was, however, neither effeminate nor snobbish. At the close of a social dinner, when the gentlemen withdrew from the ladies, he could tell and enjoy anecdotes that were a bit too Rabelaisian for mixed company. And in spite of his innate refinement, his polished manners, and his fashionable grooming, he was democratic enough to enjoy both the companionship and the earthy jests of farm-hands, wood-choppers, and stage-drivers.[8]

A little worldly he might be, but never Godless. Lifelong family influence, especially the example and the precepts of his mother, made him a pew-holder and a regular church-goer, not at the mildly idolatrous Episcopal church, but at the Congregational meeting-house. Even without the influence of family tradition, his position as tithing-man made church attendance imperative. He did, however, reserve the right, among his intimate friends, to "pick the sermons to pieces." In this connection, it is extremely probable that the offending homilies were too orthodoxly Calvinistic to please the son of Peter Bryant.

14

Successful and popular as Bryant was in Great Barrington, and greatly as he preferred that village to the hamlet of Plainfield, he was not altogether happy either in his profession or in his surroundings. As was pointed out earlier in this chapter, his enthuiasm for the law was not superlative, and, as has been hinted more than once, the town of his dreams was no village, however thriving, but the metropolitan city of Boston. Consequently, his letters, both to William Baylies and to Dr. Peter, were often querulous.

To Judge Baylies he complained that his strenuous legal practice left him neither time nor energy to cultivate the muse. Judge Baylies, being a humanist as well as a lawyer and statesman, was genuinely sympathetic, but reminded his former pupil and apprentice that one must earn a livelihood and that "Poetry is a commodity . . . not suited to the American market." [9] Writing to his father, young Bryant reverted to a theme that he had stressed off and on for several years; namely, that Boston, with its metropolitan advantages and its distinguished literary society, would afford a stimulous that was utterly lacking in such a town as Great Barrington. But Peter, as formerly, remained unconvinced. His reply was kind, but firm. If Cullen was determined ultimately to remove to the big city, all well and good. Meanwhile, however, he had better remain in Great Barrington a few more years and "lay a solid foundation." In connection with the young man's restiveness, it must be recalled that "Thanatopsis" had appeared in the September, 1817, issue of the *North American Review*.

15

During Bryant's fourth year at Great Barrington, a major bereavement caused the cup of his unhappiness to overflow. On a sunny but blustery morning in late March, 1820, the mail-coach from the north brought a missive directed to Wm. C. Bryant, Esq'r., Great Barrington. The direction, more tremulous than usual, was in the handwrting of Sarah Bryant, and the foolscap was blotched, as if by rain or snow or tears. Hastily Cullen broke the sealing-wax and unfolded the paper. The letter was terse, and it had evidently been written with difficulty. The pulmonary trouble that had beset Peter Bryant for years had finally got the best of him. He had died on March 20, in his fifty-third year. His end had been hastened by exposure in a heavy snowstorm two weeks earlier, while he was returning home from a nocturnal accouchement.

Of a certainty, Cullen Bryant must now banish all dreams of beginning a career in Boston. More than ever, he must resolve to stick to the security of a well-established practice in Great Barrington. From now on, at regular intervals, he must send a portion of his earnings to Sarah and his younger brothers and sister.

To imply, however, that his disappointment equaled his grief would be doing him a serious injustice. The death of Peter, who was still in the prime of life, shocked him beyond words. For a long time he had known that his father was "poorly," but he had not been made to realize that the doctor's condition was critical. Had he even suspected it, he would have hastened to Cummington long ago. The death of Peter Bryant meant not merely the passing of a wise and affectionate father; it meant that Cullen was henceforth deprived of the one member of the Bryant family who fully appreciated the young man's tastes and talents and aspirations.

It was with a heavy heart that the young man returned to his law books and briefs and cases. Pondering often, in those days, upon the generosity, the altruism, the fine sensibility, and the high sense of honor that had characterized his father, he could not help contrasting Peter with the sort of men whose cases he was usually called upon to prosecute or to defend. Four years of grim experience had taught him repeatedly that persons most likely to air their troubles in the court-room were, as a rule, not the most desirable neighbors or citizens. At the bottom of most "lawing" lay selfishness or pettiness or vindictiveness or sharp practice—or a combination of these unlovely traits. Persons whose social ethics was based upon the Golden Rule found little occasion either to evoke or to evade the law of the commonwealth. In short, a lawyer's clients, for the most part, seemed not the kind of people whom a respectable member of the legal profession cared to number among his most intimate friends.

Once more, as in the days when he was nursing his disappointment at having been obliged to give up Yale, Cullen found solace in communion with nature. A couple of miles to the west of Great Barrington village flowed Green River, a small but extraordinarily beautiful tributary of the Housatonic. The thing that Cullen liked best about Green River was that it "shunned to glide" through the heart of the noisy, strife-torn village, choosing rather to wind through a quiet valley "away from the haunts of [quarrelsome] men." Standing or strolling on the banks of the placid, sequestered little river, whether amid the blossoms and wild bees of spring, or amid the floral pomp of midsummer, or beneath the golden foliage of autumn, he found Green River quite the loveliest retreat within easy walking distance of Great Barrington. His reactions he recorded in a graceful lyric of anapestic tetrameter couplets, the last ten lines of which are a fair enough sample of the tone and temper of the poem.

Though forced to drudge for the dregs of men,
And scrawl strange words with a barbarous pen,
And mingle among the jostling crowd,

Where the sons of strife are subtle and loud—
I often come to this quiet place,
To breathe the airs that ruffle thy face,
And gaze upon thee in silent dream,
For in thy lonely and lovely stream
An image of that calm life appears
That won my heart in my greener years.

Of the Bryant lyrics inspired by the Great Barrington country-side, "Green River" is the most notable. Written within a short time of Peter Bryant's death, it was first printed that very year in the *Idle Man,* a short-lived periodical edited by Bryant's friend Richard Henry Dana. Soon thereafter it was given wider circulation in the *Poems* of 1821. "Green River" has always been a favorite with anthologists—and deservedly so.

CHAPTER V

Jairest of the Rural Maids

1

IN THOSE spring days of 1820, Cullen Bryant had little stomach for the more fashionable, more worldly social functions of Great Barrington. As tithing-man, however, he continued to attend the Congregational "sociables," where he found the combination of staidness and naivete restful if generally uninspiring. One such "sociable" he was destined to remember far more vividly and lastingly than any ball or whist party.

It happened, perhaps, on an evening in late April or early May. Ordinarily Cullen would have preferred a solitary country stroll in the lengthening spring twilight; but this may have been one of those rainy evenings when the candle-lighted, fire-lighted parish room of the Congregational meeting-house was more inviting than the out-of-doors. At any rate, when Cullen discovered that among those in attendance at the "sociable" was Mrs. Henderson, one of the most personable and interesting young matrons in the town, he was sure that he had made no mistake in having abandoned his stroll.

But this was not all! With Mrs. Henderson was a young girl whom Cullen Bryant had never seen before. A scant five minutes after the tithing-man had entered the parish room he found him-

self acknowledging introduction to Mrs. Henderson's sister, Miss
Frances Fairchild.

2

Within another five minutes Cullen had fully appraised the
girl, if not the situation. She was small and blonde and about
twenty-three—a little more than two years Cullen's junior—though
she looked barely twenty. She had none of the boldness or pert-
ness characteristic of Bridgewater or Great Barrington society
belles; in fact, when she addressed the handsome, spruce young
lawyer she blushed just a little. On the other hand, she had none
of the rusticity so manifest in the farmers' daughters who lived
around Cummington and Worthington and Plainfield. Dressed
quietly and unostentatiously, she yet possessed both style and
grace. Never in any ballroom or at any levee had Cullen seen
head-dress more tasteful or more becoming than the beribboned
light-brown ringlets of this young woman. Never had he seen
form or features or complexion that attracted him more. And if
this girl blushed with the bashfulness of unsophistication, at any
rate her bright gray eyes met Cullen's gaze frankly and steadily.

Moreover, Fanny Fairchild could talk—interestingly, and in-
telligently, and wittily without frivolity. Before Cullen Bryant
left the parish room that evening he knew her brief life history
as well as her lovely person and her charming personality. She was
an orphan, both of her parents having died several years before,
during an epidemic of fever. All her life she had been familiar
with Great Barrington; for she had been born and reared on a
farm out Egremont way, almost midway between this town and
the York State line. Since her parents' death she had lived mostly
with a married sister away out west, in the Finger Lakes region of
the New York frontier. Only at infrequent intervals in recent
years had she visited her other sister, Mrs. Henderson. One of
these intervals had been about a year ago, at which time she had
spent several weeks in Great Barrington. Yes, she had attended a
"sociable" then, but evidently Cullen had not been present. Perhaps he had taken one of his country strolls. Or, perhaps, he had
been dancing or playing whist with the Episcopalians; for prior
to that sobering spring of 1820, young Bryant had undoubtedly
found the parish festivities at St. James' more engaging than any
entertainment that the Congregationalists dared or deigned to

offer. Well, be that as it may, never again would he miss another Congregational "sociable"—not if he had the slightest reason to suspect that Fanny Fairchild might be there.

And Miss Fairchild—what a contrast to that Rhode Island girl!—had a lively and an intelligent interest in literature, especially poetry. Her mother, by the way, had been a Miss Pope, distantly related to the great Alexander Pope.[1] But Miss Fairchild quite agreed with Mr. Bryant that her poetic kinsman and his monotonous rocking-horse couplets were passé: art, but no heart; lacked nature and sensibility. Now take Sir Walter Scott or Mr. Wordsworth or even that wicked Lord Byron—and—oh! that reminded Miss Fairchild—Mrs. Henderson said that those beautiful lines on Death that the *North American* had printed a couple of years ago were by William Cullen Bryant.

It was Cullen's turn to blush now. For all his twenty-five years, and for all his association with the *bon-ton* of Bridgewater and Great Barrington, he was made to feel abashed in the presence of this demure little maid from the farm out Egremont way. Not that her remarks were empty, affected flattery! Quite the contrary! Indeed, that was the devil of it. Whatever the schooling of this pretty child had been, her knowledge and discrimination in the realm of poetry were truly marvelous. A most refreshing girl to meet! If church "sociables" attracted such a happy combination of beauty and brains, then more power to church "sociables." Of all the chattering, dancing, whist-playing young females to be met at the "smarter" social functions, which one ever mentioned or looked at the *North American Review?* Which one could tell whether Mr. William Wordsworth was an author, a British admiral, or a Boston victualer? But as for little Miss Fairchild, she was as engagingly frank as she was intelligent. "Thanatopsis," she repeated, was beautiful, especially in its imagery of the all-beholding sun, the rock-ribbed hills, the complaining brooks, and the meadows green. But wasn't all this dwelling upon death a bit depressing?

For a few moments the astounded, delighted Cullen found himself speechless. When he again became articulate, he stammered something to the effect that in "Thanatopsis" he had intended to stress the everlastingness of Nature far more than the transitoriness of man. In any event, it was right and proper and wholesome that healthy young folk in their teens and twenties should look forward to life, not death. Of a certainty, he and Miss Fairchild would cheat the undertaker for many years to come; the all-beholding sun should continue to cast his rays upon them for hundreds of seasons.

Turning from life and death and poetry to more immediate considerations, young Bryant expressed the hope that Miss Fairchild would stay in Great Barrington throughout the summer at least; that he might call upon her at the Henderson domicile on Taconic Street soon and often; that they might go strolling, and sometimes horseback riding, together; and that the young lady's next journey to the wilds of western New York lay far in the future and would be of short duration.

With all of these ardent words Miss Fairchild was quite manifestly pleased. In tones whose sincerity could not be doubted, she averred that she had spent a most delightful evening and that she hoped this first meeting with Mr. Bryant would be by no means the last. As for the duration of her stay in Great Barrington—well, she had come too great a distance to plan a very early departure. As regarded calls in Taconic Street (she added, with a most delectable little smile and blush), she was certain that Mrs. Henderson would be honored and happy to have Mr. Bryant come at any time he found convenient and agreeable.

3

Cullen could hardly have slept much that night. "Rural, but not rustic" was the phrase that kept running through his mind. In the parish room, a few short hours ago, the impossible had happened; he had met Mr. Wordsworth's Lucy Gray incarnate.

In the years since that first infatuation with Evelina, the girl from Rhode Island, Cullen had often wondered whether a maiden of the Lucy type could ever actually exist except in a poet's dreams—whether, in real life, rural simplicity was not inevitably accompanied by ignorance and crudeness; urbane refinement, by cynicism and affectation. Certainly the young women he had encountered during those years had not tended to make him idealize femininity. On the one hand, there were the town belles, pretty, stylish, and graceful, but shallow, heartless, and insincere. On the other hand, there were the country jades, raw-boned, snub-nosed, clumsy, harsh-voiced, and frightfully ungrammatical. Cullen Bryant had never been an ardent admirer of the poetry of George

Crabbe, but experience had forced him to conclude that the sardonic old Suffolk doctor-parson had been more than half right in declaring,

> *I paint the Cot,*
> *As Truth will paint it, and as Bards will not.*

Corydon and Chloe might do well enough in pastoral verse; but Reuben and Marthy, their Cummington counterparts, were boresome, not to say disgusting.

Fanny Fairchild, however, was distinctly different. From her lovely head to her dainty ankles, she was all charm. In her, surely, there dwelt all the grace and dignity and intelligence of Boston—heaven knew how or where she had acquired these qualities!—and the simplicity and freshness and ingenuousness of a Berkshire farm. Last night, at that never-to-be-forgotten "sociable," Dr. Crabbe had been refuted; Mr. Wordsworth had been vindicated.

Bright sunshine and the sonorous town clock reminded Cullen Bryant that it was time to prepare for another day's struggle with briefs and cases. Nervous and jaded, yet inspired and ecstatic, he arose and started dressing. Those sleepless hours just past had produced another poem, this one a "character" piece. Bell-like the simple, forthright couplets rang through his entire being:

> *O fairest of the rural maids!*
> *Thy birth was in the forest shades;*
> *Green boughs, and glimpses of the sky,*
> *Were all that met thine infant eye.*
>
> *Thy sports, thy wanderings, when a child,*
> *Were ever in the sylvan wild;*
> *And all the beauty of the place*
> *Is in thy heart and on thy face.*
>
> *The twilight of the trees and rocks*
> *Is in the light shade of thy locks;*
> *Thy step is as the wind, that weaves*
> *Its playful way among the leaves.*
>
> *Thine eyes are springs, in whose serene*
> *And silent waters heaven is seen;*
> *Their lashes are the herbs that look*
> *On their young figures in the brook.*
>
> *The forest depths, by foot unpressed,*
> *Are not more sinless than thy breast;*
> *The holy peace, that fills the air*
> *Of those calm solitudes, is there.*

[59]

A score of years later, Edgar Allan Poe was to pronounce this
lyric "a gem" and to vote it "the truest poem written by Bryant." [2]

4

On Monday, June 11, 1821, William Cullen Bryant and Frances Fairchild were married at the Henderson home. The wedding,

FRANCES FAIRCHILD BRYANT
From a Miniature by an Unknown Artist
Courtesy of The New York Historical Society, New York City

which was doubtless performed by the local Congregational minister, occurred "in the paneled southeast room" of the old Taconic Street house.[3] Apparently it was a very quiet affair. For some inexplicable reason, Sarah Bryant had not been invited—not even apprized until after the event. Quite possibly the thirty miles between Cummington and Great Barrington may have been a prohibitive distance; but, even so, it is strange that the bridegroom's mother should not have had advance notice of an event so momentous.

Not until several days after the wedding did Sarah's "affectionate son, William" break what he was pleased to call "the melancholy intelligence." This he did in a quaint letter in which he described the officiating clergyman as "a little elderly gentleman, pale, thin, with a solemn countenance, pleuretic voice, hooked nose, and hollow eyes," and the bride merely as "a young lady of the name of Frances Fairchild," whose virtues were "goodness of heart, an ingenuous and affectionate disposition, a good understanding, . . . and . . . a character . . . frank and single-hearted."[4] Between the lines of this extraordinary missive, Sarah Bryant read the assurance that when she came to know the wonderful Fanny she would be all joy and approval.

One circumstance that young Bryant neglected to mention in his letter to his mother was the embarrassment that had befallen him on the Sabbath eight days before the wedding. In his official capacity as town clerk, he himself was required to publish the banns. Frightened at the merest thought of reading them to the congregation, he had decided to emulate Martin Luther and nail his bold proposition to the church door.[5] There was, however, one exceedingly important distinction between Bryant's temerity and Luther's: Bryant was not publishing ninety-five heretical theses, but an announcement that must have evoked the warmest approbation of everyone acquainted with the estimable young lawyer and his charming little bride-to-be.

Cullen and Fanny set up housekeeping a scant square's distance from the Henderson domicile, and hardly farther from Cullen's office: in second-story rooms of the residence of a Mr. and Mrs. Ralph Taylor, at the southwest corner of Main and South Streets. How long they remained there is not known; but, at any rate, it was in the stately white Taylor house that their elder child, Frances, first saw the light of day.[6]

Those Great Barrington years were busy years—so busy that, as we have observed, Bryant sometimes complained of his lack of time to cultivate the muse.

Despite all this, the young man's pen was far from idle. Publication of "Thanatopsis" and composition of the Green River and the "Rural Maid" lyrics have already been noted. Meanwhile, Bryant was earning a modest reputation as a literary critic, a fact that may be verified by consultation of the *North American Review* for July, 1818, September, 1819, and October, 1820, respectively.

Bryant's contribution to the aforementioned 1818 issue is a critical "Essay on American Poetry," in which he appraises the work of his own poetic forerunners and contemporaries. Here he deplores the imitative tendencies of most of our early poets, especially their penchant for copying the stilted, unimaginative diction, the monotonous versification, and the unfeeling coldness of the English neo-classicists; and he pleads for the development of a national poetic literature fortified by "genius, taste, and diligence" rather than by "pompous pretensions." [7]

In the September, 1819, *North American,* Bryant expatiates "On the Use of Trisyllabic Feet in Iambic Verse," condemning the neo-classical poets for their lack of anapestic substitutions, and urging a return to the prosodic freedom and flexibility of Shakespeare, Milton, and the other great pre-Restoration bards.[8]

Bryant's essay in the October, 1820, *North American* is chiefly notable as evidence that even in those early Massachusetts days he was interested in drama; for this particular essay is an appreciative critique of an American blank-verse tragedy, *Percy's Masque,* by James A. Hillhouse. "Tragedy," opines Bryant in this review, "is a noble province of poetry," yet he finds in most modern poetic drama a diction "too florid and stately, and too far removed from the common idiom of our tongue." [9] Had Cullen Bryant, at that period in his life, ever seen a professional theatrical performance? There is no evidence that he had. But from what we have seen of his personality, we may probably venture an affirmative answer. Certainly he had never been in Boston or any other large city. Quite as certainly, however—despite the persistence of New England Puritan opposition to the theater—such towns as Bridgewater and Great Barrington were visited from time to time by strolling troupes, some of them fairly meritorious. And Cullen Bryant was much more humanistic than puritanic. Hence it would be passing strange if in 1820 his knowledge of the drama was confined to the printed page.

6

Bryant's most voluminous creative efforts of those Great Barrington years are today among the least known of his poems. They are five hymns which are much less interesting for themselves than for the circumstances under which they were written.

Among the Williams College acquaintanceships renewed by Bryant at Great Barrington was that with Charles F. Sedgwick, a young man of about Bryant's age. Sedgwick lived at Stockbridge, some ten miles north of Great Barrington; but as fellow members of the Berkshire bar, he and Bryant seem to have met a number of times in the court-room, sometimes as colleagues, sometimes as friendly if spirited rivals. In any event, it would appear that their friendship became closer in those later days than it had been at college. It would also appear that Bryant had visited the Sedgwick home and had met Charles's sister Catherine. Certainly by 1820 Cullen Bryant and Kate Sedgwick knew each other intimately and esteemed each other highly.

The friendship of Cullen and Miss Sedgwick was purely Platonic; for in 1820 the lady was thirty years old—five years Cullen's senior—and she was rather plain and a trifle spinsterly. Her charms, in brief, were of the blue-stocking variety, a circumstance at least partly attributable to the fact that for seven or eight years she had been preceptor of a young ladies' boarding-school. In no sense was Kate Sedgwick ever a rival of pretty little Fanny Fairchild.

Bryant and Miss Sedgwick were attracted to each other on two principal grounds: first, religious liberalism; second, interest in literature. Both of them were Unitarians, in belief if not by formal profession; and both of them were ardent devotees of belles-lettres. Miss Sedgwick had not yet published anything; but she was even then at work on a novel, *A New England Tale,* which, upon its publication in 1822, achieved almost immediate success. Two or three years later her second novel, *Redwood,* was to evoke from Bryant a long and enthusiastic review in the *North American*.[10] Her subsequent novels, especially *Hope Leslie* (1827), *Clarence, A Tale of Our Times* (1830), *The Linwoods* (1835), and *Married or Single* (1857), were to round out a long and a successful, if not quite a permanently distinguished career.

Our immediate interest in Catherine Sedgwick lies in the fact that in 1820 she and her brother persuaded Bryant to write five lyrics for a Unitarian hymnal compiled under the editorship of Henry D. Sewall. Although none of these five hymns have been included in regular editions of Bryant's poetry, and although none of them have become nearly so well known as the best of Whittier's hymns, they are both dignified and appealing. Incidentally, the probable reason why they do not appear in the Episcopal and other widely-used Protestant hymnals is that they are essentially Unitarian in theology; in their original form they pay no especial tribute to Jesus Christ as the divine Son of God.

7

One day in the summer of 1821, only a few weeks after the wedding of Cullen Bryant and Fanny Fairchild, our young lawyer-poet received a most astounding letter—a letter that filled him with elation and trepidation, all at the same time. It was a letter of invitation, and it was so momentous that he could not think of acting upon it without his bride's advice. It was an insistent demand that he prepare a special poem for what was perhaps the greatest American academic occasion of the entire year: the open meeting held by Phi Beta Kappa at the commencement of Harvard College. Of course if he accepted, he must go to Cambridge and himself read the poem before the assemblage.

Manifestly, the young man was elated. Going to Cambridge meant going to Boston, and going to Boston meant contact with the leading literary lights of the country, to say nothing of glimpsing metropolitan hotels, metropolitan shops, metropolitan fashions, and perhaps a metropolitan theatrical performance or two. All his life, as far back as he could remember, he had dreamed of Boston Common and Bunker Hill and Faneuil Hall, of Tremont Street and Washington Street and the Old South meeting-house, of the Charles River and the Harvard Yard and Craigie House, of the foreign sailors and cargoes and flags in the exciting, cosmopolitan region of Charlestown docks. And now, if he accepted the invitation, he would know all of those wonders at first hand. Incidentally, he would read his poem before as distinguished and as cultivated an audience as would gather anywhere on any occasion in all the three-and-twenty United States.

And yet—dared he accept? Who was he but a young country lawyer devoid of eloquence, devoid of a baccalaureate degree! All things considered, would not a man who had had four years of Harvard or Yale be vastly preferable to a reticent young man with only one year of Williams to his collegiate credit? True, Cullen Bryant, more than a dozen years earlier, had created a mild sensation as a juvenile poetic prodigy; and among readers of the *North American Review* it had become rather generally understood that he was the author of the two most meritorious American poems yet published in that excellent periodical. But, academically, Phi Beta Kappa was by far the most distinguished, the most exclusive of societies. Only a full-fledged alumnus member, one would suppose, would be called upon to display his talents at the great commencement meeting of the society. What in the world possessed Mr. W. J. Spooner (the secretary of the Harvard chapter) to invite Cullen Bryant?

But in shrewd little Fanny's opinion there was only one logical answer to Mr. Spooner's gracious letter of invitation. "Of course you will accept," she declared, kissing her favorite poet's forehead, and playfully running her fingers through his side whiskers.

8

And so in the weeks that immediately followed, whenever Cullen could spare any moments from his business with the sons of strife, he worked feverishly on the longest, most ambitious poem he had ever attempted. He called his new effort "The Ages," and when it was finished it contained some thirty-five imposing Spenserian stanzas. The theme of this poem, as William Aspenwall Bradley has accurately stated, "is the progress of man and civilization through the ages, and the object is to show the triumph of virtue and liberty and peace in the new country of America." [11]

"The Ages" appeared more than six score years ago; yet, read in the light (or the darkness) of events that have made these nineteen-forties so harrowing, some portions of this poem sound strangely modern, strangely opportune. Let us take, for instance, the two closing stanzas.

> *Europe is given a prey to sterner fates,*
> *And writhes in shackles; strong the arms that chain*
> *To earth her struggling multitude of states;*
> *She too is strong, and might not chafe in vain*
> *Against them, but might cast to earth the train*
> *That trample her, and break their iron net.*
> *Yes, she shall look on brighter days and gain*
> *The meed of worthier deeds; the moment set*
> *To rescue and raise up, draws near—but is not yet.*

> *But thou, my country, thou shalt never fall,*
> *Save with thy children—thy maternal care,*
> *Thy lavish love, thy blessings showered on all—*
> *These are thy fetters—seas and stormy air*
> *Are the wide barriers of thy borders, where,*
> *Among thy gallant sons who guard thee well,*
> *Thou laugh'st at enemies: who shall then declare*
> *The date of thy deep-founded strength, or tell*
> *How happy, in thy lap, the sons of men shall dwell?*

Subtract a few words from the second stanza of this passage, and one has a reasonably apt characterization of Europe and America as they were from the fall of France in 1940 to the surrender of the Nazis in 1945. Today, of course, no sane person believes that the "seas and stormy air" form a wide enough barrier to enable America to laugh at European or Asiatic enemies; yet as recently as the morning of December 7, 1941, every isolationist, in and out of Congress, believed it as strongly as did all Americans in 1821.

9

As soon as Cullen had completed a preliminary draft of "The Ages," he read it to his dearest critic and adviser. Pretty little Fanny, ensconced upon her husband's lap in order that she might follow the words with eyes as well as ears, listened intently and proudly to the succession of melodious iambics and felicitously colorful images. When the reading was finished she protested— ever so gently—against a few words, a few phrases, a few tropes. This and that and the other little change, she felt certain, would make the poem perfection—or as near perfection as anything can be this side of heaven. On the whole, declared the young lady fervently, "The Ages" was altogether worthy of the great occasion

[66]

for which it was being prepared. When that occasion arrived, as we shall presently observe, her judgment was amply sustained by critics much older and more pretentious than she.

In the cool of summer evenings, as Cullen and Fanny walked hand in hand among the willows that skirted Green River, the young man would recite and re-recite his newest poem, sometimes in toto, sometimes by particularly favorite passages. With each repetition the lines grew nobler and lovelier, both to him who declaimed and to her who listened.

10

The late August evening immediately preceding the day of Cullen's departure for Cambridge must have been a momentous one. Probably Fanny insisted on opening a bottle of port in honor of the occasion; and if she did, Cullen made no protest, for he was not averse to "tolerable wine." At any rate, it is pleasant to fancy the young couple drinking—soberly and discreetly, of course—to the triumph of "The Ages."

11

Bright and early the next morning Cullen was bound southward for the neighboring town of Sheffield, where he would get the Hartford mail-coach. Why he chose to travel by way of Hartford instead of by the more direct route through Springfield is a mystery. Perhaps he was satisfying a lifelong desire to see Connecticut, especially its proud capital, whose group of "Wits" had once made it a more illustrious literary center than Boston. Be that as it may, Cullen rode the few miles from Great Barrington to Sheffield "on a rough board" on top of "a crazy wagon," his traveling companions a garrulous mulatto and a dirty, tobacco-spitting old countryman.[12]

So slow was travel in those days, and so poor were the coach connections, that Hartford was not reached until six that evening, and Boston not until midnight the next. Doubtless, however, Cullen enjoyed every moment of the incredibly interminable trip. Doubtless he got a far more vivid impression of the unfamiliar Connecticut landscape than he could ever have got if his maiden journey to Cambridge had been by way of the New Haven express train of later years.

12

The rows of lighted lamps along the Cambridge and the Charlestown bridges—lamps brighter and more innumerable than he had ever dreamed of—gave him his first deep thrill upon his approach to the great New England metropolis. Within the days immediately ensuing, he was to experience a succession of thrills that were even deeper.

First came the coveted, long-anticipated meeting with Willard Phillips, the brilliant editor who had already received young Bryant's writings so kindly. Then came a drive out Waltham way in Phillips's carriage to the country estate of the great East India merchant, Mr. Theodore Lyman, who was so fabulously wealthy that at the cost of some twenty thousand dollars per annum he maintained exotic Chinese and European gardens, a tropical green-house, and a huge deer park. And then, inside the princely Lyman mansion, there was a session of small talk and fashionable tea-drinking with "several agreeable ladies," all of them indubitably more urbane than the grandest madams of Bridegwater.[13]

13

Cullen's supreme hour came a few days later, August 30, when, seated on the rostrum of the old Congregational Church in Cambridge, he faced "a very numerous and select audience," [14] which included such distinguished sons of Harvard as John Quincy Adams, William Ellery Channing, Edward Everett, John Lowell, and Timothy Pickering. It included also at least one Harvard man who was bound for future distinction; for, seated inconspicuously in about the middle of the graduating class was a quiet, introspective, self-critical youth of eighteen years, named Ralph Waldo Emerson.

Was Cullen Bryant conscious of the fact that President Monroe's Secretary of State had journeyed all the way from Washington for the occasion and now sat eagerly (and a little cynically) awaiting Cullen's performance? Probably he was; for he must have realized that a Harvard commencement without the presence of an Adams would be like a presentation of *Hamlet* with Hamlet left out. And what must have made the experience doubly terrifying was the fact that Cullen must remain seated before that brilliant assemblage while a certain John C. Gray, the orator of the occasion, delivered the lengthy Phi Beta Kappa address. If only dear, doting little Fanny could have been present—seated in a front row—to give him one look of encouragement with her bright gray eyes!

At last he stood in the pulpit, inwardly quaking, but outwardly as calm as if he were facing one of the familiar Berkshire assizes. "When in the common rest that crowns our days," he began calmly and deliberately—and within a moment all was well. No semi-hostile court-room was he addressing, but the most select of academic audiences, thoroughly polite and even sympathetic, if not prepared to be quite enthusiastic. Quietly, unoratorically, a little monotonously the young poet-reader continued; and although John Gray, seated behind him on the rostrum, kept wishing that the eloquent Mr. Everett might be rendering those truly excellent lines, the performance appears to have been a genuine success. Years and years later, Eliza Quincy recalled the handsome young Bryant's "pleasing, refined, and intellectual appearance"; his "ease and clearness of enunciation"; the "grave and elevated tone" of his poem; and, at the conclusion of the reading, the outburst of "approbation vehement." [15]

As the relieved and elated Cullen took his seat, the plaudits ringing strangely through that staid old house of worship, and John Gray grasping his hand with delighted enthusiasm, the young poet's thoughts sped westward to his "fairest of the rural maids" back home in Great Barrington. If darling little Fanny could only have been there in the Cambridge church, the expression on her pretty face would have meant more than all the "approbation vehement" of Harvard savants and ministers of state. No longer was the triumph of "The Ages" a wistful toast; it was at last a consummated reality. Day after tomorrow Cullen would hold Fanny in his arms and tell her all about it. But, at the moment, how exasperatingly remote day after tomorrow seemed!

14

In a very real sense the reading of "The Ages" marked the beginning of William Cullen Bryant's career as the most eminent poet that America had yet known. Hardly had the buzzing audience started to file out of the meeting-house when Willard Phillips and Richard Henry Dana, co-editors of the *North American Review,* had mounted the rostrum to join John Gray in congratulating the newly crowned American laureate. Of a certainty, these editorial gentlemen warmly agreed, Mr. Bryant must now publish all of his distinguished verse in a volume. Upon deaf ears fell the modest young poet's blushing, stammering protestations that his distinguished verses were too few in number for such an undertaking.

The upshot of the matter was that *Poems* by William Cullen Bryant, a forty-four page booklet bound in brown paper boards, was issued by a Cambridge press early in the autumn of 1821. Besides "The Ages" this slender volume contained "To a Waterfowl," "Translation of a Fragment of Simonides," "Inscription for the Entrance to a Wood," "The Yellow Violet," "The Hunter of the West," "Green River," and "Thanatopsis."

Of these poems the most notable that we have not yet commented upon are probably "The Yellow Violet" and "Inscription for the Entrance to a Wood."

"The Yellow Violet," written evidently at Bridgewater in 1814, is one of the most completely unpretentious of Bryant's poems; in fact, it is as simple in rhythm and diction as the Lucy poems of Wordsworth. Its eight tetrameter quatrains are as uninvolved as a nursery rhyme, and it contains scarcely a word that would be incomprehensible to a child of ten. Like Burns's "To a Mountain Daisy"—indeed, like scores of other romantic nature lyrics—it lauds a modest wild flower for the wild flower's very modesty. The only splendor that the little yellow violet has, in the mind of the poet, comes from the fact that it is almost the first flower of spring. The budding of the beech-trees; the first notes of bluebirds in fields that are still russet and still fringed with snow-banks—these are the signals for the yellow violet to peep from last year's leaves and view the pale skies of a chill, sunless New England April day. Often on such a day has the little sun-hued flower, with its tiny jet-black lip, halted the poet's steps and caused him to gaze in quiet satisfaction, if only for a moment. Soon the poor little violet will be forgotten "midst the gorgeous blooms of May, . . . the painted tribes of light." But the poet loyally resolves that he will not forget her. For was it not this modest little flower alone that brightened the otherwise dull woods and fields of April? Perhaps when Cullen Bryant wrote these lines, particularly the three moralistic stanzas with which the poem closes, his Puritan conscience was momentarily rebuking

him for his having allowed the fashionable pleasures of Bridgewater to make him forget the simpler, more rustic joys of Cummington and Williamstown.

"Inscription for the Entrance to a Wood," written in 1815,
must also have been composed at Bridgewater. In the forty-two
blank-verse lines of this poem, Bryant expresses weariness not only
with the fashionable urban world, but with the human scene in
general. It is alone in the wild wood, he declares, that man finds
calm and refreshment. It is not the haunts of men, he insists, that
are the real abodes of gladness. Rather, it is the leafy shades,
under the sunny blue sky, where green and stirring branches are
alive and musical with birds; where squirrels chirp merrily; where
throngs of insects try their wings in the shade and dance in the
sun; where even such inanimate objects as the cleft-born wild
flowers seem to enjoy existence almost as much as the wild bees
that innocently plunder their sweets. Yes, here in the unprofaned
forest, even the mossy rocks and the ponderous trunks of the pros-
trate trees breathe the spirit of tranquillity. And does not the rivulet, tripping over its pebbly bed or leaping down the rocks, laugh
for very joy at its own being? In this "Inscription" poem there is,
of course, a great deal of Wordsworth. There is also a touch of
the Puritan Snell heritage. For example, when we read in lines
11 and 12 of the "the primal curse" that "fell . . . upon the un-
sinning earth," we may be sure that however much young Cullen
Bryant may have been broadened by his life at Bridgewater, he
still took for granted one of the prime fundamentals of the Calvinistic theology.

The chorus of critical praise that greeted Bryant's *Poems* was,
if small in volume, decidedly authoritative and distinguished in
quality. Willard Phillips, in the October, 1821, *Review,* praised
the poems for their "strain of pure and high sentiment," for their
simple diction, and for the "subtle and ever varying beauties of
nature" contained in their imagery.[16] Gulian C. Verplanck, writing in the New York *American,* from the viewpoint of a critic
who had no prejudice in favor of New England authors, praised
Bryant's verses for "their exquisite taste, their keen relish for the
beauties of nature, their magnificent imagery, and their pure and
majestic morality." [17] And even that supercilious British Tory review, *Blackwood's Edinburgh Magazine,* which seldom bothered
even to mention American writers, gave Bryant's poetry a lengthy

paragraph in its September, 1824, issue. True, the *Blackwood* reviewer was far from unqualifiedly laudatory, since he averred that Bryant was not—and never would be—a great poet. The reviewer did, however, find Bryant's "few plain ideas" expressed "in a very handsome way," and he found at least one Bryant lyric ("To a Waterfowl") "very beautiful" from start to finish.[18]

When Fanny read these reviews she was thoroughly convinced —even more thoroughly convinced than Cullen himself—that destiny had stamped her husband with the mark of a great poet. In short, his days as a humble village member of the Berkshire County bar were thenceforth numbered. From this time on, his dealings with "the sons of strife" would be more and more distasteful; his dreams of national literary distinction, more and more vivid and insistent.

CATHERINE MARIA SEDGWICK

CHAPTER VI

Politics and a Bellyful

1

"I BELIEVE that Harry could help you," said Kate Sedgwick.

"I'm confident he could," agreed her brother Charles, stressing his words of agreement with a vigorous nod.

The "Harry" to whom the Sedgwicks referred was their brother Henry D. in New York. The person whom they thought Harry could help was Cullen Bryant. The time and the place of their encouraging words to Cullen are uncertain, but the conversation may well have taken place at the Bryant domicile on South Street in Great Barrington on a late winter or an early spring evening in 1824, about two and a half years after the triumph of "The Ages." Kate and Charles had, perhaps, run down from Stockbridge on business; had dropped in upon Fanny and Cullen; and had been urged to stay for tea. And now, seated before a fireplace made cheerful by blazing logs, hosts and guests were most likely discussing Cullen's increasing discontent with the law, his increasing desire to make his living with his pen.

It was the old story that Cullen, in recent months, had often poured into the willing ears of Fanny: that literature, not litigation, was William Cullen Bryant's true calling. It was not merely that the young man found "the sons of strife" increasingly distasteful in themselves. It was not merely that he derived inspiration from the peaceful woods and. fields rather than from the "subtle and loud" court-room. It was, more particularly, the intellectual dishonesty which seemed an inevitable accompaniment of his present profession. To put the matter bluntly, there had been more than a few times during the past eight years when Cullen Bryant had been obliged to prosecute or defend a case of whose merits he was extremely doubtful. And, frankly, this straightforward, idealistic young man always shrank from playing the role of Belial. If his tongue must drop manna, let it be in an honest cause; let him at least be spared the ignominy of making "the worse appear the better reason." So much for the law and all its devious, umbrageous ways! As for literature—well, at every opportunity since his earliest years of adolescence, he had proved that that was a Zion in which he was always happy, always at ease.

If, however, Bryant were to turn to his pen as a sole means of livelihood, his new profession would have to be editorial rather than authorial. When Judge Baylies, in 1817, had pronounced poetry to be a commodity not adapted to the American market, he might truthfully have substituted the phrase *creative literature in general* for the more specific term *poetry*—and his statement would have been virtually as true in 1824 as in 1817. Within those seven years—and for many years thereafter—Irving and Cooper were the only American writers to make money by their creative efforts, and neither of those two talented gentlemen pretended to live off his royalties. On the other hand, there were a few salaried editorial positions that paid as much as five hundred dollars a year.

If Henry Dwight Sedgwick was in a position to help Cullen Bryant find an editorial chair, it was because of Sedgwick's New York contacts rather than because of his literary attainments. Although Henry Sedgwick contributed occasionally to the *North American Review,* he was in no strict sense a man of letters. A lawyer by profession, he found his chief interest in public affairs. As a prominent citizen of New York, however, he had intimate acquaintance with all the Knickerbocker literary lights, and his influence among Manhattan publishers and editors was as great as that of any man of the times.

When Charles and Kate averred that Harry could help their young friend, the faces of both Cullen and Fanny must have brightened. Although both would have preferred Boston to New York, there did not happen to be an opening in the former city. And New York, as second choice, was not to be despised. Surely a city that boasted such talents as Washington Irving, J. Fenimore Cooper, J. K. Paulding, Fitz-Greene Halleck, James A. Hillhouse, and Gulian C. Verplanck was no mean literary center. And many an astute observer already regarded New York as a more promising metropolis than either of its two rivals, Boston and Philadelphia. In fact, with "De Witt Clinton's Ditch" (the Erie Canal) nearing completion, men predicted more and more that New York would one day become our indubitable national metropolis. And if commercial metropolis, why not cultural metropolis as well? Certainly the great European metropolises, London and Paris, had become as overwhelmingly pre-eminent in letters and arts as in trade and industry and politics.

But what concerned Kate Sedgwick at the moment was whether Cullen Bryant had any new manuscripts that she could send Harry to show his editor friends.

The embarrassed Cullen, we fancy, averted his gaze from Kate to the blazing logs. To tell the truth, his pen had grown alarmingly idle of late. In fact, since that glorious day in Cambridge, back in 1821, the poems that he had written were so few that he could count them on the fingers of one hand. And the best of those poems, "The Indian Girl's Lament" and "The Rivulet," were but sorry trifles compared with the most distinguished pieces in the volume of 1821.

Cullen was about to admit that he had nothing to send Harry Sedgwick; the confession was on the tip of his tongue. Fanny, however, quickly relieved matters by reminding her husband of *The Heroes.*

The Heroes? Oh, yes! But, somehow, mention of *The Heroes* made Cullen more embarrassed than ever—made his face actually redden. And when Kate and Charles Sedgwick learned what *The Heroes* was, they did not wonder at Cullen's embarrassment. What they did wonder at was what possessed the sedate author of "Thanatopsis" to try his hand at anything so frivolous as a farce. For a farce was precisely what *The Heroes* was. One night during that winter, it appears, Cullen had taken Fanny to see a troupe of strolling players do *The Rivals,* the celebrated comedy by the late Mr. Sheridan. Impressed by the ridiculousness of the duel that Bob Acres had almost fought with Captain Absolute—impressed still more with the wicked folly of duelling in general—Cullen had decided to ridicule that all too prevalent practice in a stage play of his own. The result had been *The Heroes,* the first, last, and only effort that William Cullen Bryant was ever to make as a dramatist.

When Fanny produced the manuscript from a desk drawer and placed it in the hands of Charles Sedgwick, that bewildered young gentleman "shook his dubious locks" [1] even before he had turned a single page. Well might Charles express his dubiety; for Bryant's genius, as Parke Godwin has truly remarked, "was hardly of a comic cast.' [2] Moreover, Bryant's practical knowledge of the theater and its problems, especially in those early days of his career, was virtually nil.

Nevertheless, *The Heroes* was packed off to Harry Sedgwick in New York. Whether the piece had any merit was a question that some of Harry's friends would be competent to answer, far more competent than any dweller in the bucolic Berkshire region.

2

The fate of *The Heroes* was soon known—and sealed. The verdict of the Gotham wiseacres was altogether unfavorable. A farce, they said, should be both amusing and dramatic—and Cullen's opus was neither. None of the dialogue would evoke more than the faintest of smiles, for most of its witticisms were either too stale or too subtle to be even mildly funny. As for the "business" of the play, there wasn't any; the characters just stood (or sat) around and talked. Consequently, any producer who would undertake to do *The Heroes* would be courting disaster.

Harry Sedgwick's frank letter, however, was by no means totally discouraging. Recalling Cullen Bryant's successes both as poet and as critic, he expressed confidence that Cullen could find an editorial opening in New York. Indeed, he went so far as to declare that the time for a young man of Cullen's talents to seek such an opening was "peculiarly propitious." In this connection, he pointed out that the recent establishment of the Athenaeum Library was "exciting a sort of literary rage" in New York—a rage that was reviving interest in the highly meritorious *Atlantic Magazine* and that might soon inspire the establishment of other literary periodicals, including a magazine sponsored by the Athe-

[77]

naeum itself. Even now, Harry continued, the reviving *Atlantic,* in the capable hands of Henry J. Anderson, was paying its editor the very decent stipend of five hundred dollars a year; and its publishers, Bliss and White, were already offering an additional five hundred a year for a competent co-editor—if such could be found—to assist the busy Mr. Anderson.

Moreover, a literary editor of Cullen Bryant's talents and reputation would not have to depend solely upon his salary for a livelihood. The magazine would afford his verses and essays a market which, if modest, would be by no means negligible. And he would have his evenings free for other remunerative occupations: lecturing, for instance, or the teaching of English to some of the horde of foreigners that kept pouring into America's fastest growing and most promising metropolis. On the whole, then, concluded Harry Sedgwick, it would be an excellent idea if Cullen would come down to New York and look the ground over.

3

The eager Cullen, thereupon, hastened to New York. The last week in April, 1824, found him there, as may be seen from an animated letter that he wrote to Fanny on the twenty-fourth.[3] Wretched weather, on this occasion, prevented him from seeing many of the sights of the big town; but, thanks to the efforts of Harry Sedgwick and the latter's brother Robert, Cullen was ushered into the very thick of Gotham's literary society. Dining at Robert's house he met the much lionized Fenimore Cooper, whose recent novels *The Spy* (1821), *The Pioneers* (1823), and *The Pilot* (1823), appearing in sensational succession, had made him not only the most talked-of man in town, but also the most successful fictionist that the country had yet known. At the same time Cullen met a fellow Yankee, Fitz-Greene Halleck, who had been a Gothamite for more than a decade, and whose clever "Croaker Papers" and still more clever "Fanny" had made him, for the nonce, the outstanding poet of New York. Among Bob Sedgwick's other dinner guests was Robert C. Sands, whose romantic Indian poem "Yamoden" was then at the height of its brief vogue, and whose editorial activities were soon to make him and Bryant the most intimate of associates.

Cullen's chief recollection of that Sedgwick dinner appears to have been that the egotistical Mr. Cooper, made "a little giddy" by the success of his three novels, monopolized the conversation. What Bryant's first impressions of Halleck and Sands may have been we do not know.

Of other experiences on that 1824 trip to New York, Cullen thought only two worth mentioning to Fanny. One of these was a dinner with Jared Sparks, at that time publisher of the *North American Review*. The other was a game of whist in a French household, to which Cullen had been conducted by his erstwhile Great Barrington law partner, George Ives. So far as getting an editorial position was concerned, that journey to the big city was apparently fruitless.

4

Cullen was, however, far from disheartened. The sojourn in New York, despite its failure to achieve immediate results, had proved to be more of a stimulus than a disappointment. After having dined with the great Cooper and the prominent Halleck, Cullen Bryant could never again feel utterly secluded from the literary world. As surely as fate, he himself would find a metropolitan opening for his literary talents in the not-too-distant future.

Meanwhile, substantial encouragement came to him in the form of a surprisingly generous offer from Boston—not, alas, an invitation to remove to that city, but an offer to pay him the amazing stipend of two hundred dollars a year for an average contribution of a hundred lines of verse a month. The man who made the offer was Theophilus Parsons, editor of the newly established *United States Literary Gazette*. Of course Bryant eagerly accepted. Two hundred dollars per annum for his creative efforts seemed a princely sum. Before Parsons had approached him, he would have been willing to sell any poem in his desk (or in his mind) for two dollars!

Although the Parsons-Bryant contract resulted in no really distinguished pieces, William Aspenwall Bradley is probably correct in his assertion that "this year and a half constitutes the period of Bryant's greatest poetic productivity." At least twenty poems found their way into the *Gazette*—more than twice as many as had appeared in the little brown volume of 1821.

One noteworthy poem that apparently grew out of Bryant's first visit to New York is "A Forest Hymn," written in 1825. Although this stately blank-verse effort is rightly regarded as one of Bryant's most thoroughgoing nature poems, and although its thesis does not differ materially from that of "Inscription for the Entrance to a Wood," this later poem strikes one distinct note that must clearly have been inspired by one of young Bryant's most memorable early metropolitan experiences; namely, his first visit to an elaborately liturgical church. In Bryant's extant correspondence there is nothing either to verify such experience or to identify such church, but it is not far-fetched to assume that Bryant, on the very first Sunday he ever spent in a large city, might easily have been persuaded to accompany his new French acquaintances, the Evrards, to mass. It is still more probable that during his first extensive New York sight-seeing he visited St. Peter's, the venerable and imposing six-columned Roman Catholic house of worship at the southeast corner of Church and Barclay Streets. In any event, it was hardly an Episcopal church that inspired "A Forest Hymn." A visit to a church of that faith would have been no novelty to Cullen Bryant in 1825, for of course he was already familiar with St. James' at Great Barrington; and, furthermore, the Protestant Episcopal churches of that day were decidedly pallid both in liturgy and in ecclesiastical trappings. At a time when the Oxford Movement still lay a decade or two in the future; when lighted candles and vested choirs, crucifers and servers, were almost as unfamiliar to the average Anglican as to the average Puritan; when most Episcopalians spoke of their altars as "communion tables"; and when even the service at Wall Street's famed Trinity Church would have contrasted but mildly with that in any of the large New England meeting-houses—at such a time no Episcopal church in America would have given Cullen Bryant the awed feeling that he was in a great cathedral.

No, when in "A Forest Hymn" the poet speaks of "fantastic carvings" and of adoring God "among the crowd, and under roofs that . . . [men's] frail hands have raised," he is obviously thinking in terms of a Roman Catholic church thronged with worshipers at a high mass. And when, nearer the end of the poem, he speaks of "holy men who hid themselves deep in the woody wilderness, and gave their lives to thought and prayer," he is thinking in terms of Roman Catholic monks and hermits. And when, still farther on, he speaks of other holy men—"holy men who deemed it were not well to pass life thus"—he is tacitly rebuking these same monks and hermits by comparing them unfavorably with the uncloistered Protestant saints.

The main idea, however, of "A Forest Hymn" is that Nature, the supreme work of god, is infinitely nobler, mightier, and more enduring than any of the works of man—that no man-made temple, Catholic or Protestant, Christian or Jewish, Mohammedan or Buddhist, can compare in beauty and venerability and permanence and spiritual force with God's first temples, the groves.

5

By the latter part of May, 1825, Cullen Bryant was back in New York, this time to stay. Thanks largely to the kindly efforts of Henry Sedgwick and Gulian C. Verplanck, the young Yankee lawyer-poet was at last established as co-editor of a new periodical, the *New York Review and Athenaeum Magazine*. Sedgwick's roseate predictions of a year before had not been far wrong. Although the *Atlantic Magazine* had failed, here was a more promising periodical to be issued from the same press and with Anderson as senior editor. Bryant, as junior editor, was to receive the same salary as his colleague: exactly twice the five hundred dollars a year previously mentioned. And, in this connection, let it be remembered that this was Bryant's first salaried position. A stated income, however modest, naturally appeared preferable to the uncertainties of a village law practice. Moreover, Cullen was getting into an atmosphere and an occupation that he felt certain he would enjoy—and out of an atmosphere and a profession for which his dislike had long been "augmenting daily." [4]

In those first days in New York, the future must have looked as alluring to Cullen Bryant as at any time in his life. Here in the heart of human activities and esthetic interests, and poring constantly over poems and romances and critiques, he was at last completely in his element. As for the *Review and Athenaeum*, it should certainly do better and better. To start with, it had something like a thousand subscribers: five hundred in New York itself, and several hundred more in the country at large. And the magazine had few rivals. In fact, in a rapidly growing nation of ten million people, it found only three competitors to challenge its supremacy: the *Port Folio* in Philadelphia, and the *North American* and the *Literary Gazette* in Boston. True, the circulation was small, even in proportion to the population of the country; but most contributions were correspondingly cheap. The majority of native poets and romancers were only too happy to break into print at any price; and, thanks to the lack of an international copyright law, the cream of contemporary British literature could be obtained for the price of a paste-pot, a brush, and a pair of scissors.

6

When Cullen removed to New York in that spring of 1825, he left his family (consisting now of Fanny and a very small daughter Frances) back home in the Berkshires. In a city as large and growing as New York, suitable living quarters were not to be found overnight; and, besides, Gotham summers were reputedly hot and sultry. Surely during July and August the two Fannys would be much better off if they breathed the pure air of Massachusetts in preference to the stifling atmosphere of the big, congested town at the foot of Manhattan Island.

Cullen found pleasant living quarters on Chambers Street, at the boarding-house of a French emigrant named Evrard, just a few steps from Broadway. The atmosphere of the place was indeed quaint and foreign, for all of M. Evrard's family were devout Roman Catholics, and none of them spoke anything but their native tongue. What especially impressed our rural Yankee was that the Evrards were as sincere and upright as they were devout. After all, then, it appeared that a good Catholic could be as virtuous as a good Calvinist—and more cheerful about his religion. On the whole, so agreeable and obliging were the Evrards that whatever homesickness Cullen may have felt during his first weeks in New York was a yearning for his two Fannys, scarcely at all for his native Berkshires.

And the big city afforded plenty of excitement, some of it rather tragic. In letters that Cullen wrote to Fanny during the month of June, 1825, we read of a series of events scarcely to be met in the countryside of western Massachusetts. There was, for instance, the murder of a man just arrived from Switzerland, his assassins being two ruffians who had come over on the same ship with him. There was disaster to a steamboat plying between New York and New Brunswick, New Jersey: a boiler explosion which had scalded four deck-hands and had injured many of the one hundred passengers aboard. There was the brutal (and fatal) assault upon a Mr. Lambert, who had been returning from a suburban party at two o'clock in the morning. Presumably this Mr. Lambert had been a man of wealth, for his assailants had been identified as a band of drunken apprentices. As for New York summer weather, it was torrid. Night and day the mercury scarcely dropped below eighty degrees.

Were airings in the country ever possible to a dweller in a huge town like New York? Why, yes; only the other day Cullen had called at a livery-stable, rented a nag, and ridden away up the island, far beyond the well-nigh suburban Canal Street. There was, however, one serious trouble with country roads on Manhattan Island, especially in summer. What with innumerable barouches, carts, chaises, hacks, and horseback riders, there was an incessantly stifling cloud of dust. Actually, the countryside adjacent to New York was more disagreeable than the congested city itself.[5]

7

The New York of 1825 was indeed a fascinating town—a town of great substance and still greater promise. Five years earlier the decennial Federal census had credited it with the impressive population of 123,706, a good thirteen thousand more than that of its nearest rival, Philadelphia. By 1825, with a population of at least 150,000, it outstripped the Quaker city still further. And this did not include the eight or ten thousand souls in the thriving village of Brooklyn, which lay only fifteen or twenty minutes' ride away by steam ferry. Already the ambitious metropolis, starting at Battery Park at the southern tip of Manhattan Island, had pushed its built-up portions northward to Canal Street, so that it was even then threatening to encroach upon that sequestered rural retreat, Greenwich Village. Why, in another quarter of a century, declared the proud citizens, the huge town would cover half the island. What if the old aristocracy—the Bleeckers, the Knickerbockers, the Roosevelts, the Stuyvesants, and the Van Cortlandts—still clung to their trim red brick mansions down by the Bowling Green? What if the fashionable shops still remained on meandering Maiden Lane, off Broadway below Fulton Street? The town sprawled inexorably northward. And the time was surely approaching when its most elegant districts, both business and residential, would be far uptown.

Great as were the natural advantages of the young metropolis, it owed its growth still more to a group of bold, resourceful business leaders—men like Jacob Barker, the banker; John Hone, the auctioneer; Stephen Jumel, the wine merchant; David Lydig, the flour factor; Nathaniel Paine, the money lender; John Robins, the draper; and a score of others. Anyone who stood or sauntered near the corner of Wall and Water Streets at about the noon hour on almost any week-day could see such men entering the Tontine Coffee House for "a chunk of raw codfish and a glass of spirits," [6] a friendly half hour of business gossip, and an informal mapping out of plans to make a great town even greater.

Most colorful among the group would be Philip Hone and John Jacob Astor. Hone, the auctioneer's younger brother and erstwhile business partner, newly elected mayor (in 1826), was known as the town's chief social lion, the man who entertained and dined out with more of the illustrious and the elite than any other New Yorker. Astor, far less stylish and suave than Hone, but far wealthier, was the German immigrant boy who, after years of trading Western furs for China silks and teas, had risen to the position of America's richest man—even richer than old Steve Girard of Philadelphia. And the entrance to the Tontine Coffee House was by no means the only place where the saunterer could glimpse the fascinating Hone and the fabulous Astor to good advantage. Both Hone and Astor loved to ride horseback, and both of them had a penchant for doing their riding in the main thoroughfares. During Bryant's first years in the metropolis, New York knew no more familiar sight than tall, spare, handsome, courtly Philip Hone galloping up and down Broadway, always on a spirited horse. Scarcely less familiar was the squat, rotund Astor cantering along more leisurely on a much more docile nag. And although Astor was no less fond than Hone of disporting himself on lower Broadway, the former liked also to ride farther afield. Often he would gallop for miles through the countryside, well beyond Greenwich Village, his "eyes alert for a 'For Sale' sign on some likely patch of farmland"; for John Jacob Astor, far more than any of his contemporaries, was alive to the marvelous possibilities of speculation in Manhattan real estate and within another score of years this "Landlord of New York" was to realize even greater returns from his building lots than from his furs and silks and teas.

A town with such nabobs was bound also to be a town of showy mansions—mansions "stiffly furnished with high buffets, high-backed, hair-bottomed chairs and family portraits, and silver trays with cordials for morning callers." [7] As one scans the pages of that most captivating social document, Philip Hone's *Diary* (1828-1851), one conjures a Gotham bon-ton in which people lived luxuriously and entertained lavishly. One reads of dwellings "furnished and fitted up in a style of the utmost magnificence— painted ceilings, gilded moldings, rich satin ottomans, curtains in the last Parisian taste, and splendid mirrors"; of confectioners and cooks and decorators who were "accomplished *artistes*" and who vied with one another, "each in his vocation," to produce "the *ne plus ultra*"; of quadrilles that began at nine o'clock in the evening and lasted till the wee hours of the morning; of masqueraders in magnificent, lustrous costumes that were "well conceived and supported with wit and address." [8]

8

But the New York of those days, for all its pride and its elegant bon-ton, was hardly on the whole a city of beauty. Upon its narrow, crooked, ill-cobbled streets lay heaps of refuse amid which stray cats, stray curs, and stray pigs burrowed and prowled almost to their hearts' content. At night its street corners were feebly lighted by rusty, flickering whale-oil lamps, and its citizens were ineffectually guarded and guided by a scanty band of surly, oafish constables uniformed in clumsy capes and comical leather caps.

9

Cullen Bryant, however, found old New York to be a jovial and a hospitable town. Dropping in at the Bread and Cheese Club, in the tap-room of the Washington Hotel, on Broadway between Chambers and Reade Streets, he was certain to find some of the Gothamites with whom he loved to chat: authors, actors, painters, lawyers, men-about-town. Perhaps the bumptious Fenimore Cooper would be there, or the clever Fitz-Greene Halleck, or the versatile William Dunlap, or the esthetic Samuel F. B. Morse (whose marvelous telegraph, a score of years later, was to make people forget his deftness with brush and palette). Seated at little tables that stood on the well-sanded tavern floor, most of them would be enjoying their church-warden pipes and their jugs of rum punch; and all of them would have fascinating topics of conversation. As for Cullen Bryant, he delighted in the sociability and the talk, but he cared for neither the tobacco nor the rum punch. No prude or Pharisee was he—otherwise he would have shunned the Bread and Cheese Club—but tobacco irritated his lungs, and rum punch irritated his stomach. Port and sherry, always in moderate quantities, were his drinks.

Even more fascinating for Bryant than his visits to the Bread and Cheese Club, if much less frequent, were his evenings at the theater. In those days the two prominent theaters of New York were the Park and the Bowery, which vied in offering the best theatrical fare in America. To the Park during Bryant's first winter in the metropolis came a young tragedian who, despite his exceedingly tender age, was to take New York by storm. That tragedian was a big, robustious, deep-voiced twenty-year-old boy named Edwin Forrest. Already a sensation in his home town of Philadelphia, young Forrest was to prove to Manhattan that his success in the Quaker City had been no fluke. The occasion for Forrest's New York debut was a benefit performance for an old trouper named Jacob Woodhull. The role played by Forrest was that of Othello. The triumph of the youthful Thespian was as profound as it was immediate. Old Woodhull himself, seated in the front of the house, exclaimed, "By God, the boy has made a hit!" [9] Cullen Bryant must have been in the audience that night, for he would hardly have missed so important a theatrical event as the sensational young Forrest's maiden appearance in New York. If Cullen was in the house, he undoubtedly echoed Woodhull's enthusiastic sentiments, if not quite the old trouper's words. The following autumn Forrest returned to New York, this time to play an extended engagement at the Bowery in a repertoire that included the role in which he had taken the town by storm eight or nine months before. It was apparently during this later engagement that Bryant and Forrest became intimate friends. For a quarter of a century this friendship was to last, and then it was to be broken by Forrest's outrageous treatment of his wife, the talented and adorable Catherine Sinclair.

10

Cullen's most intimate friends during those early New York days were his editorial colleagues, Henry J. Anderson and Robert C. Sands. Especially congenial did he find Sands, whose flow of wit was constantly driving dull care away. Often at week-ends Sands would invite Bryant to accompany him to the Sands parental home, which lay in the pleasant village of Hoboken, just across the Hudson from the upper reaches of the big city. Here they would compose many of their original contributions to the magazine, and often during those composings the Sands house "would ring with eloquent declamations and roars of uproarious laughter." [10]

11

As time went on, the editors of the *Review* encountered ever increasing discouragements. It was not that the magazine lacked either a respectable clientele or worthy contributors. The best and most influential people in New York made up the bulk of the subscription list, and the most promising young authors in the country submitted manuscripts. Among the latter were Richard Henry Dana, already an outstanding member of the Boston literary set; Nathaniel Parker Willis, a facile and versatile young scribbler if ever there was one; George Bancroft, a New England youth with a flair for presenting historical subjects with both charm and distinction; and Henry Wadsworth Longfellow, a precocious and exceptionally promising versifier who, although but recently graduated from an obscure little college up in the woods of Maine, already bade fair to become one of the most winsome singers of the age.

No, the difficulties encompassing the *Review and Athenaeum* were of a more material nature. In the first place, its subscription list, like that of any other magazine of the day, was pathetically small. In the second place, subscribers were often dilatory in making remittances. In the third place, advertising—the financial backbone of every successful periodical of later days—had as yet been almost unthought-of.

12

Cullen Bryant, realizing the precarious position of the *Review*

[87]

and Athenaeum, sought other employment—employment which, while not interfering with his editorial labors, would add a little to his modest stipend and, at the same time, prevent the danger of his one day finding himself entirely without a livelihood.

In this connection, we find him lecturing on poetry under the auspices of the Athenaeum Society, and on Greek and Roman mythology under the auspices of the newly formed National Academy of Arts and Design. And since these lecturings could bring him no better than a mere pittance, we find him doing one thing that must have been distasteful to him in the extreme: obtaining a permit to practice law in the city courts of New York and actually assisting Henry Sedgwick in at least one case.

13

One day early in the summer of 1826, remuneration came to Cullen Bryant in a much larger and more dependable way—remuneration that would free him permanently from worry over the imminent demise of his magazine. Seated at his desk on a pleasant mid-June morning in 1826, sniffing wistfully at a bouquet of pink roses that he had brought from M. Evrard's garden, he found himself suddenly accosted by a nervous, excited young man. The youth was a Mr. Coleman, from the office of a leading local newspaper, the *Evening Post,* who bore the tidings that his father, William Coleman, editor-in-chief of the paper, had just been seriously injured in an accident. The elder Mr. Coleman, it appeared, had been out riding in his gig and had been spilled in a runaway. His injuries were painful, perhaps dangerous; in any event, he would be confined to his room for many days, maybe many weeks. Under the circumstances, would Mr. Bryant be so obliging as to assist temporarily as editor of the *Post?* His work on the *Post* would in no way interfere with his magazine editorship.

The sudden offer rendered Cullen almost as breathless as the perturbed young man who had made it. Finally, when Cullen had collected his thoughts and mobilized his words, he promised the visitor that within one hour's time he would come to the office of the *Post* and report personally his acceptance or rejection of the generous offer. Thereupon young Mr. Coleman, mumbling some confused words to the effect that he hoped Mr. Bryant would decide to accept, departed almost as hastily as he had come.

Hardly was young Coleman out of sight when Cullen Bryant

seized his beaver hat and walking-stick, stepped out of his office, and carefully locked the door behind him. Quickly had he decided that the man from whom to seek advice was Gulian Verplanck. Gulian was eight years Cullen's senior, was an exceptionally level-headed man, and knew Manhattan from A to izzard. Gulian could tell whether the *Post* offer was a desirable one, and his counsel would be as forthright as it would be intelligent.

Cullen, threading his way northward, with briskly nervous steps, along busy Broadway, tried to analyze the situation a little further. Frankly, he told himself, he had never aspired to a position on a daily newspaper. Newspapers were mostly prose and politics; and he was fond of neither. Thievery, fraud, robbery, assault, homicide; fire, explosion, runaway; slander, adultery, divorce; allegation and counter-allegation, of and about time-serving and venal public men! Why, these were the very things with which he had been surfeited in his practice at Great Barrington. And in a great cosmopolitan town such as New York they would be intensified a hundredfold. Even at this very moment a dirty, ragged, shrill-voiced urchin of about fourteen was trying to thrust into his hand a morning paper, in which he could "read all about the scandal in Beaver Street."

But the earnest young Mr. Coleman had impressed Cullen Bryant very favorably—had flattered Cullen's sense of dignity and importance by coming to see him in person instead of sending a messenger boy. And, besides, Cullen was at this precarious time in no position to look a gift-horse in the mouth. Up at Great Barrington he had had security at least—security for himself and for his growing family. Down here in New York, even so recently as half an hour ago, he had seemed threatened with disaster.

Over a glass of wine at the Bread and Cheese Club, Verplanck unhesitatingly advised Bryant to accept young Coleman's offer. The *Evening Post,* he reminded Bryant, had been functioning successfully for a quarter of a century, and it had always succeeded in maintaining the prestige that its founder, the great Alexander Hamilton, had given it at its very inception. Unquestionably it was the newspaper of the influential class in New York. As for its financial profits, Verplanck happened to know that they amounted to about thirty thousand dollars a year,[11] surely a handsome sum indeed. And a temporary position on the *Post* would in no way interfere with Bryant's editorship of the *Review and*

Athenaeum. Why, ever since Bryant had come to New York he had wished that he might have fewer idle hours and more dollars.

14

And so Cullen Bryant, on that pleasant June day of 1826, hung up his beaver hat and walking-stick and found a desk in the office of the New York *Evening Post.* Although he could not have dreamed it at the time, he was not to see the last of that desk for more than half a century.

What stipend Bryant drew originally from the *Post* we do not know, but we have several evidences that it was a lucrative one. In the first place, having become convinced that he could now afford to keep his two Fannys in New York, he went back to Great Barrington to get them at the earliest opportunity. In the second place, the final demise of the *Review* in October, 1827, evoked scarcely a murmur of regret from him. In the third place, within a score of months after he had taken the *Post* position he was defending his decision with an enthusiasm the genuineness of which cannot be doubted. Writing on February 16, 1828, to his good friend Dana, who had expressed regret at his having taken up anything so prosaic as newspaper work, he had replied: "I do not like politics any better than you do; but they get only my mornings, and you know politics and a belly-full are better than poetry and starvation." [12]

From the start, Bryant was virtually editor-in-chief of the *Evening Post;* for Coleman never completely recovered from the runaway accident. And when Coleman died, in mid-July, 1829, Bryant became editor in name as well as in fact.

15

Although Bryant still loved the muses as dearly as ever, his grasp of politics had become so thorough that he was admirably qualified for his newspaper editorship. At the promptings of the Sedgwicks, he had read Adam Smith's *Wealth of Nations* and David Ricardo's *Principles of Political Economy and Taxation,* and thereby he had become convinced that both he and the *Post* had been wrong about some of their economic views. Particularly was this true of the tariff. Dear to the Federalist hearts of Alexander Hamilton and William Coleman and Peter Bryant had been a high protective tariff; but now Cullen Bryant had reached the conclusion that high protection was an abomination to everyone but the plutocratic industrialist, an everlasting burden upon the consumer, a pregnant cause of friction between nations.

Bryant thus came to identify himself and the *Post* more and more with that group of Jeffersonian Republicans who leaned leftward and who called themselves Democrats. To these liberals, headed by that bluff frontiersman, General Andrew Jackson, almost everything connected with the incumbent administration in Washington was anathema. The high tariff, however, was by no means their only aversion. Quite as much did they detest the Bank of the United States, which they said was like the tariff in that it aided the rich industrialists at the expense of the laborers and the farmers. Then, too, the administration was constantly asking for Federal funds with which to build roads and canals—projects which ought to be taken care of by the several states. As for President John Quincy Adams himself, what was he but a Boston-Harvard aristocrat whose sympathies were all with the privileged class? Moreover, Adams's election in 1824 had been the most tainted in the history of the republic. Far from having had a majority of the electoral votes, Adams had run well behind Jackson; and had not the unprincipled Henry Clay venally released his votes to Adams, Jackson would now be President.

About Jackson's chief supporters, Bryant undoubtedly had his misgivings. John C. Calhoun and William H. Crawford were Southerners—with irritating Southern prejudices—and, besides, Calhoun was a bit shifty, and Crawford was tactless and dogmatic. Martin Van Buren, the squire of Kinderhook, was a good New Yorker; but, so far as President Adams's abominable policies were concerned, Van Buren had blown hot and cold in the Senate. On the whole, however, Calhoun and Crawford and Van Buren all espoused the kind of liberalism that Bryant and the *Post* chose to sponsor. And however much a refined gentleman might deplore Andrew Jackson's manners and diction and spelling, the fact remained that the old Indian fighter and hero of New Orleans was the consummate champion of the people.

16

A concrete example of Bryant's defense of the common man is afforded by an event that occurred in the spring of 1836. In May of that year twenty-one New York journeyman tailors banded together for the purpose of obtaining higher wages. The move was indeed a bold one; for in those days trade unions were few and feeble and isolated. No single group had ever been organized upon more than a local scale, and there was little interrelation of groups representing the different trades. The first single group to organize successfully and permanently on a national scale would be the locomotive engineers, whose Brotherhood was effected in 1860. The American Federation of Labor would not become a going concern till 1881. Even in the 1820's and 1830's, however, labor was trying repeatedly, if sporadically, to get organized. In 1827, for instance, some workmen in Philadelphia, largely carpenters, had formed the Mechanics' Union of Trade Associations. This union had lasted barely two years, but it had given rise to other unions, most notably the New York Trades Union, formed in 1833, and the National Trades Union (which was far from truly national) in 1834. All such organizations proved to be short-lived, for influential public opinion was strongly against them.

What the "better element" thought of these organizations may be seen from Philip Hone's comments on the twenty-one refractory New York journeyman tailors. Writing in his *Diary* for June 6, 1836, Hone dilates scathingly "on the spirit of faction and contempt of the laws" evidenced in "the conduct of the journeyman tailors, instigated by a set of vile foreigners (principally English), who, unable to endure the restraints of wholesome law, well administered in their own country, take refuge here, establish trades-unions, and vilify Yankee judges and juries," and he goes on to rejoice that "twenty-odd of these were convicted . . . of a conspiracy to raise their wages and to prevent any of the craft from working at prices less than those for which they struck." [13]

But Cullen Bryant, convinced that the tailors had a genuine grievance, was not to be cowed, even by the most influential men in New York—men in a position to damage seriously the prestige and the circulation of his paper. Writing in an *Evening Post* editorial he demanded, "Can anything be imagined more abhorrent to every sentiment of generosity and justice, than the law which arms the rich with the legal right to fix, by assize, the wages of the poor? If this is not slavery, we have forgotten its definition. Strike the right of associating for the sale of labor from the privi-

leges of a freeman, and you may as well bind him to a master, or
ascribe him to the soil." [14]

17

Not quite always, however, did Cullen Bryant side with the
radicals. When Fanny Wright lectured in New York in 1829, Bryant derided her in one of the very few satirical poems of his
career. Miss Wright, a brilliant but eccentric young Scotch woman
who had steeped herself in the writings of such revolutionary
philosophers as Helvetius and William Godwin, went from rostrum to rostrum championing all sorts of unconventional isms:
atheism, Owenism, Abolitionism, racial equality, women's rights,
the "Dirty Shirt Party," and "moral" (as opposed to "legal") marriage. She was, moreover, as unconventional in deportment and
outward person as in the things that she advocated. Her short
hair, her sensationally mannish garb and gait and gestures, and
her oratorical propensity—in an age when no ladylike "female"
would take to the public platform—did quite as much as her radical views to evoke the wrath of decorous people wherever she
appeared.

Bryant, wisely deciding to be amused rather than angry with
this Caledonian virago, paid his respects to her in a few sprightly
tetrameter couplets in the *Evening Post* of January 29, 1829:

> *Thou wonder of the age, from whom*
> *Religion waits her final doom,*
> *Her quiet death, her euthanasia,*
> *Thou in whose eloquence and bloom*
> *The age beholds a new Aspasia!*
> .   .   .   .
>
> *O 'tis a glorious sight for us,*
> *The gaping throng, to see thee thus*
> *The light of dawning truth dispense,*
> *While Colonel Stone, the learn'd and brave,*
> *The press's Atlas, mild but grave,*
> *Hangs on the words that leave thy mouth,*
> *Slaking his intellectual drougth,*
> *In that rich stream of eloquence,*
> *And notes thy teachings, to repeat*
> *Their wisdom in his classic sheet. . . .*

Incidentally, the Colonel Stone in the foregoing lines, as we shall very soon observe, was a rival editor for whom Cullen Bryant had little admiration. Bryant's ode to Fanny Wright must have won the hearty approval of every conservative gentleman in New York, including the meticulous Philip Hone. Hardly, however, did it stamp Bryant as a "Lost Leader," a renegade from the ranks of the liberals. For as Mr. W. E. Woodward, one of the most liberal of our present-day historians, declares, the rabid Fanny Wright "seems to have been crackbrained, to say the least, and she may have been definitely insane." [15] Cullen Bryant, like every other sane progressive, naturally objected to having progressivism brought into disrepute by lunatic devotees.

18

Bryant, in promulgating his liberal political views, had a vigorous, aggressive lieutenant in the person of William Leggett. Called to the office of the *Evening Post* upon the death of William Coleman, young Leggett, then in his twenty-eighth year, brought with him a dynamic personality and, withal, a remarkable background of experience for one of his youth. Leggett was no novice in journalism, for he had served the *Morning Chronicle* as well as a short-lived weekly called the *Critic*. More interesting, however, was the fact that he had knocked about a great deal, both on land and on sea. Erstwhile a midshipman in the navy, he had found naval discipline intolerable and had turned to the freedom of frontier life on the prairies of Illinois. His varied experiences had inspired him to write tales and verses—none of which, however, had been conspicuously meritorious or successful.

Returning to his native city of New York, young Leggett quickly became an editorialist whose writings were the envy of his friends and the terror of his enemies. Fearless, irascible, pugnacious, and uncompromisingly democratic, he wielded both the rapier of satire and the cudgel of outright denunciation. To hostile editors' charges that every *Evening Post* leader began with a stale joke and ended with a fresh lie, Leggett responded with such picturesque epithets as "detestable caitiff," "craven wretch," "hireling slave," "blustering, bullying sheet." [16] No wonder the newspaper readers of New York declared William Leggett to be possessed of every qualification of a good journalist except moderation and discretion!

19

Strangely enough, however, it was Cullen Bryant, not William Leggett, who became a party to the most spectacular altercation involving an *Evening Post* representative since the days of Alexander Hamilton.

It happened on a mild April morning in 1831. For some time before that memorable morning, the *Post's* particular *bete noire* had been the violently anti-Jackson New York *Commercial Advertiser,* which was edited by the able but dogmatic and pugnacious William Leete Stone.

Except for disagreements over Fanny Wright, except for the ever torrid controversial issue of President Andrew Jackson, and except for the fact that both Bryant and Stone had rather quick tempers, there was no very good reason why the two should have quarreled violently. Of approximately the same age and of similar New England Calvinistic background,[17] the two men shared many commendable views in common. For example, Stone was as much opposed to slavery as Bryant; and Stone, like Bryant, had championed such liberal causes as Greek independence, and such decent causes as honest municipal government, improved living and working conditions, and the proper kind of civic pride. But Stone, who had spent all of his working years in newspaper offices, probably looked resentfully upon Bryant as an upstart in the journalistic field. And Stone was a dyed-in-the-wool Federalist who refused to recognize the patent fact that the Federalist party, as a national influence, had been dead for fifteen years. To him there was only one thing more utterly vile than Jeffersonianism; and that was Jacksonianism. In editorial after editorial he ferociously abused the bluff frontiersman in the Executive Mansion. Finally he went so far as to declare that no gentleman would or could support the coarse, crude, profane, gambling, duelling blatherskite from the back country of Tennessee.

This last declaration was too much for Bryant. Arming himself the next morning with a cowhide whip, which he carefully concealed under his coat, he set forth for the office of the *Post*. On his way, as he had anticipated, he met Stone, whose path usually crossed his as the two were *en route* to their respective offices to begin their day's work. The meeting occurred on Broadway, opposite City Hall Park, and directly in front of the residence of former Mayor Philip Hone. Some heated words were exchanged. Perhaps Bryant demanded to know whether Stone did not consider him a gentleman. Perhaps Stone, forgetting the moral precepts of his pious ministerial father, had replied that he considered Bryant a deity-cursed male offspring of a feminine canine. In any event, Bryant quickly unsheathed his cowhide whip and rained blow after blow upon his astounded insulter.

The thrashing was not of long duration. Stone was much the larger, stronger man of the two, and as soon as he had recovered from his astonishment he lost no time in wresting the whip from the hands of his furious assailant. The crowd that had gathered as if by magic broke up the very fight that it had come to witness. Of course no constable appeared on the scene of action; New York constables in those days rather consistently managed to be several blocks away from any first-class fracas.

The next day, in the columns of the *Post,* Bryant apologized for the impetuous manner in which he had taken the law of libel into his own hands. He could not refrain from adding, however, that Stone had given him "gross provocation." [18]

PARK ROW, NEW YORK CITY, 1831

CHAPTER VII

Realms That Lie Afar

1

THE NEW YORK *Evening Post,* during the early years of Bryant's editorship, grew steadily both in size and in prestige. To one who thumbs through its yellowed files today, it looks small and thin and quaint; for, a century ago, it never boasted more than four pages to the issue, and not until Bryant had been editor for almost a decade was its page widened from six columns to seven. Among its contemporaries, however, it was one of the great metropolitan papers, quantitatively as well as qualitatively. Its headlines, all of them amazingly small to the twentieth-century eye, tended to stress local events; for prior to the coming of the telegraph, the only really fresh news was perforce local. And many of those old headlines look strangely inexpressive to us. For instance, CONFUSION AMONG THE JUDGES means little to us until we read that at ten o'clock on a certain morning, six New York city courts attempted to meet in four rooms. FOUL AFFAIR AT SEA is equally vague until we read that the mate of a certain brig at sea had thrown a sailor overboard. CASE OF MME. RESTEL means nothing to us; to New York readers of a century ago it meant an account of new developments in a notorious murder case. FIRES— A CHILD BURNED TO DEATH is, on the other hand, exceptionally and painfully expressive.

But discriminating newspaper readers of little old New York and its wide sphere of influence liked the *Evening Post*. Even when they disagreed with its editorial opinions, they respected its frankness and integrity, as well as the fact that it was the most decorous of all New York daily journals. By 1834 the paper could boast of a circulation well over two thousand, and a quarter of a century thereafter it could point proudly to a fivefold increase over that figure. Indeed, by the beginning of the Civil War some twenty thousand copies of the *Evening Post* were being issued daily. And although even this last figure looks modest compared to the seventy-seven thousand claimed by the cheaper, more sensational New York *Herald*, it suggests two impressive facts: in the first place, the *Post* circulation increased tenfold within a third of a century; in the second place, the *Post* always catered to the best element, the most intelligent and judicious readers.

In those days the New York *Evening Post* did not grow rich in advertising. No newspaper did. If the old headlines were relatively small, the old advertisements were even smaller. Display "ads" were undreamed-of, and retail shops almost never advertised. Fifteen or sixteen short columns encompassed the entire advertising in an average issue, and the reader who bothered to scan those columns found quaint information about such diverse activities and commodities as auctions, lotteries, St. Croix rum, and Negro wenches.[1]

As for advertising rates, they were unbelievably low, even for the slightness of the advertising. In the early years of Bryant's connection with the *Post*, regular daily advertisers were paying a flat rate of forty dollars a year, regardless of the number of words used.[2]

2

Despite all this, both the *Post* and Bryant prospered. What with cheap labor and cheap materials, the overhead was so small that the few cents charged for each copy of the paper constituted a real profit, regardless of any advertising. In 1829, the year that Cullen became editor-in-chief, his one-eighth share brought him an income of thirteen hundred dollars. In 1834 his one-third share yielded almost forty-seven hundred.[3] And in the 1830's a stipend of forty-seven hundred dollars a year was indeed princely. Hardly a score of men in all New York were doing better.

No wonder Cullen and his growing family—consisting now of baby Julia as well as the two Fannys—moved to more and more fashionable quarters. No longer would the modest boarding-house of M. Evrard do. For a time the Bryants lived in a handsome brick house on Hudson Street, with a pleasant garden of roses and sweetpeas, nasturtiums and hollyhocks. Later they removed to a handsomer brick house on Varick Street, just below Canal, with a pleasanter garden of more fragrance and color and variety. And ere long they were ensconced in a mansion on Carmine Street, away uptown among the nabobs of Greenwich Village.

3

These constant raisings of the Bryant standard of living ate but little into the mounting income. Finer mansions might demand costlier carpets and draperies and furniture. Dinners might become more lavish, clothes more numerous and elegant, and trips to the theater and the opera more frequent. But still the Bryant balance at the bank grew apace.

And with the wherewithal to travel, Cullen yearned to see far more of the world than the pathetically few miles that he had traversed. Rural Massachusetts and metropolitan New York were all very well; but, after all, they constituted but a tiny nook in the habitable globe. Strolling at the Battery or at the foot of Rector Street on a fine summer evening, Cullen would gaze fascinatedly at the incoming and outgoing ships that flew the flags of a score or two of nations. Sloops, brigs, whalers, swift clippers, and now even an ocean-going steamboat or two, they carried varied folk and varied cargoes to and from a thousand exotic ports, almost any one of which the affluent Cullen Bryant could now afford to visit. Especially did he grow wistful as he noticed the Union Jack of Great Britain and the tricolor of France. The ships flying those flags would take one to the places that seemed richest in historical and literary lore. And Cullen Bryant, being a modern young man, thought that a trans-oceanic voyage by steamboat would be the greatest thrill of all. The graceful clippers were surely fleet, but, just as surely, the time was soon coming when the steamers would outstrip even them in speed. Only a few years ago—in '27, to be exact—the Dutch steamship *Curacoa,* using steam power and none other, had traversed the four thousand miles between Antwerp and Paramaribo in a mere month; and now there was talk of a still greater, faster steamboat, the *Royal William,* which would soon be launched in Montreal for swift passage to England. Yes, Cullen Bryant must take a long voyage one of these days. Had not Peter Bryant visited Africa in days when travel was much more difficult than now?

4

But Cullen did not go abroad posthaste. There were too many obstacles, too many complications, too many special considerations militating against an immediate voyage. In those days, when the crossing from New York to Liverpool was a matter of weeks instead of days, one did not go to Europe for a mere summer; one planned to remain abroad for at least a year or two. And a year or two was a long time to be away from one's home and one's office. If the children had been several years older, the entire family might have made the trip to the advantage of all concerned, but now little Fanny and little Julia were quite too young sprouts to be transplanted, even temporarily. As for the affairs of the *Evening Post,* could William Leggett carry on without his superior for even twelve months? Might not that impetuous young man, left for so long to his own devices, ruin the fair name of the paper by some act of characteristic rashness?

On sober second thought, would not a much shorter trip—a trip within the bounds of one's own country—be more desirable at this time? After all, there was little enough of the United States that Cullen Bryant had yet seen. Philadelphia, Baltimore, and the whole region south of the Potomac, as well as the great Western frontier country, were all virgin soil to him. Throughout the summer and autumn of 1831, Cullen pondered much upon these obvious facts.

5

The result was that in February, 1832, Bryant paid a ten days' visit to the young capital city, Washington. Of his reactions to that strange town he has told us very little, but he must certainly have noticed two especial things about it: first, its striking contrast to the older, more metropolitan New York and Boston; secondly, its own amazing self-contradictions.

Here was a village (or a group of villages) whose thirty thousand inhabitants were spread rather unevenly over an expanse of a hundred square miles. (The Federal government had not yet given back to the state of Virginia the territory on the south side of the Potomac.) It was a city of broad and long and numerous streets and relatively few buildings; a city where swamps and red mud were more in evidence than lawns or gardens or cobblestone pavements; a city whose stately Capitol and dignified white Executive Mansion stood in startling juxtaposition with the squat brick dwellings of government clerks and the squalid wooden hovels of Negro laborers; a city where all the thoroughfares were as straight as taut strings, but where some of them followed the points of the compass and others radiated from the Capitol or the President's house like the spokes of two gigantic wheels; a city whose rustic little shops and stores were more suggestive of Great Barrington than of New York.

Cullen seems to have been far more interested in the social and political life of Washington than in its physical appearance. Writing to his brother John, then located in Illinois, he tells the reader that Washington—presumably in contrast to New York—is a simple, Spartan, early-to-bed community, whose fashionable balls begin at eight and break up at eleven, and where refreshments are light and late suppers are unknown. As for President Jackson, Cullen finds him a sensible old gentleman of "agreeable" manners. And Cullen goes on to relate that while in Washington he "heard a few words from most of the distinguished men in Congress, but no speeches of length or importance." [4]

6

Cullen's next trip, made some three months later, took him much farther afield. Two of his brothers having recently migrated to Illinois, and having become extremely enthusiastic about the rich soil and glowing future of that new commonwealth, Cullen himself felt the urge to see the great West. Not only would it afford a pleasant relief from the dirty, crowded, noisy metropolis; it would mean novel and exciting modes of travel. The long journey by stage across the Appalachians to Pittsburgh would be succeeded by still longer journeys by steamboats thence to Cairo and St. Louis, and a short stage journey from St. Louis to Jacksonville, in those days the chief town of Illinois. It would, indeed, mean ten days or perhaps a fortnight "on the move."

Especially beautiful would be the stage journey across the

Pennsylvania mountains, which, at this season of the year, would be gorgeous with tender forest verdure offset by flaming redbud and snowy dogwood. Scarcely less beautiful—and, in many ways, much more fascinating and novel—would be the long voyage down the Ohio in one of those "floating palaces" which, within barely a decade, had completely revolutionized travel in the great interior of the country. And at no roadside inn were Ohio and Mississippi steamboat voyagers compelled to pause for rest or refreshment. By night they slept comfortably in ornate staterooms; by day they breakfasted, dined, and supped sumptuously in a magnificent "social hall," or regaled themselves on the spacious deck with the ever-changing panoroma of luxuriant woodland, lush bottom land, green pasture, brown ploughed field, placid village, and bustling new city. Meanwhile the huge paddle-wheels sped them incessantly on and on, often at a rate as high as fifteen to eighteen miles an hour; for paddle-wheels, unlike horses, never wearied. Wheeling, Marietta, Parkersburg; Gallipolis, Ashland, Portsmouth; New Albany, Owensboro, Evansville! Although these village names on the new maps bore no such historic associations as Salem or Norwich or Morristown or Princeton, they were none-the-less names to conjure with. To Cullen Bryant they suggested, in particular, strange new human types: sweating wharf-hands, curious loiterers, industrious woodsmen bringing fuel for the boat. And many of these, no doubt, would be clad in outmoded coonskin caps and moccasins and leggins, in linsey-woolsey breeches and jackets.

But no longer was the great West all raw frontier. In these progressive, aspiring 1830's no river voyager ventured many hundred miles into the interior without passing or putting in at some city of amazing growth and rare promise. There was, for instance, Cincinnati, whose population had expanded in twenty years from a scant two thousand to an impressive twenty-five thousand, and which already quite equaled Richmond and Charleston in size and importance. Nor was the importance of Cincinnati merely commercial; already, thanks to the influence of such men as Timothy Flint, James Hall, and Hiram Powers, the young "Queen City of the West" was becoming devoted to some of the "finer things of life." Farther downstream there was the thriving city of Louisville, which, if considerably smaller and less impressive than Cincinnati, was just as ambitious and perhaps as promising. And at the end of the river voyage there would be the old French town of St. Louis, quaint and foreign, yet modern and American and energetic—in many ways the most interesting of them all.

Cullen made his memorable Western trip in May, 1832. At the end of the journey he found his Illinois brothers, Arthur and John, as hale and hearty and enthusiastic as their letters had indicated. Already they were full of plans to unite the entire Bryant family in the great prairie country. Poor Austin! how foolish he was to cling to the old place back at Cummington, trying to eke a decent living from that rocky Massachusetts soil that God had never made for agriculture. At the earliest opportunity he must sell or rent, and bring his mother west with him. Wiry, alert Sally —bless her heart!—was by no means too old to be transplanted; in fact, her declining years would be healthier and happier in the dry climate of Illinois than in the humid, catarrh-ridden Westfield valley. And Cyrus must be pried away from his school-mastering job at Northampton—which, like school-mastering jobs in general, offered neither lucre nor promise. If Cy must continue to teach, there were plenty of uninstructed urchins here in Illinois, and many more of them were coming in every year. And if Cullen himself would come, the whole family would be reunited— all except poor dear young sister Sarah, who had died eight years ago, soon after her marriage to the estimable Mr. Shaw.

Well, what about it, Cullen? Of course Arthur and John realized that Cullen was the big man, the conspicuously successful man, of the family—editor-in-chief of a leading newspaper in the greatest city in America. True, Illinois had no great newspapers, no great cities. But Illinois, with her opulent soil, her splendid waterways, and her broad and level domain, was humming and teeming with promise. Why, up at the foot of Lake Michigan, on the site of Fort Dearborn, lay a bustling village with a manifestly tremendous destiny—a little place called Chicago. Far-seeing sages declared that the very location of Chicago assured it of being a great metropolis tomorrow—perhaps the equal of Boston or Philadelphia or even New York!

But Cullen smilingly shook his head in response to his brothers' ardent pleadings. Poet of nature though he might be, dear, sordid, clamorous New York had got into his blood. Blue skies and boundless green fields were all very well as a respite and a retreat. To a man of the world, however, libraries and lectures and theaters and concerts, to say nothing of the everlasting human stream along Broadway, were indispensable. And one who had strolled in the Battery on fine summer evenings could never long be happy without sight of strange foreign ships and strange foreign faces. Frankly, Cullen Bryant had become so incorrigibly metropolitan that he could never quite appreciate the Illinois of 1832.

Buy land in Illinois? Well, possibly. Bureau County, where the Bryant brothers had settled, was unquestionably rich in bituminous coal deposits, and within barely a decade its farmers had made it one of the most productive corn and wheat regions in all the great West. But if Cullen decided to buy land there, it would be only as an investment, not at all with a view to migrating thither.

Touring wide expanses of the Illinois country on horseback, Cullen found what he had expected to find: a huge, rich, raw frontier region whose limitless expanses of grass-grown plains and opulence of wild flowers and wild life accentuated the relative paucity of trees and human habitations. Woods and villages, the former mostly scrubby, the latter small and mean, hugged the banks of the rivers; and the intervening open country appeared stupendous. Well, pondered Cullen, here was a commonwealth whose fifty-six thousand square miles lacked a scant ten thousand of equaling all New England, yet whose one hundred sixty thousand scattered inhabitants comprised a smaller population than that of tiny Manhattan Island. Only fourteen years before, Illinois had been admitted to statehood. If fertile and abundant land meant wealth, then here was opulence unbelievable; for here were millions of acres whose black fecundity would be the envy of any Eastern farmer. Yet what privations, what countless hours of toil and tillage, would be required to bring this land to cultivation!

As for the towns— No wonder Jacksonville, the "metropolis," was an unimpressive village, less metropolitan in every way than the Great Barrington whose rusticity Cullen had found so depressing! And no wonder Jacksonville's young rival Springfield, with its log-cabins and "dirt and discomfort," [5] was even more unprepossessing than poor, raw little Jacksonville! Not in generations could the urban dweller in the Illinois country enjoy the comforts and conveniences and "advantages" that had long been commonplace on the northern and middle Atlantic seaboard.

Most of the Illinois settlers, however, pined far less than did Cullen Bryant for the flesh-pots or the urbanities of the East, for few of them had ever made even remote acquaintance with luxury or culture. Shouting Methodists from the infecund upland regions of Virginia and Kentucky, unlettered "High Dutch" from the Susquehanna valley of Pennsylvania, ne'er-do-well Yankees from Massachusetts and Connecticut, and barefoot women with dirty, shaggy children from parts unknown, they almost all of them sought—and found—on the undeveloped frontier much greater opportunities than the meager ones they had enjoyed on the other side of the Appalachians. Consequently, if they lived on hominy and corn-bread and wild game and buttermilk; if they ate largely with their fingers and their knives; and if they made a single pewter spoon "do" for the entire family—they did not have a sense of "roughing it." True, not all of them were dolts or oafs or yokels; a few of them had as much native intelligence as the most urbane citizen of Boston or New York. For instance, there was a tall, lank, ungainly young militia captain who, at that very time, was serving valiantly in the Black Hawk War. Cullen met him and was much impressed with the captain's good sense, well-chosen diction, and keen wit, to say nothing of the fact that the fellow's numerous earthy anecdotes were never pointless. The big boy's name was Abraham Lincoln—and Cullen Bryant was to know and respect him far more in years to come. But, of course, the Illinois country boasted few Abe Lincolns, and even the clever, witty Captain Lincoln would hardly have been as congenial a dinner companion as Gulian Verplanck or Richard Henry Dana. In short, a man of Cullen Bryant's background could not help finding Illinois impossible as a place of residence.

7

For all that, however, the Illinois country furnished Bryant with the inspiration for one of his noblest poems, "The Prairies," a blank-verse effort of over a hundred lines. In this poem he speaks of the Illinois prairies as "the gardens of the Desert," and in these boundless and beautiful and unshorn gardens he finds the vault of heaven to be somehow nearer and of a tenderer blue than the sky back East. What impresses him most, however, is that in these unpeopled expanses, as in the busy streets of New

York, there is almost continual motion—the motion of sweeping clouds, of breeze-blown wild-flowers and wind-crisped brooks, of leaping marmots and flapping prairie-hawks and fluttering insects. And once upon a time these prairies were peopled too: first with the disciplined, industrious mound-builders, and then with their conquerors, the warlike red men, who, in turn, have been driven to regions farther west. It is the old, old story, the burden of so many of Bryant's songs: the transitoriness of man in contrast to the permanence of nature. Yes, races of men come and go, but the woods and the hills and the prairies remain forever. In this poem, however, the final human note seems more concerned with life than with death; for in the closing lines the poet envisions "that advancing multitude" which will soon fill these deserts with all the amenities of civilization.

This note of optimistic enthusiasm contrasts strikingly with the sentiments expressed in the closing stanzas of an earlier Bryant poem, "An Indian at the Burial-Place of His Fathers" (1824). In the 1824 poem, Bryant has a wise old Indian envisaging the time when the westward advance of civilization will prove a curse rather than a blessing to the white man. The pale-face, says the red man, may prate of his superior arts of husbandry, of his sheep and cattle and horses, of his efficient laborers and well-tilled fields; but in felling the mighty forests, in order to make room for his civilized pursuits, he has unwittingly invited his own doom. Thanks to the destruction of the trees, the rivers have shrunk, the brooks have disappeared, and the time may come when the white man's ill-gotten land may become a barren desert. When Bryant wrote this earlier poem, however, he was thinking in terms of his native Massachusetts. Obviously, the pioneer white settlers of Illinois destroyed no mighty forests.

8

Civilization has its pestilences as well as its amenities. Of this fact Cullen was painfully reminded upon his return to New York. In our growing metropolis, sanitation had failed to keep pace with population, and finally the inevitable had happened. Early in the summer of 1832 an epidemic of cholera had broken out in Manhattan. Shallow wells and neighborhood pumps might be acceptable in a country village, but not in a community of two hundred thousand. Pigs might be tolerable scavenger on the farm, but not in America's greatest city. The flow of slops through gutters might be a mere nuisance in Great Barrington; in New York it was a menace. The inevitable happened. On June 26 the first case of cholera appeared, and by early August nearly half of the people of Gotham had fled in terror. Despite the fact that the pestilence was striking down its thousands of victims "on the right and the left, often at noonday but mostly in darkness";[6] despite the feverish comings and goings of doctors and (untrained) nurses and clerics and undertakers; despite the rumbling of death-carts and the digging of incredibly numerous graves—the merchants labored valiantly to save themselves and the town from utter ruin. And the newspapers lied valiantly—if unconscionably—in the town's and the merchants' behalf. As late as July 13—the day after Bryant's return to New York—the *Evening Post* declared that there was no real epidemic, and ten days later it was angrily accusing its more candid rival, the *Courier and Enquirer,* of spreading alarmist lies.[7]

But, epidemic or no epidemic, Cullen Bryant was thankful that he and his family had removed to a cottage across the Hudson in wholesome little Hoboken. Amid this ghastly scourge it was indeed a satisfaction that the two Fannys and little Julia might live apart from the plague in relative security. And thanks to the steam ferry, Cullen too could nightly breathe the pure air of Castle Point.

With the advent of cool autumnal weather the plague abated and then disappeared. By early October Richard Henry Dana, writing from Newport, could grimly surmise that New York must once more be "as gay as ever, and in full dance over the graves of the thousands who had gone down to death since the plague entered it."[8] And Bryant could recall the calamity as a nightmare from which he had awakened at long last. The memory of the nightmare, however, remained poignantly vivid; for he could not forget that day after day, during those terrible summer weeks, he had been afflicted with "a feeling in the stomach like that produced by taking lead or some other mineral poison."[9]

9

Cullen's affliction, caused largely no doubt by anxiety, disappeared with the demise of the epidemic. His health fully restored, he found himself imbued with a new energy—an energy that by no means spent itself at his busy desk in the office of the *Evening Post*. His political worries were few and slight, for long before November it had become apparent that General Jackson would be triumphantly and decisively re-elected. The plain people—thank heaven!—would have none of Nicholas Biddle's Bank, or of Mr. Biddle's tool, the sleek, smooth, time-serving Henry Clay. Moreover, the one great social scandal of the Jackson administration had been laid at rest. No longer need the old General waste his precious energy in trying to defend the rather dubious virtue of Margaret Eaton. For Secretary of War John Henry Eaton had conveniently resigned from the cabinet, and taken his Peggy back to Tennessee, where she would be far from the snubs and sneers, the whispers and raised eyebrows, of squeamish Washington ladies. And New York's own Martin Van Buren, who had proved to be the staunchest Jacksonian in the administration, was safely on his way to the chair of heir apparent.

And so in the crisp, clear evenings at Hoboken, after Cullen had romped for a few minutes with little Fanny and little Julia, he could mount to his study and read and write. A cultivated editor must not allow himself to grow rusty or Philistine. He must not even be content to re-read the ancient Greek and Latin classics, invaluable as these classics were. All of the principal modern languages, too, had their great literatures. He must pick up a reading knowledge of Italian and Spanish and Portuguese, and he must make metrical translations of such poets as Vellegas and Iglesias and Semedo.

He must likewise try his hand at short prose fiction—fiction somewhat in the manner of Washington Irving. Four of Cullen's most intimate friends—William Leggett, James Paulding, Robert Sands, and Kate Sedgwick—had decided to collaborate in a volume of tales, and they had invited Cullen to join them. The result, *Tales of the Glauber Spa,* was published before the end of the year. Cullen's contributions to the volume proved little, beyond the fact that his narrative gifts were decidedly inferior to his descriptive.

By all odds, however, the most notable literary achievement of William Cullen Bryant in 1832 was a volume of eighty-nine poems published first in New York and subsequently in London. The London edition, sponsored (at Bryant's request) by Washington Irving and dedicated (shrewdly enough) to wealthy, influential

[108]

old Samuel Rogers, had all kinds of interesting repercussions. For one thing, it evoked an enthusiastic eighteen-page review in *Blackwood's* by that prince of British critics, Christopher North (John Wilson). For another thing, it started a mild quarrel, a tempest-in-a-teapot affair, between Bryant and Irving. The cause of the quarrel was a single line in a five-stanza poem, "Song of Marion's Men."

> *The British soldier trembles*
> *When Marion's name is told,*

Bryant had written. But Mr. Andrews, the London publisher, had declared that such an aspersion upon British valor would not do. Accordingly, the tactful Irving had changed the offending line (without Bryant's permission) to "The foeman trembles in his camp." And Bryant, only too happy to have a volume of his work published in London, would probably have let this high-handedness pass without protest. Not so, however, Bryant's hot-headed friend and assistant, William Leggett. Bursting into print with his characteristic impetuosity, he denounced Irving as a craven Anglophile truckler and an impertinent meddler. And Irving, supposing his assailant to be Bryant, replied with more heat than the genial Knickerbocker was usually capable of generating. And so a nasty verbal brawl seemed to be brewing. Fortunately, however Leggett was as honest as he was choleric. Sensing the mess that he had stirred up, he lost no time in explaining to Irving that Bryant had had nothing to do with the denunciation. And so Bryant and Irving became and remained friends.

10

Literary recognition on the other side of the Atlantic revived Cullen Bryant's desire to see Europe—fanned it, indeed, into flames. In two more years he would be forty, and yet in all his life he had traveled only as far as Illinois! Of literary shrines he had seen none more venerable than those of Boston and Cambridge. Yet Fenimore Cooper had gone abroad at thirty-seven; Washington Irving, at thirty-two. Well, in two more years the Bryant children would be old enough for a European voyage, and then the whole family could set forth. Of course the affairs of the *Evening Post* were still to be considered; but Leggett seemed to be growing a little more discreet. Perhaps the unfortunate little rumpus with Irving had at least partially cured young Hotspur of his propensity for rushing into print where angels would fear to tread. At any rate, Leggett would hardly wreck the *Post* in a year or eighteen months. On the whole, indeed, his trenchant editorials were more of an asset than a liability; the intelligent reading public admired an editor with backbone.

And so, on a fine June day in 1834, the four Bryants set sail for Havre. The voyage over was not quite so pleasant as its rosy, sunshiny beginning. Much of the way across, the good ship *Poland* was buffeted and tossed by frigid gales from the north, and it was nineteen days before she docked at the mouth of the Seine. But if the Atlantic had been cold and hostile, the kingdom of "Citizen" Louis Philippe proved warm and genial. A little steamboat took the Bryants up the river, past busy Rouen and quaint little Vernon, past luxuriant vineyards and lush green meadows and poppy-crimsoned fields, and landed them in Paris in time for Bastille Day and the other July festivals. Then on they proceeded, always leisurely, to Lyons, Marseilles, Genoa, Rome, Naples, Florence, Pisa.

France and Italy, for all their antique charm, were a little disappointing to Cullen Bryant. In every city, it appeared, idleness and filth rubbed elbows with grandeur. At the entrance to every cathedral, ragged beggars, many of them repulsively deformed or disfigured, loitered and whined and offered worthless trinkets for sale. In taverns and shops, large and small, rapacious publicans and merchants drove sharp bargains with gullible tourists. Through main thoroughfares echoed the tramp-tramp-tramp of French or Sardinian or Roman or Austrian soldiery, a stern warning against democratic uprisings. At every frontier stood pompous, officious wearers of epaulets and brass buttons who inquisitorially demanded to know each newcomer's nationality, his business, and the purpose and probable duration of his stay in the kingdom of France or Sardinia or the Two Sicilies. Even nature seemed more deformed than embellished by the hand of man. Certainly the scrubby olive trees and the still more scrubby maples, pruned within an inch of their feeble lives, afforded an ugly contrast to the majestic woods back home along the Hudson or in the Berkshires or the Appalachians.

Not until Cullen reached the classic town of Heidelberg, in the grand-duchy of Baden, was he really happy about his sojourn in Europe. And even here his happiness seems to have been caused less by the charm of the old country than by his meeting and becoming intimate with a fellow Yankee. During that autumn of 1834 one of the students at Heidelberg's famed university was a young Mr. Longfellow, who, at the callow age of twenty-seven, had already been promoted from a professorship at Bowdoin to one at Harvard. Bryant somewhat vaguely remembered the young man as a valued contributor of mellifluous lyrics to the late lamented New York *Review and Athenaeum Magazine*. Henry Longfellow, a slightly rakish-looking youth with curly hair, smooth-shaven face, and "rosy cheeks and china-blue eyes," [10] was some twelve or thirteen years Cullen Bryant's junior; but the two men had so very much in common that they quickly became as brothers. Both were a little foppish in dress. Both loved literature and philology, and Henry at least was an enthusiastic admirer of Cullen's poetry. (Henry's own maiden poetic volume, *Voices of the Night*, lay four years in the future.) Both liked to get away from their families occasionally—not at all through lack of domestic devotion, but because kindred, mutually understanding spirits must sometimes hold close communion. Even so, the Bryant-Longfellow intimacy might have become much more a family affair except for one unfortunate circumstance: pretty young Mrs. Longfellow was too much of an invalid to go about a great deal. Like so many delicate young New England women of the day, she was a victim of incipient consumption. Within a little more than a twelvemonth (although Henry could not realize that the end was quite so near) poor Mary Longfellow would breathe her last— in Rotterdam. And so Cullen and Henry often strolled and talked together, sometimes along the Hauptstrasse, sometimes among the ivied halls of the venerable university, sometimes up the Jettenbuhl hill toward the castle. And occasionally they would drop in at a *bierstube* in the Carl Platz to sip a bit of dark Bavarian lager, the epicurean Henry always drinking a little more than the abstemious Cullen.

Soon after New Year's, 1835, Bryant's stay in Heidelberg was rudely interrupted. A letter from William Leggett, scrawled in an unsteady hand, brought bad tidings. No, Leggett had not been printing rash, inflammatory editorials. He had not been assaulting any rival editor, either physically or metaphorically. The fact was that Leggett was a sick man—too sick to continue his editorial duties unaided. Indeed, Leggett must have been in this condition for weeks, for in those days no message crossed the Atlantic faster than sails and uncertain winds could bear it.

Cullen must pack his carpetbag and depart at once. A packet, he learned, would sail from Havre for New York on February 2. Toward Havre, then, he must proceed by the fastest diligence. His family, for the time being at least, would stay in Heidelberg and keep the Longfellows company. Arrived in Havre, Cullen found such vile winter weather that his boat, the *Francis I,* could not leave port for another week. And when she finally sailed, she could not get beyond the fierce English Channel; head winds drove her into Plymouth for another week's delay.

And so, after all, Cullen was to see England. It was good to hear one's own language spoken on every hand once more, even if with a broad West Country accent; good to find one's self in a tidy old town much more like Boston than any other he had seen for a year and a half; good to rub elbows with people much less "foreign," if more reserved, than the French or the Italians or the Germans; good to be away from militarism and priestcraft and mendicant shopkeepers. But the Devon landscape, under the leaden January sky, was bleak and forbidding; and the air bit shrewdly. The mutton at the inn was poorly seasoned; the coffee was insipid (and, at breakfast, unobtainable); and there would be no fresh fruits or vegetables for months. Merry England, in other words, would not be really merry until April or May.

11

Cullen Bryant's first truly happy experience with England was not to come for several years—not till 1845, to be exact. In that year, and in several subsequent years, he was to have foreign travels that would remain vividly—and, on the whole, delightfully —in his mind to the close of his long life.

For instance, there was that 1845 trip to England. What precious and what enduring memories! Visiting in Liverpool with that idealistic philosopher and Unitarian preacher, James Martineau! . . . Attending the theater and the opera in London with his compatriot Edwin Forrest! (One wonders why Forrest, at the time, was not himself busy on the bright side of the footlights.) . . . Breakfasting repeatedly with Samuel Rogers, whose own poetry might be mediocre, but whose mansion and breakfasts were superb! Listening to old Rogers's caustic but always brilliant remarks! Hearing old Rogers ridicule a poet who had breakfasted at his table only yesterday or last week! (Fanny Kemble had expressed a world of truth when she had declared that Sam Rogers had "the kindest heart and unkindest tongue" in England.) . . . Going down to Cambridge by train, and dining in commons with Henry Hallam and Michael Faraday! . . . Journeying to the Lake District to meet old Wordsworth in the venerable Laureate's own garden! Recalling Wordsworth's "white broadbrimmed, low-crowned hat" and his squinting near-sighted eyes! Being irritated by the old man's dogmatic Tory politics, and bored by his egotistical insistence upon reciting some of the most banal of his *Ecclesiastical Sonnets!* . . . Crossing the border to pay homage to good Sir Walter's memory at Abbotsford, and being insulted at the gate by a tipsy, crusty care-taker who would not let him see the inside of the house! . . . Forming warm friendships with individual Englishmen, but hating the eternal class-consciousness and snobbery of English society! [11] Finding the landscapes and landmarks of old England more interesting, even, than her great men!

12

Equally abiding were the memories of the later trips abroad: most of them to western Europe, but a few of them to countries not so much frequented by American tourists in those days.

In the spring of 1849, for instance, there was a visit to our island neighbor Cuba—a visit that left in his mind a host of luminous images, some of them beautiful, some of them revolting. Acres of coffee trees near Matanzas! . . . Acres of sugar cane at Los Guines! . . . And then a giddy week in Havana! Before the week was over, he had shaken hands with the haughty, black-mustachioed Castilian governor-general; had witnessed a blood-curdling Spanish melodrama and a bawdy Spanish farce; had followed the agile pirouettes of spangled harlequins at a masked ball; had seen a boatload of African slaves landed "almost openly" on the quay; had shuddered at the brutalities of a cock-fight. And —ironically, most memorable of all—he had watched the public execution of a wretched mulatto peon: strangulation by an unspeakably horrible iron collar known as a garrote.

13

The other trips, for the most part, evoked fewer unpleasant recollections. In the autumn of 1849, some five or six months after the Cuban trip, there was a third voyage to Europe. In the winter of 1852-3 there was a tour of the Near East, which included a steamboat trip on the Nile, a camel-back ride in the desert, a swim in the Jordan, and a stroll among the ruins of the Parthenon. There were meetings with Robert and Elizabeth Browning, first in Florence and later in Paris. There were the days of roughing it among the swarthy Bedouins—days when Cullen found shaving so impossible that he grew a full beard. (And he loved that beard so well that he was never to part with it; thereafter the public was never to see him, in person or in portrait, without that gray beard.) There was a fifth sojourn in Europe, in 1857-8— a sojourn chiefly notable, perhaps, for the fact that in Naples he finally embraced Unitarianism in a formal way, being baptized by an American clergyman friend, the Reverend R. C. Waterston. (This, doubtless, was a second baptism. Sarah Bryant, with her Calvinistic belief in the damnation of unbaptized infants, could hardly have neglected having William Cullen baptized at the earliest opportunity.) There was a final voyage to Europe—a voyage made with his daughter Julia just after the death of Mrs. Bryant. And then in 1872, when he was almost an octogenarian, there was a trip down into Mexico. The high light of this trip had been an official reception in his honor in Mexico City, and the old gentleman had apologized in excellent Spanish for feeling obliged to address the assemblage in English.

Like most eminent American men of letters of the nineteenth century, therefore, William Cullen Bryant was an inveterate globe-trotter. Though the woods of New England might be his favorite theme for poetry, he became incorrigibly, irrevocably a citizen of the world. Whatever his verses might say, he was a spirit much less nearly akin to Thoreau than to Chaucer or Shakespeare or Dickens. The human scene, whether in New York or in London or in places where strange folk babbled in strange tongues, became such a passion to him that he could not long dwell happy apart from it.

CHAPTER VIII

The Rose Trees Droop

1

IT WAS 1842.

John Tyler, last of the line of Virginia patricians to occupy the White House, was President of the United States—not, however, by first choice of the electorate, but by virtue of the death of "Old Tippecanoe" Harrison barely a month after the aged Indian-fighter's inauguration. Washington and Congress were in a turmoil; for by opposing the Spoils System on the one hand and the scheme to restore the United States Bank on the other, the stubborn Tyler was antagonizing both the Democrats to whose tradition he belonged and the Whigs who had inadvertently put him at the head of the government. Over in the State Department, however, sat plausible, persuasive Daniel Webster, ironing out with Her Britannic Majesty's special envoy, Alexander Baring, Lord Ashburton, the disputed points regarding our northeastern boundary.

In the Governor's mansion at Albany dwelt a sleek young lawyer and politician named William Henry Seward, whose liberal attitude toward immigrants and Roman Catholics had endeared him to the cosmopolitan urban element downstate—and had correspondingly alienated the people of the farms and villages. Incidentally, the latter group of citizens could not forget Seward's prominence in the anti-Masonic movement of a decade earlier.

[115]

Up in Rhode Island two rival claimants to the Governor's chair, Thomas Dorr and Samuel King, were maintaining their claims so strenuously that finally King was put in office and Dorr in prison.

In Boston Ralph Waldo Emerson, the Sage of Concord, was editing a highbrow literary-philosophical quarterly, the *Dial*, which was read (and written) by some two or three hundred intellectuals who called themselves Transcendentalists. And on a rocky, infertile plot of ground nine miles southwest of Boston a group of Emerson's disciples (without much moral support from their leader) were trying to lead a communal life of "plain living and high thinking" at an establishment which they called Brook Farm.

In July of that year the Old Manse, former Concord home of Emerson, was ready to receive as inmates a newly wedded couple, Nathaniel Hawthorne and Sophia Peabody. Nathaniel at the time was chiefly known for his *Twice-Told Tales*. Sophia was the brainy and artistic sister of the still brainier if less artistic Elizabeth Peabody.

Those were the days when fashionable folk were reading *Godey's Lady's Book;* taking therapeutic baths at Saratoga Springs; getting mildly tipsy on wine or cider syllabubs; flocking to charlatan exhibitions of spiritualism or animal magnetism. They were the days when gentlemen wore top hats and neckerchief stocks and swallow-tailed coats for all occasions; when ladies, laced and crinolined to look like hour-glasses, plastered their front hair with pomades and let their back hair hang in luxuriant curls; when well-attired little girls wore calf-hiding, ankle-hiding pantalets; and when a few ultra-foppish young blades, just back from London or Paris, sported little square chin beards (sans mustaches)—the kind of beards that we always associate with Abraham Lincoln and Jefferson Davis and Mennonite farmers.

By 1842, in the thickly populated portion of the Atlantic seaboard—the region bounded on the north by Boston and on the south by Richmond—people were riding more in railroad cars than in stage-coaches. Farther south and farther west the quickest as well as the most luxurious mode of travel continued to be the steamboat. Particularly impressive were the floating palaces— much finer and a little faster than the ones that Cullen Bryant had ridden in in 1832—which traversed the Ohio and the Mississippi, serving such ports of call as Pittsburgh, Cincinnati, Louisville, Cairo, St. Louis, Memphis, Vicksburg, Natchez, and New Orleans. Smaller and less gorgeous were the lake steamers that connected, more or less desultorily, the little towns of Buffalo, Cleveland, Detroit, Milwaukee, and Chicago. But in those days only the most venturesome spirits had any desire to go to Cleveland or Detroit or Chicago.

In 1842, thousands of the more emotional religious folk became excited over the Reverend William Miller's prophecy that the world would come to an end the following year. There was much praying and exhorting and soul-searching, and in many cities and towns—sophisticated Gotham included—white ascension robes would soon be placed on sale in the dry-goods stores.

2

New York, in 1842, was a great metropolis of more than three hundred thousand inhabitants, not counting the fifty thousand who lived over in Brooklyn. No longer did she have a real rival; for Philadelphia (plus Frankford and Germantown) boasted a scant two hundred thousand. Baltimore and Boston and New Orleans were still smaller, and behind them trailed the ambitious Western metropolises, Cincinnati and St. Louis.

The immense growth of New York, both in population and in area, was continually aggravating the problem of local transit. Steam ferries, some of them large enough to carry horse-drawn vehicles, connected Manhattan with Long Island and New Jersey; and a ceaseless stream of omnibuses and hackney-cabs clattered along Broadway and other principal streets at all hours except the wee ones of the morning. But people grumbled more and more about the discomfort of being jolted over cobblestones. In the 1830's a queer horse-drawn omnibus christened the *John Mason* had run on iron rails along the Bowery and Fourth Avenue; and although the *John Mason* had finally been abandoned as a commercial failure, there was now an increasing demand for transit by tramway. Three years later, in 1845, New York would see the beginning of a permanent street-railway system.

From the standpoint of public utilities, the big event of 1842 was the opening of the Croton Aqueduct, which gave the metropolis the water supply that she had sorely needed for many years. Theretofore, New York had never had a waterworks system

[117]

worthy of the name, but not until a twenty-million-dollar fire had ravaged the business district late in 1835 had people realized the importance of municipal waterworks. Appropriately and dramatically, the opening of the new Aqueduct was set for July 4, with huge paradings of brass bands, blue-coated constables and red-shirted firemen; with voluble oratory by Mayor Robert H. Morris and other city dignitaries; and, as the shades of night fell, with fireworks and illuminated fountains.

The New York theatrical season of 1842 was not a notable one—at least in the realm of legitimate drama. William Charles Macready, the great English Shakespearean tragedian, would be over in '43, but New York drama lovers in '42 would have to be content with less distinguished fare. The 1842 play-bills of New York's three legitimate theaters (the Park, the Bowery, and the Olympic) list nothing more outstanding than Park Benjamin's *Fiscal Agent,* a play so mediocre that Professor Quinn does not give it even one sentence in his definitive *History of the American Drama.*

Lovers of esthetic dancing, however, enjoyed a rare treat in the performances of Fanny Ellsler, dainty Viennese danseuse, who had long been the sensation of Europe and whose every American appearance was the signal for a fresh ovation. The beautiful Fanny could dance divinely, and the broken English in which she acknowledged the thunderous plaudits of the audience was utterly charming. As for her sylphlike capering, especially unforgettable and unsurpassable was her rendition of the Spanish *cachuca.*

At the corner of Broadway and Ann Street, opposite old St. Paul's church, was a series of attractions that drew far greater crowds than all the theaters combined. The place was known as the American Museum, and its proprietor and manager was a young Connecticut Yankee named Phineas Taylor Barnum. In 1842 the Museum was still a decided novelty, for Barnum had started business there only the year before. Among the attractions that he offered there were a model of Niagara "with real water," a family of trained fleas, and a "Feejee" mermaid that was guaranteed to be the real thing. Before 1842 was out, Barnum would be displaying a genuine dwarf from his own home town of Bridgeport, tiny Charles Stratton, whom the world was to know as General Tom Thumb.

[118]

To New York book-lovers, however, the really great event of 1842 was the visit of Charles Dickens. And here the term *book-lovers* refers not merely to highbrows who awaited eagerly each issue of the *North American Review* or the *Southern Literary Messenger;* indeed, it refers less to the intellectuals than to the entire novel-reading public. The furore created by the American visit of this young Englishman was in many ways as surprising as it was tremendous. Only thirty years of age at the time, and with a literary reputation scarcely half a decade old, Dickens had not yet written any of his supremely great novels except *Pickwick Papers.* Such masterpieces as *David Copperfield, Bleak House, A Tale of Two Cities,* and *Great Expectations* still lay years in the future. Already, however, "Boz" was, on both sides of the Atlantic, by far the most read, most talked-of novelist that had appeared since good Sir Walter Scott. Thackeray, it must be remembered, was as yet virtually unknown: his *Vanity Fair* would not appear until almost the end of the decade, and his *Pendennis, Henry Esmond, The Newcomes,* and *The Virginians* would all come still later. George Eliot was a girl of twenty-three who had not yet written so much as a paragraph for publication. And Bulwer-Lytton, as a fictionist, was internationally known solely for *The Last Days of.Pompeii;* for the rest, he was famed as a playwright rather than as a novelist. And so in 1842 "Boz" was decidedly the novelist of the hour.

Dickens came to our shores for a variety of reasons. In the first place, he was young and venturesome. In the second place, he was curious about our great experiment in democracy—eager to observe a social system in which a man of his own humble origin might hope to rise as high as any patrician. In the third place, he had been greatly flattered by American enthusiasm for his books; he wanted to rub elbows and shake hands with men and women who were avidly spreading his fame in the New World. About this American adulation, however, there was one disappointing feature: the wide circulation of his writings on this side of the Atlantic brought him almost no royalties. Since no international copyright law existed, his books could be pirated as fast as they came from the press. As a matter of fact, the overwhelming majority of his innumerable American readers had come to know and love *Pickwick* and *Oliver Twist, Nicholas Nickleby* and *The Old Curiosity Shop* and *Barnaby Rudge,* not through authorized editions, but through cheap piratings that sold for as little as twenty-five cents a copy. There was, however, hope for betterment. As Dickens well knew, many distinguished American authors and editors, including William Cullen Bryant, were as eager for an international copyright law as was Dickens or any other British writer. Perhaps Dickens, during his American sojourn, could get the Bryants and the Washington Irvings and the Fenimore Coopers to join with him in arousing public sentiment for international copyright.

The Dickens visit to New York occurred in February. Its high lights were a sumptuous banquet at the Astor Hotel and a huge reception-ball at the Park Theater. At the former the toastmaster was the genial Washington Irving, and one of his most prominent fellow hosts was Cullen Bryant. At the latter the guest of honor was treated to graphic representations of scenes and characters from his novels—scenes and characters that his illustrators, Cruikshank and "Phiz," had helped to imprint in the imagination of every Dickens lover. There were alcoves fitted up to look like the Old Curiosity Shop, and there were tableaux presenting such immortals as Mr. Pickwick, Mrs. Bardell, Sam Weller, Fagin, Squeers, Madame Mantalini, Dick Swiveller, and Dolly Varden. As for the crowd, it taxed the large theater to the very limit; so vigorously did the three thousand ebullient receptionists push and nudge and tramp upon each others' toes that dancing became utterly impossible.

To Cullen Bryant the most abiding memories of the Dickens visit were of neither the glamorous banquet nor the still more glamorous ball. What Cullen best remembered was an intimate little breakfast at the Carlton Hotel, at which Dickens was the host and Bryant one of the three guests. The other two guests were Fitz-Greene Halleck, the Gotham satirical poet, and Cornelius Conway Felton, the "jolly giant" Professor of Greek at Harvard. (What a Dickensian contrast big Felton and little Dickens must have made!) Altogether, it was a most delightful breakfast. Dickens, in one of his most flattering moods, declared (with profuse apologies to Halleck and Felton) that, next to the incomparable Washington Irving, Bryant was the one man in America that he had most desired to meet. And he went on to describe a cherished volume of Bryant's poems that he had thumbed and fondled so much as to wear the gilt inscription almost completely off the cover.[1] And Bryant, in his turn, avowed that although he himself had no propensity for telling a story or depicting the human scene, he had few greater pleasures than the reading of good novels—particularly those of the greatest living English novelist.

Off the record, Dickens and Bryant did not altogether approve of each other. In later days, Dickens reported to an intimate friend that he had found Bryant to be "a little sad and very reserved."[2] And Bryant confided to a few cronies that Dickens's dandyism was too obviously Cockney: his waistcoat too flashy, his jewelry too profuse.

All this, however, did not prevent Bryant from writing a most enthusiastic Dickens editorial for the *Evening Post* of February 18. Why had this little Englishman so completely taken New York by storm? Well, for one thing (Bryant explained), Dickens wrote in a style that could be appreciated by stable-boys as well as by statesmen; for another thing, he knew human nature and human speech, and he could recreate them more vividly than any other living mortal; for another thing, his matchless humor and pathos were based upon the warmest of sympathy, especially for the poor and oppressed; and, finally, his claim to distinction was not rank or title, but exceptional genius.[3]

Yes, little "Boz" had captivated Bryant and the rest of New York. It was, then, doubly unfortunate that "Boz" went home to satirize our country and its metropolis so caustically in *American Notes* and *Martin Chuzzlewit*. But, as Bryant pointed out in a *Post* editorial on November 9, there was a modicum of truth in the unpleasant things that Dickens wrote about America. To be perfectly frank, the habit of tobacco chewing and spitting *was* a "national abomination"; our party spirit *was* ferocious and malignant; much of our press, especially in New York, *was* lacking in "morality and decorum"; many New York society women *were* over-dressed and over-rouged; and many of our public men *were* windy and boastful and truculently Anglophobe.

What Bryant might well have added was that Dickens always had as keen an eye for the evils of his own country as for those abroad. Never did he satirize offensive Americans or American institutions more severely than he satirized offensive Englishmen and English institutions. Surely Jefferson Brick and the New York

Rowdy Journal are no more disgusting than Wackford Squeers and Dotheboys Hall. But the America of 1842, like any other adolescent, was very, very sensitive. Besides, Dickens had been an honored guest of guests; he had been received as cordially as any European who had ever set foot on American soil—not even excepting the Marquis de Lafayette.

4

In the summer of 1842, Cullen Bryant began expressing dissatisfaction with the cottage at Hoboken. Seated on the east veranda with Fanny, on a torrid July evening after a sweltering day at the office, he would complain about Hoboken and the whole Jersey shore. Either there was not a breath of air stirring, or there was a sultry breeze from the south—a breeze that brought with it the stench of the Jersey City slaughter-houses. There was never a cooling breeze except from the Hudson—and not one wind in ten was an east wind.

When Fanny, perplexed at Cullen's unwonted querulousness, would protest that they had a lovely view from up there on Castle Point, Cullen would grudingly admit that the view was good enough. Certainly, as he himself had often remarked, the Hudson was beautiful, and the pageant of ferry-boats, tugs, lighters, Albany river-boats, and barges was everlastingly fascinating. But after one had worked hard in the big city all day, why should one sit on one's veranda in the evening and gaze down upon the scene of one's labors? Of course Cullen was proud of New York, and he found there a stimulus that could have been found nowhere else in all the land. There can, however, be a surfeit of even the best things.

The truth of the matter was that Cullen had been thinking for months that it was about time the Bryants were leaving Hoboken. Certainly, they had been very happy there; so far as that was concerned, they would have been very happy anywhere. And the little village house had not been a bad place in which to bring up the young ones. But as for Hoboken now—well, it had never seemed the same since poor Bob Sands had died. And as Fanny herself had often remarked, the Bryants *could* do with a larger house. Even with Fan away from home—Fan having married Parke Godwin in the spring of that very year—the cottage at Hoboken had begun to cramp and crowd the three Bryants that remained. And, of course, they could well afford a bigger house. But where, demanded Fanny, had Cullen thought—

Long Island was the place he had thought of; by all means, Long Island. Truly it would be pleasant to spend one's summer evenings and nights and one's year-round week-ends in some quiet retreat where bustling Manhattan could be neither seen nor heard. And as the girls had grown to young ladies and Cullen and Fanny had widened their circle of distinguished friends, it would be equally pleasant to have a commodious mansion instead of a modest cottage. If only Cullen had had a large country house in which to entertain Mr. Dickens last winter!

Just the other day Cullen had run into Gulian Verplanck at the club, and Gulian had been all enthusiasm for Long Island— had called Cullen's attention to a number of things worth pondering. So far as Gulian himself was concerned, he was well satisfied with his ancestral farm at Fishkill, in Dutchess County; but he certainly would not advise a townsman in quest of a suburban retreat to settle as far away as Fishkill. There were plenty of other country seats, quite as lovely, within far easier reach of Park Row. The sum and substance was that the Brooklyn ferry had long ago made the western tip of Long Island as convenient to New York as any place along the Jersey shore, and now that the Long Island railroad was being built, there would be plenty of island villages of easy access to the metropolis. Indeed, twenty or thirty miles would not be too great a commuting distance. Moreover, the Sound would be much more refreshingly cool than the Hudson, and from one's veranda one would see—not the welter of New York, but the trees and the fields and the tidy houses of the placid white villages of Connecticut.

5

A tour of western Long Island revealed to the Bryants just the place they wanted, and in the spring of 1843 they moved into it. It was a forty-acre farm bounded on the north by Hempstead Bay, and since the farm-house was handsome and commodious, there would be no tedious dealings with architects and building contractors. The house, a large, substantial Dutch colonial with dormer windows and a two-story front veranda, had been built in 1787 by a well-to-do Quaker named Richard Kirk. Its greatest charm, perhaps, was the beautiful view of the bay; but there were numerous other attractions. The farm was picturesquely rolling and well wooded, and, because of the rich green abundance of tall cedar trees, Cullen and Fanny decided to christen the place

CEDARMERE

"Cedarmere." [4] To the rear of the house stood a spring-fed pond, along the near shore of which grew rose-bushes so lovely and luxuriant that in early summer this became Cullen's favorite spot of spots. As he was to express it later, in his autobiographical poem "A Lifetime,"

> *I see him again at his dwelling,*
> *Where, over the little lake,*
> *The rose-trees droop in their beauty*
> *To meet the image they make.*

Cedarmere was twenty-three miles from lower Broadway, and only a few minutes' walk from the village and the railroad station. The village was a new one, and, because of the profusion of roses in its gardens, the new squire of Cedarmere gave it the name Roslyn. The region as a whole, however, was venerable; for within a radius of a few miles stood such villages as Oyster Bay, Huntington, and Hempstead, whose history dated back to the seventeenth century. Particularly rich in historical associations was Hempstead, a scant eight miles to the south of Roslyn. So desirable a dwelling place had the site of that town been considered that as early as the 1640's it had been a battle-ground of rival settlers: Lynn Yankees, New Amsterdam Dutch, and Stamford Yankees. As for the coves that punctuated the jagged north shore of the island, they were replete with memories of whalers and oysterers, pirates and smugglers, Tories and patriots. And in a score of graveyards Cullen could find gray slate tombstones as old (with inscriptions as quaint) as any he had ever seen at Bridgewater.

Thanks to new modes of travel, a person living at Cedarmere could eat his cake and have it; while remaining close to the conveniences of the city he could bask in the joys of the country. An hour's ride from the hubbub of Park Row, by steam ferry and steam cars, would take him to a rural retreat as tranquil as any Berkshire village. Then let omnibuses clatter along Broadway and Nassau Street; let tug-boat sirens shriek on the East River; let hawkers scream their wares; let countless feet shuffle and scurry on countless serious or trivial errands. Come evening or come Saturday, Squire Bryant would be oblivious of all this commotion; for him the fire-bird and the song-sparrow would be warbling in the fragrant locust trees just across the rose-girt pond.

Incidentally, the line of demarcation between Editor Bryant

and Squire Bryant was complete; for Cullen steadfastly refused to take his office cares with him.[5] When he stepped from the sooty suburban train at Roslyn, he knew that for a few hours or a few days he was free to do as he pleased: sit before the cherry woodfire in the library and chat with Fanny; ensconce himself beneath a lamp with an English novel or a book of Spanish poems; loll on the north veranda and gaze out upon the Sound; row on the pond with Julia or with Fan Godwin; potter among the geraniums and sweet-peas in his garden; visit his stables and exchange anecdotes (some of them, perhaps, a little ribald) with the coachman and the gardener; prune his fruit-trees; pick out his choicest apples for a winter's supply of cider; stroll alone or with Fanny through his woods; compose, perhaps, a short lyric or two; retire to the summer kitchen and brew a vat of beer (since the beer that was sold in New York tap-rooms did not quite suit his palate).[6]

6

Bryant's pride in Cedarmere caused him to do a great deal of entertaining there. Despite a natural reserve, even a cold formality, in his greeting of strangers, Cullen Bryant had a surprisingly large circle of intimate friends; and he delighted in showing them his hospitality. Especially during his early years at Cedarmere it was indeed a rare Friday or Saturday when the train from Brooklyn failed to bring him at least one or two over-Sunday guests. As for Fanny, she soon became accustomed—even reconciled—to having guests come on short notice.

7

On a mid-week, mid-summer evening in 1843, Fanny received one of those characteristic notices that she had well learned to expect. Cullen announced abruptly that Fan and Godwin were coming out for the week-end, and that they were bringing with them the Forrests; that is, Edwin Forrest, the most celebrated American tragedian of the day, and his brilliantly accomplished English wife and co-star, Catherine Sinclair.

Fanny smiled. And her smile was such that Cullen read in it something more than good-naturedly ironical amusement at the suddenness of the announcement.

When Cullen offered a penny for his lady's thoughts, she answered that she was only wondering what poor Mother Bryant would have thought of their being host to play actors.

Cullen frowned, ever so slightly, and muttered something about *autre temps, autres moeurs*. Sarah Snell, he reminded Fanny, had spent her life in an age and a place that obviously had no use for plays or players or play-houses. Of course she never saw a theater—inside or outside. All she ever knew about the theater was that good people said it was a work of the devil. Well, Cullen and Fanny happened to belong in a more tolerant age, if not a better one. Mother Bryant had lived according to her lights; Cullen and Fanny were living according to theirs.

Fanny had no intention of arguing. She merely wanted to have her little tease, she explained. Actually, she quite agreed with Cullen that the theater at its best was a great cultural force; that Mr. Edwin Forrest, who always chose meritorious plays both old and new, was a prime honor to his profession; and that Miss Catherine Sinclair (Mrs. Forrest) seemed as sweet and refined and ladylike as she was beautiful and talented. Certainly, agreed Fanny, the narrow old idea that all player folk were vagabonds must go by the board—go the way of John Calvin's and Jonathan Edwards's harsh theology. Why, that evening at the Park Theater —a couple of years ago, wasn't it?—when she and Cullen had seen Mr. Forrest and company in *Jack Cade* was one of the most memorable, most delightful evenings of the Bryants' New York years. Yes, Fanny thoroughly approved of Fan's and Godwin's friends, especially those as charming and as gifted as Edwin and Catherine Forrest. She was delighted that they were coming out to Cedarmere.

Cullen, not to be outdone by his wife in enthusiasm, started praising Mr. Forrest's staunch Americanism. It did his soul good, he declared, to see Forrest encourage a native American dramatic poet like Mr. Robert Conrad. Of all nonsensical notions that too many of our American players had, one of the worst was the notion that when we wanted a new play we had to depend on such English chaps as Henry Milman and Sheridan Knowles and Edward Bulwer-Lytton. Frankly, our Yankee Conrad was as good as any of those Britishers, and so were Nat Willis and Robert Bird and John Howard Payne. And Forrest had been patriot enough to sponsor all of them.

At the moment Cullen Bryant was all zeal for a native American theater; for American players in American plays. And since the appreciative Fanny was his only audience at this particular time, he probably ended the colloquy by rising from his chair and declaiming, in stentorian, Forrest-like tones, one of his favorite passages from *Jack Cade:*

> *The wren is happy on its humble spray,*
> *But the fierce eagle revels in the storm.*
> *Terror and tempest darken in his path;*
> *He gambols 'mid the thunder; mocks the bolt*
> *That flashes by his red, unshrinking eye,*
> *And, sternly joyful, screams amid the din:*
> *Then shakes the torrent from his vigorous wing,*
> *And soars above the storm, and looks and laughs*
> *Down on its struggling. Safety still*
> *Reward ignoble ease:—be mine the storm.*

8

What a variety of guests came out to Cedarmere!—poets, painters, actors, linguists, pathologists, clergymen! There were, for instance, Fitz-Greene Halleck and Richard Henry Dana; Asher Brown Durand, the landscapist, and Daniel Huntington, the portraitist; Edward Robinson and his wife, Therese, who knew more about Oriental languages than any other living Americans; Dr. Samuel H. Dickson, one of the greatest medical authorities of the day, and at the same time, a courtly Southern gentleman, a charming and brilliant conversationalist, a "devoted Unitarian," and a lover of literature and art; Rev. R. C. Waterston and Rev. Orville Dewey, Unitarian clergymen; James H. Hackett, supreme Yankee character actor; and, of course, the Forrests. (When first the Forrests visited Cedarmere, no one dreamed that a few years later they would be contestants in the most sensational divorce trial that New York had ever known.) And while Cullen and Fanny were extending invitations to Cedarmere, they did not forget their old Berkshire friends Kate and Charles Sedgwick.

9

Of the celebrities mentioned in the preceding paragraph, two —besides the Forrests—deserve special consideration. Those two are Asher Brown Durand and the Reverend Orville Dewey.

Durand, who was about two years Bryant's junior, was the son of a New Jersey watchmaker. At the age of sixteen he had been apprenticed to an engraver, and within a few years thereafter his work of engraving had inspired him with ambitions to become a painter. By the time he had reached his forties, he had become the eminent portraitist of many of our most noted public men, including several Presidents of the United States. In 1840 he had gone abroad to study the old masters at first hand, and upon his return to the United States he had forsaken portraiture for land-scapes.

The thing about Durand that appealed especially to Bryant was Durand's appreciation of the distinctive beauties of American scenery. As Professor Norman Foerster has well said, "For a long time [after the first European settlers came] the distinction of America, the new world, was simply nature." [7] The people were transplanted Europeans, and their handiwork was perforce largely European in design and inspiration; but the hills and the plains, the streams and the woods and the flowers, the birds and the wild beasts, were peculiarly and gloriously American. To take but one phenomenon for example, our American autumnal foli-age had a chromatic splendor to which the more somber au-tumnal foliage of England could never offer anything approach-ing a parallel. And just as Bryant was the first American poet to record that fact, so was Durand the first American painter to do likewise. Or, at any rate, he was *almost* the first; for the real pioneer American landscapist was Durand's friendly rival, Thomas Cole (whom Bryant made the subject of one of his most eloquent sonnets).

Durand's most famous paintings are as woodland-inspired as Bryant's "Inscription" and "Forest Hymn." They are "Woodland Brook," in the Stuart Collection, New York Public Library; "In the Woods," in the Metropolitan Museum, New York; and "Mountain Forest," in the Corcoran Gallery, Washington. Al-though these canvases may appear harsh and over-literal and over-detailed in comparison with the subtler, more delicate work of Inness or Wyant or Martin, they are still as impressive as they are authentically American. Moreover, they entitle Durand—along with Cole—to be known as forerunner of our most famous group of landscape painters, the Hudson River School.

Whenever Durand came out to Cedarmere, we may be sure, host and guest spent joyful hours in animated conversations on the subject of their supreme common interest: the native woods that both had learned to paint with such loving fidelity.

10

To Cullen and Fanny Bryant, the name of Orville Dewey came to connote two quaintly incongruous things: cigars and sermons. For Dewey was both an inveterate smoker and a brilliant preacher. If he had been a Roman or an Anglican priest, his devotion to Lady Nicotine would have been no cause for comment; but as a Unitarian he was something of an anomaly.

Dewey's background was, in many ways, strikingly similar to Bryant's. Born the very same year as Bryant, in western Massachusetts, Dewey had attended Williams College—had, in fact, been one of Bryant's classmates and boon companions there. Incidentally, Orville Dewey does not appear to have been a near relative of Bryant's favorite Williams instructor, Chester Dewey. Although the two Deweys were natives of the same town (Sheffield), no biographical sketch of either of them makes mention of any kinship. After graduation at Williams, Orville Dewey had attended Andover Theological Seminary with the intention of becoming an orthodox Congregational minister. Near the end of his course at Andover, however, he had met and come under the spell of the eloquent and magnetic William Ellery Channing, that greatest and best-loved of all pioneer Unitarian preachers. As a result, Dewey had renounced Calvinism and had become Channing's assistant at the theologically liberal Federal Street meetinghouse in Boston. From 1835 to 1848 he was pastor of the Second Unitarian Church in New York, the church that the Bryants most frequently attended in those days. In 1848 he returned to his native Massachusetts, but both before and after that time he was a frequent and ever welcome guest at Cedarmere.

Whenever Fanny Bryant saw Cullen bringing home a box of "segars" she knew that they were about to have a visit from "Three D's" (Dear Doctor of Divinity, as they playfully called the reverend gentleman). Dewey was the one man whose stench of tobacco the non-smoking Cullen Bryant positively enjoyed.

But if Bryant found great vicarious enjoyment in Dewey's "segars," he and Fanny found still greater direct enjoyment in Dewey's sermons. Whenever Dewey came to Roslyn the local Presbyterian minister felt obliged to have him serve as guest preacher, and, of course, Dewey always preached much more liberal sermons than any Calvinistic divine. The thing the Bryants said they liked about Orville Dewey's sermons was that Dewey always preached good Unitarian doctrine: the dignity, rather than the depravity, of human life. Both Cullen and Fanny, in their younger days, had been subjected to an overdose of Calvinism. They welcomed a happier, more rational theology.

There were, however, plenty of other things that Cullen Bryant liked about Orville Dewey. He especially liked Dewey's catholicity of tastes and interests—a catholicity that ranged from politics to science, from philosophy to the arts. Hosts and guests at Cedarmere marveled at the topics that the bald, broad-faced, benign, smoke-wreathed parson could discuss with both intelligence and enthusiasm. All agreed that if there was one man who could most illuminatingly talk drama with Forrest, painting with Durand, poetry and Abolition and the tariff with Bryant, that man was Orville Dewey.

11

It was, however, not merely the great and the famous and the specially privileged who flocked to the Bryant country home. From time to time the villagers came to garden parties—fetes such as an English lord and his lady might have given their tenants, except that Cullen and Fanny were too democratic to assume a patronizing attitude toward even the humblest. In this connection, one of the happiest of all functions at Cedarmere was the annual "pear party," an occasion on which the children of the village were invited to romp about the grounds, play all manner of games, and eat as many of the wind-fallen Cedarmere pears as they could hold.

Everyone who ever breakfasted or dined or supped at Cedarmere agreed that the cuisine was excellent. Though Cullen Bryant himself was no epicure, he was determined that his guests should have the choicest of comestibles and potables. And most of the delicacies served at his table came from the farm itself; in general, only the sugar, the spices, the tropical fruits, the coffee, the tea, and the wines came out from New York. Among the homemade refreshments was the cider, which Cullen always insisted should be made from hand-picked apples. Then there was the beer!—judging from the way in which Cullen bragged to Kate Sedgwick about his home brew, one may be sure that it really was better than the New York brewers made. The wines, however— served in what Caroline Kirkland called "the cheerful hour over which moderation presides" [8]—were imported. A brewer Cullen Bryant might be; but he did not set himself up as a vintner.

Guests who came to Cedarmere for more than the week-end understood that in the daytime they would do much of their own entertaining. If the library or the billiard table or the front view palled upon them, they could stroll in the grounds or row on the pond; and if they tired of strolling and rowing, the family coach was at their disposal for a tour of the surrounding country. It was Cullen's idea that the average guest did not care to be dragged about the place and shown things that might interest him far less than they did his host.

In the evenings, however, Cullen was usually the master of revels. Apropos of this, one thing about which he was singularly (and justly) vain was his histrionic talent. Often—when captious professionals like Hackett and the Forrests were not present—he would regale his guests with impersonations of individuals whom he had observed closely during his travels abroad. Often, for instance, he would be vain old Wordsworth, unctuously reciting an Ecclesiastical Sonnet; and often (after he had returned from the Orient with his famous beard) he would don turban and gown, jabber in broken English, and throw the young folk into gales of laughter by his playing of an Arab sheik. In this latter role, indeed, he even fooled one young lady into believing that there was a distinguished Oriental guest in the house.[9] There was, then, something of the Puckish in Cullen Bryant, even in his riper years.

12

Bryant's poetical output during these middle years of his career was not extensive. In fact, the decade of his removal to Cedarmere witnessed the publication of but two slender volumes of verse from his pen: *The Fountain and Other Poems* (1842) and *The White-Footed Deer and Other Poems* (1844). And these were the last verses that he was to publish in book form until near the close of the Civil War. The title poems of the two volumes issued in the 1840's are undistinguished. Perhaps the most notable pieces in the two volumes are "The Battle-field," "The Antiquity of Freedom," and "Oh Mother of A Mighty Race."

"The Battle-field," inspired by Bryant's own editorial conflicts, reminds the reader that physical battles are soon over, whereas moral and intellectual battles endure as long as men of integrity are willing to fight for the truth as they see it. Moral and intellectual courage, therefore, are quite as important as physical courage, and may require more stamina. "A friendless warfare" the poet calls this moral struggle, and he adds that "a wild and many-weaponed throng" hang on the front and flank and rear of the man who dares to espouse a just but unpopular cause. Had not Bryant himself, in his outspoken fidelity to such causes, antagonized the wealthy and the influential and jeopardized the prestige of the *Evening Post?* What had the spokesmen of the business community had to say about his championing of low tariffs, collective bargaining, almost the whole program of Jacksonianism? And, except for a few such hardy liberals as the Sedgwicks and George Bancroft, what did his respectable fellow New Englanders think of his apostasy from the Federalism of his forefathers? The consolation that the poet finds is that "Truth, crushed to earth, shall rise again."

"The Antiquity of Freedom," as the title indicates, depicts Freedom not as "a fair young girl with light and delicate limbs," but as "a bearded man, . . . scarred with tokens of old wars." The central idea of the poem is that although Freedom is as ancient as the human race, Tyranny is only a little younger, and, if weaker, more subtle and wily. Freedom, therefore, can never rest upon its laurels; it must wage an everlasting battle with Tyranny, which all too frequently appears in the tempting guise of demagogy. Incidentally, this poem sounds strangely modern. For did not Hitler's New Order promise men "freedom" from the evils, real and alleged, of a "decadent" democracy? And have not the people of the democratic nations taken the permanency of their blessings too much for granted?

"Oh Mother of A Mighty Race," written just after Bryant's return from his second trip to Europe, hails young, progressive, democratic America, and contrasts her with effete, weary, tyrant-ridden Europe. More petulant in tone than most of Bryant's poems, this lyric stresses the idea that America's older sisters, the nations of Europe, are forever taunting her and sneering at her, and that their taunts and sneers are born of downright jealousy. Perhaps, when Cullen Bryant was in England, he had heard some Britisher speak more bluntly than tactfully about the United States. Perhaps the shafts and barbs loosed by the ungrateful little "Boz" still rankled. At any rate, this short poem is further evidence of a fact mentioned earlier in the present chapter; namely, that in the 1840's the United States of America was a self-conscious, hypersensitive adolescent.

CHAPTER IX

Iron Tempest

1

MOST OF Cullen Bryant's
time was, of course, spent
in New York rather than at Cedarmere. Even after the purchase
of Cedarmere, Bryant always maintained a town house: in his
middle years, a red brick dwelling on Carmine Street in Greenwich Village; in his later years, a brownstone-fronted mansion at
24 West Fifteenth Street. And during most of the week-days in
winter, his town house was his real lodging.

Consequently, whereas a score or two of fortunate friends and
country neighbors knew Bryant as the hospitable squire of Cedarmere, the public at large knew him as the able, forceful, colorful
editor of the New York *Evening Post*. And Cullen Bryant, despite
his reserve and dignity, was a truly colorful figure. In this connection, everyone who ever frequented the office of the *Post* remembered certain things about the very memorable, very individual-
istic editor. To be sure, Bryant was not nearly so eccentric as
Horace Greeley, of the *Tribune*, or nearly so sensational as Gor-
don Bennett, of the *Herald;* but, in his way, he was just as unforgettable as either Greeley or Bennett.

People who saw Bryant sitting at his desk, or emerging into
Park Row or Broadway, or lunching on milk and fruit and
graham bread at his favorite chop-house, got the impression of a

middle-sized, middle-aged man whose fastidious dress, conservative in cut and quiet in color-scheme, just escaped foppishness. And if the day happened to be rainy or cloudy or threatening, they could not help noticing one startlingly incongruous accouterment of the dapper editor: a faded blue cotton umbrella that might well have belonged to a chimney sweep or a charwoman. So ashamed were the Bryant women of this ugly old umbrella that they often tried hiding it and replacing it with a decent new silk one—and always with such unpleasant results that the beloved old "rain-stick" was speedily restored to its accustomed place.[1] But if the disreputable old umbrella looked strangely incongruous, the well-trimmed side whiskers, now turned a little gray, always harmonized with the spotless white cravat and the perfectly fitting navy-blue or black coat.

Bryant's big office desk was as unprepossessing as his umbrella. Always littered with manuscripts, documents, memoranda, clippings, pencils, quill pens, paste-pots, and what-not, it was made doubly chaotic by its owner's penchant for scribbling his editorials on the backs of old letters and envelopes. Once when Bryant was out of town for a protracted stay, a fastidious colleague, John Bigelow, tried to tidy the desk up a bit; but on Bryant's return there was such a scene that never again was the desk molested.[2]

But if Bryant's unkempt desk matched his shabby blue umbrella, his stately office deportment matched his neat, correct attire. Dignity was the rule of the *Evening Post* editorial staff—a dignity so unbending that every member was invariably addressed as Mr. So-and-so, never as William or John. Even Parke Godwin, who had married Fanny Bryant, and who, after 1837, had been chief assistant editor, knew better than to address his "in-law" and superior during office hours as anything but "Mr. Bryant."

2

Bryant's editorials were the most distinguished of their day. Not only were they models of excellent sentence structure and apt diction; they abounded in allusions such as only an extraordinarily well-read person could command. Plato and Aristotle, Horace and Marcus Aurelius, Cervantes and Goethe, were quoted and cited as readily as Shakespeare or Milton. There was, however, no pedantry about Bryant's references to the ancient and the modern classics; each allusion was presented in such a way that any intelligent reader could get its point.

Bryant, then, set a high standard for journalistic writing, and he expected all of his subordinates to follow that standard to the best of their ability. Slovenly English he would not tolerate, either in the editorial or the reportorial columns of the *Evening Post*. Such inflated words as *inaugurate* (for begin); such improprieties as *balance* (for remainer) and *loan* (for *lend);* such vague generalities as *banquet* (for *dinner* or *supper)* and *juvenile* (for *boy);* and such inane phrases as *in our midst* and *devouring element—* these were as strictly taboo as the vulgarisms *gents, pants, Darkey,* and *Secesh.*[3]

But if Editor Bryant was a purist, he was by no means a humorless prig. Witticisms he practiced and encouraged, always with the proviso that they be apt and in good taste. So barbed, indeed, was some of his editorial wit that it evoked counter-blasts from rival editors—many of them more ill-natured and less witty than the quips that had provoked them. In this connection, it must be remembered that mid-nineteenth-century editors in general were much more abusive than any reputable editor of today. During most of the Bryant journalistic era Editor Pot and Editor Kettle seldom hesitated to call each other black.

3

Never, of course, did Bryant lack for editorial topics. When he was not inveighing against the tariff, or the Bank of the United States, or the paper currency, reckless speculation, and other unsound financial practices that brought on one serious business depression in 1837 and another in 1857, he could find plenty of local municipal conditions that needed improvement. In a great and rapidly growing commercial and industrial community like New York, new evils were constantly arising, and old evils were constantly being aggravated. There were dangerous and insanitary working conditions, excessive hours of labor and inadequate wages, crowded and noisome dwellings, exploitation of immigrants by demagogues, sharp practices of shop-keepers, paucity and smallness of public parks, lack of a free library, and—almost above all—a spirit of rowdyism that made New York a byword among cities. In this last connection, there had been the horrible Astor Place riot of 1849, in which an insanely angry mob had besieged a theater, stones and bullets had filled the air, windows and doors and lamps had been smashed, and thirty-four persons had been killed. And all because a famous English tragedian, William Charles Macready, had dared to enact *Macbeth* in rivalry of an American tragedian, Edwin Forrest! The fact that there had long been mutual jealousy and ill-will between Macready and Forrest was inconsequential. The important thing was that the ruffianly "b'hoys" of New York, with their customary criminal stupidity, had tried to turn a petty personal rivalry into an international issue.

Fortunately, however, those years provided a number of pleasant editorial topics, both in New York and in the nation at large. There was, for instance, the concert of Jenny Lind at Castle Garden in September, 1850, an occasion which showed that Americans could appreciate great music superlatively rendered. There was the completion of the New York Central Railroad from New York to Albany in 1851. There was the Crystal Palace exposition of 1853, the first fair of nation-wide interest that this country had ever known. And there was the laying of the trans-Atlantic cable, over which the first messages were sent in the summer of 1858.

4

But all through those years there were increasing evidences that, sooner or later, one editorial topic would come to outweigh all others; namely, the relation of the Union to the institution of slavery. As early as the 1830's it became manifest that there were prominent, active Americans, in all sections of the country and in all walks of life, who either loved or hated slavery more than they loved the Union of the several states. Fanatical young editors such as William Lloyd Garrison and fanatical young poets such as John Greenleaf Whittier were demanding the abrogation or nullification of all pro-slavery laws, even though such action might wreck the republic. Angry Southern politicians and planters were showing much more concern about states' rights and property rights than about the solidarity of the nation. Then came the annexation of Texas, 1845; the Mexican War, 1846-1848, and with it the Wilmot Proviso; Clay's Compromise and the Fugitive

[138]

Slave Law, 1850; *Uncle Tom's Cabin*, 1852; the Ostend Manifesto and the Kansas-Nebraska Bill, 1854; the Lecompton Constitution and the Dred Scott Decision, 1857; John Brown's raid of Harper's Ferry, 1859.

Bryant's editorials through this succession of crises presented the Northern point of view at its best. The first agitations of the Abolitionists displeased and disquieted him, as they displeased and disquieted thoughtful Northerners generally. There were several reasons for this perturbed state of mind. In the first place, the Abolitionists, like any other fanatics, were people of one-track minds; they could see no great evil but slavery, no great panacea but Abolition. In the second place, Bryant believed that slavery, "though an unmitigated evil, was [already] in the process of extinction" [4]—that it was slowly but surely becoming so unprofitable from an economic standpoint that ultimately it would be abandoned. In the third place, Bryant's views on the tariff and the Bank had long ago committed him to the Democratic party, and it happened that the Democratic party was drawing more and more of its strength from the South. Consequently, in the presidential election of 1844 Bryant supported the pro-slavery James K. Polk against both the compromising Henry Clay and the anti-slavery James G. Birney.

Support of Polk for the presidency, however, did not mean that Bryant had any enthusiasm for Polk's views on slavery. Everyone who had followed the *Evening Post* editorials over a period of years was well aware of that fact. As early as 1837, in one of the most vigorous of leaders, Bryant had praised unstintingly those Abolitionists who had had the courage to suffer persecution and even death for their convictions. Speaking in particular of the mobbing and murder of Elijah P. Lovejoy, a young Abolitionist editor at Alton, Illinois, he had declared:

> We approve, then, we applaud—we would consecrate, if we could, to universal honor—the conduct of those who bled in this gallant defense of the freedom of the press. Whether they erred or not in their opinions, they did not err in the conviction of their right, as citizens of a democratic State, to express them; nor did they err in defending their rights with an obstinacy which yielded only to death. [5]

It is, then, not surprising that by 1848 Bryant was becoming less and less interested in the Democratic party, more and more concerned about slavery. In his opinion, the choice offered by the two major parties in the presidential campaign of that year was not a happy one. Lewis Cass, the Democratic nominee, though a Northerner and a man with an excellent record both as territorial governor of Michigan and as Minister to France, had consistently tried to conciliate the slave-owning interests, and his stand on important national issues generally had shown him to be a time-serving politician rather than a high-minded statesman. Zachary Taylor, the Whig nominee, had neither political training nor political knowledge; his sole claim to the nomination had been his record as a successful and popular Mexican War general. Moreover, Taylor, a Louisiana plantation-owner, was one of the largest slave-holders in the nation. And of course the Whig platform, like Whig platforms generally, was either silent or evasive on all important controversial questions. Consequently, Bryant lent the support of the *Evening Post* to ex-President Van Buren, who ran on what was called the Free Soil ticket, and who had at least the merit of taking a firm stand against the extension of slavery into the territories.

The election of 1852 found Bryant and the *Post* back in the regular Democratic camp. Certainly Franklin Pierce, the dark-horse nominee of the party, was neither a strong man nor an anti-slavery man. But Pierce was, at any rate, a New Englander and a Unionist. Moreover, he was on intimate and amicable terms with Bryant's friend Henry Longfellow, with whom he had attended Bowdoin College some thirty-odd years earlier. And Pierce's Whig opponent, the senile and elephantine General Winfield Scott, had no more qualifications for the presidency than the late Zachary Taylor had had. As for John P. Hale, the Free Soil nominee, there was no evidence that he was anything but a one-track-minded Abolitionist. Consequently, in November of that year, Bryant and the *Evening Post* took at least a negative satisfaction in the very sweeping electoral returns: Pierce, 254; Scott, 42; Hale, 0.

By 1856, however, Bryant and the *Evening Post* had deserted the Democratic party for good. Two years earlier a group of anti-slavery members of the two major parties had formed a new party, the Republican, and Bryant had cast his lot with the new organization. In consequence, when the Republican party presented its first presidential ticket, Bryant and his paper were among its foremost supporters.

[140]

About the first Republican nominee, John C. Fremont, Bryant could have had no great illusions. He must have realized that Fremont was an adventurer and an engineer rather than a statesman—a man whose dubious background and checkered career gave little promise that he would be either a dignified or a sagacious chief executive. Certainly, as "Pathfinder" Fremont's supporters pointed out, his daring and resourcefulness as explorer and frontier warrior had been of incalculable service in opening the country clear through to the Pacific coast, and as the son-in-law of the able and influential Senator Thomas Hart Benton and the husband of the charming and vivacious Jessie Benton he had acquired invaluable connections with official and semi-official Washington. But, as his opponents demanded, was he not the illegitimate son of a French *emigre?* Had he not been expelled from college? Had he not been defendant in one of the most sensational court-martial trials in our national history? Had he not been almost criminally reckless in some of his financial transactions? In short, the "Pathfinder of the Rockies," for all his intrepidity and colorfulness and prestige, was hardly a man whose presence in the White House would inspire widespread respect and confidence. At any rate, however, John C. Fremont stood upon a forthright Free Soil platform.

His Democratic opponent, James Buchanan, though an experienced legislator and diplomat, had done nothing to win the approval of the anti-slavery element; in fact, Buchanan had been prominent both in support of the Ostend Manifesto and in opposition to the Wilmot Proviso. Moreover, at the time of his nomination he was sixty-five years of age. If he were to be elected, he would become—with the single exception of the pathetic William Henry Harrison—the oldest President ever to take office.

As for the poor old Whig party, it was so badly emasculated that in 1856 it did not even put up a ticket. Its followers rallied largely to the support of the comparatively new American (or Know-Nothing) party, which presented both a candidate and a platform that were utterly unattractive to Cullen Bryant. Its standard-bearer was ex-President Millard Fillmore, of whose policies Bryant had always been "a strenuous opponent." [6] Its platform showed far less concern over slavery and the Union than over what it considered the twin menaces of unrestricted immigration and Roman Catholicism.

And so William Cullen Bryant and the New York *Evening Post* became a powerful factor in getting the Republican party off to a good start in its first presidential race.

Fremont ran a very good second in the election, polling thirty-three per cent of the popular vote as compared to Buchanan's forty-five and Fillmore's twenty-two. The Electoral College gave Buchanan 174 votes; Fremont, 114; and Fillmore, only eight.

Displeasing as was the election of Buchanan to Bryant and his fellow Republicans, the strong showing made by Fremont greatly buoyed their hopes for triumph in 1860. So thoroughly had the seeds of discord been sowed in the Democratic field that Fremont had drawn about as much support from erstwhile Democrats as from erstwhile Whigs. The vacillating President Buchanan had all the earmarks of a one-termer; yet the Democrats had no acceptable man with whom to replace him. Aggressive young Vice President John C. Breckenridge was so utterly pro-slavery that if he were to head the ticket every Free Soiler in the Democratic ranks would desert. And Stephen A. Douglas, the brilliant, magnetic little senator from Illinois, was so pro-Union that he would get scarcely a handful of votes south of the Mason and Dixon line. Meanwhile the Whig party, whether under an old or a new name, might as well be forgotten; for the Whigs simply would not take an unequivocal stand upon the one vital issue of the day.

Next time, however, the Republicans must put up a more statesmanlike candidate than the erratic and somewhat besmirched Fremont. In that connection, many supporters of the new party looked with favor upon the able, cultivated, dignified William H. Seward, who had given an excellent account of himself both in the Governor's chair at Albany and in the Senate at Washington, and whose attitude toward both slavery and the Union was eminently satisfactory. The more closely one examined Seward, however, the less he approximated the ideal candidate. For one thing, in 1861 he would be sixty years old—surely a bit advanced in age for a man just entering the most arduous of all public tasks. For another thing, Seward was too Whiggish to please such erstwhile Democrats as William Cullen Bryant; his sympathies were more with the moneyed classes than with the laborers. Worst of all, Seward, for all his undoubted personal respectability, had slept with some suspicious-looking political bedfellows: notably the crafty Thurlow Weed, whose political methods were, to say the least, rathɔr Jesuitical. Weed, for example, had thought it a good idea to grant the New York street-railway franchise to whatever capitalists would be willing to pour the most money into the Republican organization coffers; and Seward, apparently, had approved of Weed's stand in this matter.[7] But was there any other really promising candidate for the Republican nomination in 1860?

5

On a crisp February evening in 1860, Cullen Bryant stood before the large mirror in his bedroom that looked out upon Carmine Street into Greenwich Village. It was the twenty-seventh of the month, and although the air outside was sharp and the streets were blanketed with white, there were more than a few hints of coming spring. The days were growing noticeably longer. On the last sunny afternoon—the afternoon just before the most recent snowstorm—Cullen had seen some boys playing marbles on the sidewalks, and some other boys flying kites in Washington Square. Back in the Berkshires, the maple sap must have been dripping into buckets throughout the sunny hours; innumerable New England sugar camps must have been sending up their incomparable incense .It was almost time for bluebirds and crocuses, and Easter was only a little more than a month away.

As Cullen stood before his mirror, however, his chief thoughts were not of approaching spring. They were not even of his own immaculate image in the glass, his perfectly tailored black evening suit, his spotless white frilled linen. Still less were they of his clean, shining bald head, his keen, lustrous gray eyes, or his luxuriant but well-groomed gray beard, which, ever since his trip to the Holy Land seven years earlier, had covered his chin as well as his cheeks.

No, the question that Cullen was asking at the moment was not, "Will *I* do?" but, "Will *he* do?" That very afternoon he had asked Fanny and Julia Bryant and Parke and Fanny Godwin the same question, and they had been no more able to answer the question than had he.

After giving his beard and his bushy brows a final touch of the comb, and his white bow cravat a final twitch, Cullen descended to the dining-room for a glass of sherry—the strongest bracer that he would ever allow himself.

A few moments later he was clattering eastward behind an old cab horse, bound for Peter Cooper's Institute at the confluence of the Bowery and Third and Fourth Avenues. Under ordinary circumstances he would have walked the few short blocks, but this was a very special occasion.

Upon entering the brilliantly gas-lighted auditorium, Cullen observed that at least two thousand other persons were as expectant as he; for three-fourths of the seats were already taken, and people were still pouring in. Certainly the legitimate theaters would do a poor business that evening—and not because Lent had started, but because for this one night the cultivated ladies and gentlemen of Gotham were promised a more engaging attraction than any play or opera. Originally this program had been booked for Henry Ward Beecher's Plymouth Church in Brooklyn, but later its promoters had wisely decided in favor of the more spacious, more centrally located Cooper Institute.

Cullen Bryant, being the chairman of the evening, made his way to the platform, where he was almost immediately shaking hands with the man whom the hundreds had come to hear. Twenty-eight years earlier, Cullen had first met this man, though under very different circumstances and in very different surroundings.

The star performer of the evening did not look at all prepossessing. His shock of dark hair had resisted the discipline of the comb, and his nose and ears and mouth were much too large for an Adonis or a Lord Byron. His black evening suit, wrinkled by too long confinement in a carpetbag, was excessively abbreviated both at the sleeves and at the trousers. The gestures of his lanky arms and big hands, as well as the shufflings of his huge feet, were unremittingly clumsy. All in all, he looked like an overgrown frontier farmer who had somehow blundered into the wrong attire and wrong surroundings.

As dapper, gray-bearded Cullen Bryant escorted the uncouth, beardless[8] rustic giant to the speaker's chair, his sense of humor must have been quietly tickled by the incongruity of the scene; the raw frontiersman towered a good eight inches above the polished metropolitan editor.

But Bryant was too greatly worried to be more than very mildly amused. The speaker of the evening was a man in the prime of life, some fourteen years the junior of the sixty-five-year

[144]

old Bryant. So far, so good; fifty-one was an ideal age for a presidential candidate. This man's career, however, had been generally undistinguished. His one contact with the national capital had been a single term in the House of Representatives, during which he had never set the Potomac aflame. For the rest, he had been an Indian fighter, a small-town lawyer, a member of the legislature of his home state, and an unsuccessful candidate for various public offices, including a seat in the United States Senate. The reasons why Republicans all over the nation were tremendously interested in him at the moment were twofold. In the first place, his pronouncements about both slavery and the Union had been eminently sound; in the second place, he had acquitted himself surprisingly well in a series of debates with the brilliant Stephen A. Douglas. As for this man Lincoln's rusticity—well, had not rusticity been a positive political asset to Andrew Jackson and William Henry Harrison?

Still, Bryant was worried. Tonight Abe Lincoln was not debating before a crowd of farmers and store-keepers at Decatur or Peoria or Galesburg or Kankakee; he was addressing what Horace Greeley's *Tribune* tomorrow morning would pronounce as large "an assemblage of . . . intellect and culture" [9] as America's greatest city had ever known. And even though these cultivated ladies and gentlemen had manifested their interest by filling the largest auditorium in New York to capacity, they had come at least as much out of curiosity as out of enthusiasm. If their mood was receptive, it was likewise critical. However strongly many of them hoped that the bucolic statesman from the West might "do," the vast majority of them had grave doubts. Rumor declared that this lanky rustic sometimes tried to cover his awkwardness by acting the clown. Would he do it this evening? Would his gestures be more those of a frontier rail-splitter than of a polished orator? Would he, in the heat of his discourse, upset the water pitcher? Would he intersperse his talk with cheap jokes and anecdotes of a kind that were popular in Illinois country stores on Saturday nights? Would he even fall into solecisms that would make every Harvard gentleman and female-seminary lady in the audience wince? (Certainly his speeches read well enough in print. But who knew how extensively they had been edited? At any rate, it was understood that Abe Lincoln's formal education had not extended beyond a few winters in a country district school.) All of these uncomfortable thoughts must have run through the mind of Cullen Bryant—and through many other minds as well.

Fears and doubts, however, proved utterly groundless. Before Lincoln had been speaking five minutes the only unhappy Republicans in the vast auditorium must have been the friends and supporters of William H. Seward. Not one cheap joke or anecdote did Lincoln tell. Not one solecism did he commit. And if his voice was somewhat nasal and his presence a bit ungraceful, these defects were more than offset by eloquence, moral earnestness, even dignity. His diction and phraseology were not merely correct; they were positively masterful. And if he employed no classical allusions, he did show an intelligent familiarity with such European historical events as the Gunpowder Plot in London and Orsini's Conspiracy in Paris. His tone, though forceful, was constantly marked by sweet reasonableness. Manifestly, rumor had maligned this country lawyer from the prairies. Here was no lout, no ignoramus; far from it! No wonder "the vast assemblage frequently rang with cheers and shouts of applause, which were prolonged and intensified at the close." [10]

It was a happy Lincoln who returned to his room at the Astor House at a late hour that night; for there could be no shadow of a doubt that he had magnificently triumphed. It was an equally happy Bryant who returned to Carmine Street to dream of words of encomium with which to fill his leading editorial the next day. The Sewardites might sulk; and Henry J. Raymond, in the *Times,* might try to belittle both speaker and speech. But tonight New York knew, as Cullen Bryant knew, that the Republican party had an admirable candidate for election in the coming autumn. And tomorrow, when the papers published the full text of the address, the country at large would know it.

6

During the next two years Bryant's enthusiasm for Lincoln waned considerably. After wielding his editorial pen to get Lincoln nominated and elected, Bryant began to wonder, more and more, whether he had done the wise thing. About his opposition to Seward he had no regrets. But had Lincoln proved to be the right man? Might not Salmon P. Chase, the liberal and idealistic but sound and business-like statesman from Ohio, have been better? As a native of New Hampshire and a graduate of Dartmouth College, Chase had a thoroughly good Yankee background. As a long-time resident of the Buckeye State, he knew the mind and the problems of the Western frontier almost as well as Lincoln. And as a dweller in the border city of Cincinnati, he had acquired an intelligent if never quite a sympathetic understanding of the Southern point of view. Lincoln had been very well advised in making Salmon P. Chase his Secretary of the Treasury. But would not Chase have been still better in the chair that Lincoln himself now occupied?

Of course Bryant did not blame Lincoln for the secession of the eleven Southern states. Better disunion than craven compromise! As Bryant had written in a spirited lyric, "Our Country's Call," in the summer of 1861,

> *The arms that wield the axe must pour*
> *An iron tempest on the foe.*

But Lincoln appeared to be a bewildered weakling, pulled hither and yon by his cabinet, by Congressional leaders, and by bickering military strategists. And, now in the saddle, he failed to give the war that ethical character that a forthright declaration against slavery would have given it.

Meanwhile, the war was going very badly for the North. Despite its immense superiority in man-power and resources, its military leaders were being constantly outgeneraled by the Confederate trio, Lee, Jackson, and Johnston. Northern armies had twice been routed at Bull Run, first under the incompetent General McDowell, and subsequently under the still more incompetent General Pope. Fussy, over-cautious General McClellan, commander of the Army of the Potomac, was spending most of his time drilling and retreating; even when he won an occasional tentative victory, as at Antietam, he permitted the good results to be largely nullified by the blundering of some nincompoop subordinate such as General Burnside. Only in the western theater of war were the Union forces meeting with any appreciable successes; and there the commander was a shabby, disreputable, bibulous fellow named Grant, whose past life had branded him as a besotted ne-er-do-well, and whose intimate acquaintances derisively declared that his Christian name ought to be "Useless" instead of Ulysses. And meanwhile the man in the White House apparently

[147]

sat twiddling his thumbs and trying to amuse his cabinet with crude anecdotes.

Clearly, something drastic must be done. If the administration and the Congress and the generals were indisposed to act vigorously, then the citizenry must speak out in no uncertain terms. Caustic editorials appeared in the New York papers, especially Bryant's *Evening Post* and Greeley's *Tribune*. Indignation meetings were held. Prominent New Yorkers, such as Mayor George Opdyke and Dr. Charles King, President of Columbia College, went to Washington to remonstrate with Lincoln. Finally, since New York editorial diatribes seemed to be getting no results on Capitol Hill or on Pennsylvania Avenue, it was decided that some outstanding gentleman of the press must do as Mayor Opdyke and Dr. King had done. If Mr. Lincoln did not bother to read editorials in New York papers—even papers that had supported him for nomination and election—perhaps he would at least be willing to grant some responsible editor a few minutes' interview.

But which gentleman of the press was to undertake this delicate mission? Certainly not Raymond of the *Times,* or Bennett of the *Herald,* or Marble of the *World;* for all of these editors had been consistently inimical to Lincoln. In fact, Bennett and Marble had shown decided "copperhead" leanings; they were not nearly so much interested in Northern victories as in a possible compromise that would restore New York's erstwhile prosperous trade with the South. By the process of elimination, that left Greeley of the *Tribune* and Bryant of the *Evening Post.* And Greeley, though his heart was in the right place, was an utter impossibility! The eccentric Greeley would be neither dignified nor tactful, and, as likely as not, he would propose to President Lincoln some chimerical scheme that would be even worse than inaction.

Bryant, then, must make the trip to Washington. It was not a pleasant thing to contemplate; for the month was August, a time when railroad journeys were mostly heat and cinders, and when the sprawling town on the Potomac would be a veritable Turkish bath. And, to a man of Cullen Bryant's delicate sensibilities, the idea of telling the President of the United States how to conduct his own business was far from alluring. Moreover, Cullen was no longer a young man; in November he would be sixty-eight. Although he was still surprisingly active and vigorous,

[148]

he found it increasingly necessary to take vacations in the country. Even now, when this particular call to Washington came, he was relaxing among his flower beds and his fruit trees at Cedarmere. But of course he must go on the thankless journey. The Bryant women folk said so; Parke Godwin emphatically agreed; and, in his heart of hearts, the aging but energetic editor knew that they were right.

7

The train trip from Jersey City to Washington proved not so bad as Cullen had anticipated. True, the weather was increasingly torrid; the car was stuffy and ill-smelling; the fresh air let in by the few open windows was largely offset by gusts of cinders from the huge funnel-shaped smokestack of the locomotive; the waits at "depots" were hot and tedious; and the farms and towns and villages, especially those below Chester and Wilmington, were shabby and untidy. For all that, however, what an agreeable contrast to the journey that Cullen had made to Washington just thirty years earlier! In '32 he had had to travel by stage-coach and steamboat, touching such out-of-the way places as Perth Amboy and Havre de Grace; and the trip had consumed three or four days. Today it was but a morning-to-night journey, all by steam cars, and with changes only at Philadelphia and Baltimore. Moreover, what a wonderful improvement were these big, commodious, eight-wheeled, leather-upholstered railroad cars of these 1860's over the tiny slow stage-coaches of yesteryear! Truly these later days were wonderful times. And after the war there would be still further improvements. Already there was talk of adopting a standard track gauge, which would make it possible for a single train to run all the way from Jersey City to Washington—or, for that matter, from New York to the new Western metropolis, Chicago. The cars, too, would be made more spacious, more comfortable, more elegant. In fact, just within the preceding two or three years a young man by the name of George Mortimer Pullman had designed and built a palatial sleeping-car at the stupendous cost of eighteen or twenty thousand dollars, and the car was now being successfully operated on some Western railroad—Cullen could not remember which one. Perhaps if Cullen Bryant lived till about 1870 he might have the enjoyable experience of going to bed in Jersey City, sleeping as soundly as in a good hotel, and

[149]

waking refreshed in Washington. He might even be able to order a delicious breakfast on the train. For, if sleeping-cars, why not dining-cars? As early as 1838 the Baltimore *Chronicle* had predicted both of these luxuries.[11] Thirty years later both of them would be in rather general use.[12]

8

Cullen found the city of Washington as much improved as the means of travel thither. Even riding from the "Depot" in the humid Southern August dusk, behind a scrawny cab horse driven by an aged Negro, he could notice a few improvements. The shops, for instance, were much larger, more elegant, and more metropolitan than those of a generation earlier. Substantial red brick dwellings were much more numerous. A few main thoroughfares, such as Pennsylvania Avenue and Seventh Street, were paved with cobblestones and lighted with gas lamps as luminous as those along Broadway. Commodious horse-cars rattled and jingled up and down the Avenue. And, as Cullen would very soon discover, the hostelry toward which he was bound was as fine and modern as any in New York. Yes, he was going to Willard's for two reasons: in the first place, it was the newest of Washington's great hotels, built no longer ago than the administration of Zachary Taylor; in the second place, it was only two squares from the Executive Mansion, a comfortable walking distance even in hot weather.

The metropolitan appearance of Washington recalled to Cullen Bryant that our national capital was now a great city of some seventy-five thousand inhabitants—in fact, the ninth largest city in the United States (not counting rebel New Orleans). Tomorrow, if his conference with the President did not take too long, he must go on a sight-seeing tour. Especially must he see the greatly enlarged Capitol building, to which two huge wings had been added in '48. When the dome was completed, the structure would be as impressive as any parliament house in the world.

Strolling the next morning from Willard's to the Executive Mansion, Bryant realized that this was his first trip South in mid-summer. The somnolent odor of honeysuckle, wistaria, and catalpa in Lafayette Square, and the fetid odor of Negroes all around, reminded him that he was far from New York, far from Roslyn. So did the everlasting presence of blue uniforms, of hale

[150]

soldiers and crippled soldiers—though in a different way. Here now was a city that several times during the past twelvemonth had been in imminent danger of beleaguerment. And tomorrow or next week the danger might recur.

Quite apart from the danger of beleaguerment or even capture, the national capital, in these war-time years, had become a singularly undesirable place in which to live. It was not merely that the town was swarming with war-workers, many of whom were obliged to spend both their working hours and their sleeping hours in cramped, ugly, inflammable, jerry-built temporary structures. No, the worst thing about war-time Washington was that it had become a moral cess-pool. Cullen Bryant, on his brief walk from Willard's to the White House, encountered no painted women, for ladies of easy virtue would hardly be disporting themselves on Pennsylvania Avenue at that hour of the morning. Nevertheless, he had been told on excellent authority that since the spring of '61, prostitution had become far more rampant in Washington than it had ever been in New York or Philadelphia or even the rough, rowdy young Western city of Chicago. Nor was sexual vice in the District of Columbia confined by any means to professional prostitution. Government clerkships, in innumerable cases, were said to be held by the mistresses of politicians and "graceless petty officeholders," and many of the clerks were said to be foolish young girls who had come to the capital city without funds and been forced to choose between sin and destitution. In May, 1864, Samuel Bowles's Springfield *Republican,* one of the most reliable, least sensational newspapers in the country, would report that fallen women were "believed to constitute a quarter of the civilian population of Washington." [13] Some day, when the war situation became a little less critical, Cullen Bryant must write an editorial on this appalling affront to decency and morality. Or he must ask Parke Godwin to do so.

9

Bryant's visit to the White House that day, in its immediate effects at least, produced no surprises. The President received the distinguished editor courteously, even cordially, and after a few pleasantries and a bad pun or two, assumed a properly serious air. Oh, yes, indeed, Mr. Lincoln remembered that Mr. Bryant was the *Post* man and was therefore well "posted" on the affairs of the nation. He also recalled Secretary Stanton's peevish remark that the New York papers must be reliable. For did they not keep on lying and *relying?*

As the President lapsed into seriousness, Bryant noticed that the man had aged considerably since that memorable February evening at Cooper Institute. Looking much older than his fifty-three years, Mr. Lincoln now wore a graying square chin beard. His mouth and forehead had gathered many wrinkles, and his tired eyes were a little bloodshot. Obviously, being chief executive in times like these was no sinecure. Moreover, the President's domestic life was known to be far from happy. Within recent months one of the Lincoln children, a twelve-year-old boy, had died. And rumor persisted that Mrs. Lincoln was an extremely difficult woman to live with. Silly, extravagant, vain, and shrewish, she was said to make life miserable for her easy-going spouse. It was even whispered—though Cullen Bryant did not believe these ugly whispers—that Mary Todd Lincoln was disloyal to the Union. At any rate, however, it could not be denied that she had both brothers and brothers-in-law in the Confederate army. Cullen, who had known more than forty years of unalloyed connubial bliss, and whose lovely and devoted daughters had given him nothing but pride and joy, could pity a man whose home life was infelicitous; he did not, however, quite know how to sympathize.

The President listened patiently, even appreciatively, to what Bryant had to say. Truly, there could be no question of "the excellence of his [Lincoln's] intentions" or "the singleness of his purposes." [14] Yes, of course the war must go on until the Union had been completely re-established—and on a Northern basis. But Lincoln was exasperatingly vague and indecisive about methods.

Back in the sanctum of the *Evening Post,* a few weeks later, Bryant was again inveighing editorially against "the weakness and vacillation of the Administration." [15]

10

And then, for some reason or variety of reasons, things began to happen. On September 22, 1862, President Lincoln announced the forthcoming Emancipation Proclamation (as of January 1, 1863), thus making the war the moral crusade that Bryant had repeatedly insisted it should be. On the third day of July, 1863, after three days of ferocious fighting at Gettysburg, Pennsylvania, General Meade sent Lee's army reeling back into Maryland with some forty per cent of its men killed, wounded, or missing. On the very next day Grant celebrated the Fourth by capturing Vicksburg and thus wresting the all-important lower Mississippi from the hands of the Confederacy. In the November election the following year, the discredited General McClellan, running on a peace-without-victory platform, was overwhelmed by President Lincoln at the polls, the electoral vote being 212 to 21, and the President's popular plurality well over four hundred thousand in a vote of barely four million. A few days before Christmas, General Sherman's army, after having scourged Georgia from end to end, marched triumphantly into Savannah. Meanwhile, the diplomatic position of the South had been rendered hopeless by the fact that no European power would officially recognize the existence of the Confederate States of America. Even after the turn of the tide, Napoleon III, arch-enemy of democracy, was eager to recognize the Confederacy. But without the support of England, Napoleon dared not act; and the British government was too realistic, the British people too anti-slavery, to establish official dealings with a "nation" that was now fighting hopelessly for the right to hold three million human beings in bondage.

11

There remained, however, a few sore spots, one of the ugliest of which erupted at almost the moment when the North had passed the crisis. On July 13, 1863—just ten days after Meade's victory at Gettysburg, and nine days after Grant's triumph at Vicksburg—New York began witnessing the bloodiest, most disgraceful series of riots in her history: the Draft Riots. These disorders resulted from a tardily enacted and clumsily conceived conscription act.

The Civil War was almost two years old when, on March 3, 1863, Congress finally decided that an adequate army could not be maintained without a Federal draft law. By this law all able-bodied male citizens between the ages of twenty and forty-five were declared liable to military service. There were, however, two loopholes which made this law exceedingly vulnerable. The first of these was that any drafted man could obtain exemption by providing a satisfactory substitute. The second was that any drafted man, by paying the sum of three hundred dollars, could purchase exemption outright.

In view of this latter proviso, it is hardly surprising that demagogic politicians and editors of "copperhead" leanings raised the cry that Abe Lincoln's war was a rich man's war, but a poor man's fight. This cry was not slow in producing baleful results. On Saturday, July 11, the law went into effect. On Monday, July 13, fierce rioting broke out in New York. Draft headquarters and armories were looted and wrecked; stores, dwellings, and a Negro orphans' asylum were burned; newspaper offices were attacked; and some four or five hundred persons, guilty and innocent, were killed. Not until the following Thursday did the police, the firemen, and the soldiery succeed in restoring order.

Down in Richmond a high official of the Confederate government exultantly declared the tidings of the "sedition at New York" to be "very, very good news." Up in Albany the Democratic governor, Horatio Seymour, while deploring the destruction of life and property, laid the blame for the riots upon "an unjust and unconstitutional law." In New York such anti-administration papers as the *World,* the *Herald,* and the *Daily News* condoned the great mass of the rioters as poor men "with a burning sense of wrong toward the government" and toward "a war mismanaged almost into hopelessness, perverted almost into partisanship." [16]

But Bryant's *Evening Post,* like Greeley's *Tribune,* condemned the Draft Riots in the most scathing terms. Without undertaking to pass judgment upon the merits of the Conscription Act, the *Post* denounced the ring-leaders of the mob as "a small band of cutthroats, pickpockets, and robbers" who were amenable to no suasion but "an abundance of grape and canister." And of the cowardly policemen who had attempted to dispel the mob by the firing of blank cartridges, it declared succinctly, "They ought to be shot."

The work of the mob proved as futile as it was nefarious. Within a month after the Draft Riots, a bi-partisan state commission pronounced the Conscription Act to be fully valid; on August 19 the New York draft was permanently resumed; and even the recalcitrant Governor Seymour advised "peaceful submission to conscription." [17]

On a mild, sunny April afternoon in 1865, Cullen Bryant strolled through his Cedarmere orchards, now pink and white and fragrant with blossoms foretelling a bountiful yield of fruit in the coming summer and autumn. It was a Sunday, the ninth day of the month, and that morning he had attended services at the little Presbyterian church at Roslyn. Ordinarily, on a Sunday so early in spring, he would have gone to All Souls Unitarian Church in New York—partly because, under ordinary circumstances he would still have been in town; and partly because he preferred the liberal sermons of Dr. Henry Whitney Bellows to the Calvinistic orthodoxy of the Roslyn Presbyterian preacher. But that spring the Bryants had returned to Roslyn unusually early, and Cullen had become such an inveterate church-goer that he preferred being suckled in a creed outworn to having the world too much with him.

Events of the past few years, both in his own immediate family and in the nation at large, had made him increasingly spiritual. This afternoon he was strolling alone for the reason that his beloved Fanny had become too delicate to stroll with him; and he had taken Fanny out of town in the hope that the quiet and the pure air of the country would strengthen her.

As he walked among the blossoms, he was doubtless thinking a little sadly of human frailty—of the physical frailty of advancing age; of the moral frailty that caused the slaughter and maiming of countless strong young men on fields of battle. It was the old, old story that Cullen Bryant had repeated so often in his poetry: the weakness and transitoriness of human life; the strength and permanence of inanimate nature. These lovely orchards would bloom for a generation as yet unborn, and for generations after that one.

We may be sure, however, that Cullen's thoughts were not entirely sad; on so beautiful an April afternoon they could not be. The state of the nation was, on the whole, wonderfully encouraging. Abraham Lincoln had grown so tremendously in spiritual stature that he had become perhaps the noblest statesman that the country had ever known. And Ulysses Grant, the erstwhile ne'er-do-well, was winning victory after victory in the Wilderness of northeastern Virginia. The South was near exhaustion; surely, before many months the Confederacy would be an evil thing of the past.

Cullen, in the midst of his meditations, was surprised to hear footsteps behind him. On turning around, he was still more surprised to see his son-in-law and chief assistant, Parke Godwin, striding toward him with unwonted alacrity. What could be amiss? Parke and Fanny Godwin often came out to Roslyn for Sunday dinner, but this week-end they had planned to stay in town. In fact, events had been occurring so rapidly in the region of the Potomac that Godwin had expected to spend at least part of that Sabbath day at his desk. Evidently something most unusual had happened—something that had caused Godwin to hurry out to Roslyn on the only afternoon train that ran on Sundays. Godwin looked flushed and excited; but the expression on his face was one of joy, not sorrow. In his hand he waved a yellow telegram. Yes, the great event had happened! Lee had surrendered to Grant at Appomattox Court House. Of all the once proud Confederate armies, none now remained with the single exception of a small, depleted corps under the command of General Joseph E. Johnston; and so mercilessly were Joe Johnston's ragged, weary, footsore little band being harassed by the superior forces of General Sherman that the end had been in sight for weeks. On this bright Sunday afternoon the South, as well as the North, knew that to all intents and purposes the great war was over.

Tomorrow, from the Mason-Dixon line to the Canadian border, there would be scenes of wild rejoicing in every city and town: flag-wavings, fireworks, torch-light parades, carousings in taverns. In sedate places, such as the Union League Club in New York, there would be patriotic speeches—one of which, as Parke Godwin announced, would be made by the dean of New York editors, William Cullen Bryant.

13

One short week later the country was in the deepest mourning. A crazy actor by the name of John Wilkes Booth had shot and mortally wounded President Lincoln. The President had died within a few hours. Of the numerous poetic tributes to the martyred chief, the two most famous, of course, are "When Lilacs Last in the Dooryard Bloomed" and "O Captain! My Captain!"— both of them by Walt Whitman. Not even these, however, are more deserving of immortality than a simple, unpretentious four-stanza lyric, "The Death of Lincoln," by William Cullen Bryant.

> *Oh, slow to smite and swift to spare,*
> *Gentle and merciful and just!*
> *Who, in the fear of God, didst bear*
> *The sword of power, a nation's trust!*

> *In sorrow by thy bier we stand,*
> *Amid the awe that hushes all,*
> *And speak the anguish of a land*
> *That shook with horror at thy fall.*

> *Thy task is done; the bond are free:*
> *We bear thee to an honored grave,*
> *Whose proudest monument shall be*
> *The broken fetters of the slave.*

> *Pure was thy life; its bloody close*
> *Hath placed thee with the sons of light,*
> *Among the noblest host of those*
> *Who perished in the cause of Right.*

14

During the entire Civil War period, Bryant published only one book—a little volume with the self-explanatory title *Thirty Poems*. That was in 1864, the year of his seventieth birthday. To the reader who thinks of William Cullen Bryant as having written and published all of his most notable verse in the early part of his career it is interesting to mention the fact that the 1864 volume contained Bryant's two longest original poems, "Sella" and "The Little People of the Snow," and two of his most memorable lyrics, "The Planting of the Apple Tree" and "Robert of Lincoln."

Most notable of all the *Thirty Poems*, perhaps, is "The Poet," a nine-stanza lyric in which Bryant answers a question that must often have been asked: Why did William Cullen Bryant, foremost citizen among American poets, not write many more occasional poems than he did? In the light of stirring events, what silenced the muse of this gifted poet-editor, who was a greater public figure than any other American bard except Lowell, and who was much nearer to the public pulse than the aristocratic Lowell could ever have been? How did it happen that this eloquent maker of memorial tributes in prose, this layer of corner-stones and dedicator of monuments, was so seldom moved to record noble occasions in rhyme?

The answer, to Bryant, was simple. As he so beautifully declares in "The Poet," the framing of an immortal lyric is not "the pastime of a drowsy summer day." Only the poet who has actually clung with terror to the tossed wreck of his sinking ship can sing with true spontaneity of a disaster at sea. Only the poet who has actually scaled the ramparts and fought hand-to-hand with "the assaulting host" is fully qualified to sing of a battle. In other words, great poems are not made to order; they come from the poet's heart, from his own burning experience, or they do not come at all. Cullen Bryant knew well that whether amid the hubbub of lower Manhattan or in the quiet of Cedarmere, he was far removed from the vicissitudes and dangers and carnage of the "iron tempest" at Antietam or Gettysburg. So far as the tempests and the great tumult were concerned, he was only a bystander— an interested and a sympathetic and a tremendously helpful bystander, it is true—but still, only a bystander. Too old to don a uniform himself, he had neither son nor grandson to send into battle. Who, then, was he to tell the soldier or the soldier's kinfolk what their emotions really were?

CHAPTER X

O Goddess, Sing the Wrath

1

ON THE whole, the advancing years dealt kindly with Cullen Bryant. The "delicate child and slender" of the 1790's evolved into the small but wiry and agile old man of the 1860's. Very seldom was his work interrupted by illness. Never did he have to wear spectacles, either for reading or for observing distant objects. And even at three score years and ten, he scorned the elevator leading to his ninth-floor office; he preferred to climb the long and numerous flights of stairs. In short, at seventy he was as well and active as his fifty-year-old colleagues. As for his personal appearance, although his bald head, his bushy gray beard, his shaggy brows, and his long, flowing back-locks gave him a patriarchal look, his skin remained surprisingly young and fresh and unwrinkled and free from sallowness, his gray eyes surprisingly luminous and alertly expressive. In dress, moreover, he continued as fastidious and dapper as when he had arrived in New York forty years earlier.

Bryant attributed his excellent physical condition to his habits. Whether in town or in the country, he sought the open air at every opportunity, and, both in speed and in distance, he could outwalk—even outrun—most of his middle-aged associates. But this was not all; every morning and every night he exercised religiously for a few moments with dumbbells and Indian clubs. His eating and drinking habits were as regular as they were ascetic. Whatever the press of business, he ate his meals both punctually and leisurely, regaling himself far more upon fruits and vegetables than upon meats. Graham bread he much preferred to white bread; milk and cocoa, to tea and coffee. Tobacco in all forms he eschewed entirely, not in any prudish or Pharisaical spirit, but because he felt sure that whatever pleasure or relaxation an occasional cigar or pipe might have given him, it would have been unkind to his heart and his constitutionally delicate lungs. Indeed, his only dissipation was a glass of wine now and then or—less frequently—a glass of lager beer. And the glasses were always small, and seldom refilled at the moment. As for late hours, only an exceptionally tempting lecture or concert or play would keep him out of bed later than ten o'clock at night.

Old Cullen Bryant was fortunate, also, in another way: the friends whom he had known most intimately and affectionately through scores of years were as long-lived as he. Kate Sedgwick and Richard Henry Dana and Gulian Verplanck and Orville Dewey all remained in the land of the living, and although Bryant seldom saw any of them except his fellow-townsman Verplanck in New York, he carried on a constant correspondence with all of them.

The Bryant family, too, stayed happily intact. The younger daughter, Julia, having remained unmarried, dwelt under the parental roof—or roofs. The elder daughter, Fanny, wife of Parke Godwin, was a near neighbor to her parents and a frequent visitor both to West Fifteenth Street and to Cedarmere. And Fanny Godwin's children had much more frequent contact with "Papa and Mamma By," as they affectionately called the old people, than most grandchildren have with their grandparents. The family of Cullen and Fanny Bryant were never to be scattered and separated as the family of Peter and Sally Bryant had been.

As an editor, the aging Bryant was singularly fortunate in having for his chief lieutenant a man of the calibre of Parke Godwin. Godwin, a native of New Jersey and a graduate of Princeton, had come to the *Evening Post* in 1837, as a youth of twenty-one, and had grown up with the paper. At the close of the Civil War he was a vigorous man in his fiftieth year, admirably equipped to relieve his father-in-law, more and more, of the bur-

[160   ]

dens and responsibilities of chief editorship. Although Godwin's editorials, as Professor Nevins has said, "had not the eloquence or finish of Bryant's," [1] they were quite as scholarly, quite as well informed, as those of the older man. But Godwin was not merely an able editor; what was even more satisfying to Bryant was the fact that upon every important question, political and economic and social, Godwin saw eye-to-eye with the old gentleman. Like Bryant, Godwin had joined the Republican party because of its attitudes toward slavery and the Union. Like Bryant, on the other hand, Godwin viewed with alarm certain post-war Republican tendencies: notably protectionism and the waving of the bloody shirt. Like Bryant, Godwin had the utmost contempt for carpet-baggers, scalawags, and South-hating politicians such as Thaddeus Stevens. Like Bryant, Godwin upheld the honest (if crude and tactless) President Andrew Johnson in the latter's quarrel with the intolerant Edwin M. Stanton. And, to move our narrative forward momentarily to 1872, Godwin fully agreed with Bryant on the relative merits of the rival presidential nominees Grant and Greeley. To Godwin, as to Bryant, the General's administration in Washington had been a dismal disappointment: inept, inefficient, even corrupt. But the very unsatisfactory Grant would have to be preferred to the erratic, eccentric, uncouth, boorish Greeley; for, as Bryant declared with unwonted asperity, a candidate for the office of President of the United States "should be, at least, a gentleman." [2] And Godwin had uttered no protest against the use of exactly these words in the editorial columns of the *Post*.

Yes, Parke Godwin was a man and an editor after Cullen Bryant's own heart. Except for the trifling fact that Parke was constitutionally a bit lazy, the younger Fanny had made an excellent matrimonial choice; her father, an equally good choice of junior partner. To old Cullen Bryant it was the greatest of comforts to know that when he finally laid down his editorial pen it would be taken up by a man who would implicitly maintain the best Bryant-*Post* traditions in every way.

2

The winter of 1865-6 found Cullen very much occupied with domestic affairs. The continued delicate state of his wife's health—no better than on that memorable April Sunday eight or nine months before—impelled the old gentleman to a new project.

[161]

Since even Cedarmere, with its refreshing breezes from the Sound, was hardly bracing enough for an invalid in mid-summer, he would seek a summer dwelling farther north.

In this connection, naturally, his thoughts turned to his beloved Berkshires. Great Barrington, with its broad elm-shaded streets and its chaste white Dutch colonial houses, was indeed a pleasant little town—much pleasanter when viewed from the distance of many miles and many years than in the old days of restless, unsatisfied ambition. No longer was Great Barrington to be thought of as the rustic, Philistine home of "the sons of strife"; it was to be remembered as the village in which Cullen Bryant had met, courted, and wed his "fairest of the rural maids."

But, no! Great Barrington, with all its beauty, all its salubriousness, all its precious memories, was not quite the place for Fanny now. Complete rural quiet was what she needed—and Great Barrington was much noisier, much more populous than Roslyn. What with the New Haven Railroad and the droves of summer tourists, not to mention the flourishing paper mill, it would be especially bad in July and August.

Then what about Cummington? What about the old Peter Bryant homestead? Alas! the cottage in which Cullen had first seen the light of day had long since passed out of the hands of the Bryant family. Well, perhaps it could be purchased back. New England farmers, still lured by dreams of fertile lands to the west, were by no means reluctant to sell their stony acres, especially if they could get a generous sum. Yes, there was an idea worth considering. The very next time Cullen ran into town, he must ask his lawyer to investigate.

A little correspondence revealed the fact that the old homestead could be bought. Of course the house, only a story and a half in height, was much too small for comfort. But it could be enlarged and remodeled. The addition of a story and perhaps a wing or two could make it positively commodious. The next time Cullen was in town, he would tell his lawyer to lose no time in closing the deal. He would also consult an architect.

The old farm was repurchased, and the process of remodeling the house proceeded forthwith. The plans pictured a beautiful two-and-a-half-story Dutch colonial house of white clapboards, with a new wing on each side. As for the location, it was ideal: a good mile and a half from the center of the village.

BRYANT'S CHILDHOOD HOME

The prospect aroused Fanny's enthusiasm quite as much as it did Cullen's. In the brisk, delightful air of Cummington she would become a new woman; by autumn she would be stronger and more energetic than in years. Writing to a friend in May, she spoke fervently of the happy, healthful weeks that lay ahead in "the dear old homestead where my husband passed his childhood and earlier youth." [3]

The new-old house was to be ready for occupancy in June, and the house-warming was to be a joyous family reunion; for Arthur and John Bryant, who had long hungered for a sight of the old place and a renewal of the old associations, had gladly accepted an invitation to come back from Illinois and bring their families. One regret of all concerned was that Sally and Austin had not lived to join in the happy occasion. Another regret was that Fanny Godwin and her children were in Europe.

3

June arrived, and with it the Illinois Bryants. But Cullen and Fanny and Julia lingered on at Cedarmere. The sad truth was that Fanny Bryant's condition had grown steadily worse; in fact, so feeble had the aged woman become that the journey from Roslyn to Cummington would certainly have proved fatal to her. Cullen, who had become an ardent convert to homeopathy, had summoned one of the leading New York homeopaths, Dr. John F. Gray. Doubtless many of Cullen's friends and relatives regretted that he did not call an orthodox allopathic practitioner; but Fanny was fully satisfied with her husband's choice.

Bryant's devotion to homeopathy was truly that of a zealot. As early as 1842 he had delivered public lectures in defense of that relatively new and decidedly heterodox school of medicine.[4] Sixteen years later, in referring to a serious illness suffered by Fanny during the Bryants' European sojourn of 1857-8, Cullen had written to his brother John: "I am inclined to think that if she had had an allopathic physician I should not have brought her alive out of Naples, and that for her recovery I have to thank the gentle methods of the new system."[5]

At first glance, Cullen Bryant's espousal of homeopathy appears surprising for at least two reasons. In the first place, Cullen was the son of a better-than-average practitioner of the old school. In the second place, he was a man of too keen and too well disciplined a mind, too rich an intellectual background, to fall an easy prey to sensational new fads and "isms."

As for homeopathy, it *was* generally regarded in Bryant's day as a fad rather than as a substantial contribution to the advancement of medical science. Among the intellectually respectable, it had scarcely any higher standing than spiritualism, Millerism, or animal magnetism. Of its very founder, Samuel Christian Friedrich Hahnemann, an erratic eighteenth-century German doctor, it had been remarked: "That man would have been a great chemist, had he not been a great quack." And as late as 1893 Dr. Edward Berdoe, a leading light in the British medical profession, could say of the disciples of Hahnemann: "The sciences of anatomy and physiology are quite superfluous to the homeopathist."

When homeopathy was first practiced by a few daring experimentalists among American physicians, they "were expelled from the medical societies, and were avoided by their former friends and companions."

Bryant's zeal for homeopathy was probably not inspired by either the dubious Hahnemannic theory that "like cures like" or the patently absurd Hahnemannic theory that "all chronic maladies proceed from the itch." What probably impressed Bryant was the fact that homeopathy came to be a consistent and persistent protest against the time-honored but stupid practice of administering strong and disgustingly unpalatable drugs in enormous dosages.

As for the sneers and raised eyebrows of the intellectually respectable and influential, Cullen Bryant was far from the sort of man to be intimidated by such signs of disapproval. A man who could renounce Trinitarianism, Federalism, protectionism, Bankism, and appeasement of the cotton interests was hardly to be bullied into conforming to the conventional thought of the "better element." And, as in his other apostasies, Bryant lived to see his faith in homeopathy justified in no small measure; for, although comparatively few outstanding physicians ever became willing to wear the badge of homeopathy, the medical profession as a whole came gradually to adopt all of the most sensible of the homeopathic practices. Indeed, long before Bryant's death the phrase "allopathic doses" came to be a phrase of unqualified derogation.

Dr. Gray pronounced Fanny Bryant's ailment a liver obstruction, complicated by water on the heart, which neither drugs nor the surgeon's knife could cure. Through ten weeks of suffering the unfortunate woman lingered at Cedarmere, with Cullen or Julia almost constantly at her bedside. On July 27 the end came.

Fanny's death proved the inspiration for Cullen's most beautiful memorial poem—though not immediately. At the moment, and for some three months thereafter, the bereaved old man was so overwhelmed with grief that he was inarticulate. For forty-five years his beloved wife had been his constant companion, his constant helpmeet. And although two-score years of metropolitan residence punctuated by foreign travel had made her, in the very best sense, a charming and gracious woman of the world, she had always remained to Cullen his "fairest of the rural maids." On every important problem he had sought her advice, and invariably he had found it helpful. Every poem that he wrote he repeated to her; and, as he confided to his daughters, he had "found its success with the public to be precisely in proportion to the impression it made upon her." [6] Now this beautiful, wise, kindly, loving wife was gone, and for weeks Cullen felt a sorrow too deep for words.

In the autumn, however, a memorial poem shaped itself in his mind. Here was a lyric that the author of "The Poet" could write from the heart; for here was no second-hand theme; no vicarious experience, but a devastating tempest in which he himself had been most cruelly tossed and buffeted. The result was "October, 1866," a threnody in the stately quatrain measure of Gray's "Elegy." The spontaneity of the poem may be observed partly from the fact that it is totally free from Bryant's penchant for contrasting mortal man with immortal nature. The only striking contrast in this poem is that between the beauty of the July weather and the somberness of the occasion. For the rest, the piece is very, very personal. And since Bryant's Unitarianism was of the right-wing variety, his elegy expresses no Emersonian vagueness on the subject of personal immortality. Cullen firmly believed that Fanny's immortality was no mere shadow or monument, no mere memory to her loved ones and friends who remained on earth. He felt certain—as certain as any orthodox Trinitarian—that Fanny now abode in "fields of unwithering bloom," yet that at the same time she continued to stand near to the members of her family, serving them "with loving ministrations" and directing their wandering thoughts away from every treacherous and evil path.

Cullen and Julia spent August and September at Cummington —not very happily, of course. Naturally, renewed association with the Bryant brothers was a satisfaction. And the renovated house was beautiful—even more beautiful than the architect's plans had pictured. Yet to Cullen this very beauty was as a draught of worm- wood. Had he not planned this renovation largely for Fanny's sake? No wonder he remarked sadly to his brother John that his interest in this new-old place had been "greatly diminished."⁷

As the summer wore on, Cullen found himself confronted with a new worry: the ordeal attendant upon Fanny's illness and death had seriously impaired Julia's health. A New York homeopathist, called from his summer cottage at Lenox, prescribed a complete change of scene, especially a sea voyage. Julia's sad eyes bright- ened perceptibly; to her the prescription meant Europe. In the mind of the tired, heart-broken old father, the thought of another trip to Europe aroused no enthusiasm; but now his main concern was the happiness and well-being of Julia. In October they sailed from New York on one of the fast new "screw-steamers" of the day, the *Periere.*

Cullen's letters from abroad, in the ensuing months, show how little pleasure he derived from that last trip to the Old Country. Writing to Dana on December 17, 1866, from Amelie-les-Bains, a French Pyrenees resort, Bryant was still harboring unpleasant memories of the voyage across. The passage, he admitted, was breathtakingly fast—only nine days—and relatively smooth; but so incessantly did the new-fangled "screw-steamer" roll from side to side that Bryant suffered the most enduring fit of sea-sickness in all his experience. In the same letter he complained of the dark- ness and chill and rain of Paris in late autumn.⁸

Writing to a Mrs. Moulton, a Roslyn neighbor, on January 22, from Seville, he roundly berated the Spanish winter climate, the Spanish winter landscape, and the Spanish people. The days, it seems, were too short; the mornings and the evenings, benumb- ingly cold. The landscape at that season was "in its undress." As for the people, they were mostly a half-civilized, bull-fighting, gambling, indolent, inhospitable, ill-bred lot—especially the young men, who seemed to have nothing better to do than stand or sit loafing in the sunshine, staring rudely at foreign ladies and making uncivil remarks about them.[9]

Writing to his brother John, on February 27, from Florence, he expatiated upon the unsettled political condition of Italy, its discontented people, its high cost of living, its omnipresent militarism, its grasping and arrogant priests.[10] Indeed, not even the satisfaction of meeting and conversing with the great Garibaldi seemed to atone for Cullen's generally unfavorable impression of the entire peninsula.

As for Germany, it was in that country that the aged poet-editor suffered a severe cold which was accompanied by a touch of fever. It was there also—in Dresden—that he received a telegram from Geneva, informing him of the death of his six-year-old grandson, Walter Godwin.[11]

Nor did Great Britain, the last country on the itinerary, give the querulous old man much greater satisfaction than the Continent had given him. Writing to Miss Julia C. Sands (presumably a daughter or a maiden sister of the long-deceased Robert Sands), Cullen declared that for "striking mountain scenery" North Wales was no better than the White Mountains or the Adirondacks or the Alleghanies; that the Welsh inn where he and Julia stayed served no fresh fruit, "not even a gooseberry"; and that the British July weather was even more disagreeably chilly than ever.[12]

Only after he had returned to the comforts of his "very beautiful" Roslyn did he admit, somewhat grudgingly, that he and Julia had had "a rather pleasant time" in England.[13]

7

Even in the winter of Cullen Bryant's discontent, however, a new inspiration was beginning to ferment in the old poet's mind. In the months following Fanny's death he had often thought vaguely of some sort of *magnum opus,* some creative project so strenuous and exacting that its execution would leave him neither time nor energy to brood over his bereavement. But what sort of project? For a long time he could think of nothing at all suitable. For lengthy poetic romances such as Professor Longfellow's *Evangeline* or *Hiawatha,* or Mr. Tennyson's *Idylls of the King,* he had no talent whatsoever. Still less could he do anything in dialect, like Professor Lowell's wise and witty *Biglow Papers*. As a reviewer of his 1864 volume, *Thirty Poems*, had pointed out in the *Independent*, "No great poem—using the word 'great' in the sense of size—has illustrated his [Bryant's] career—no mighty epic flight, no grand dramatic masterpiece, no long narrative of heroic deeds, or of crime and sorrow and woe." [14]

No, his poetic genius was essentially lyrical and reflective; almost never could he go much beyond a hundred lines in a single poem.

One day in London, however, an inspiration came to him quite by chance. On rainy summer mornings in the British metropolis, when the weather was too inclement for a pleasant stroll in Hyde Park, he and Julia would often saunter through the museums or browse in bookshops. On one such morning, apparently, after an hour's communion with the Turner Collection in the National Gallery, they had wandered into a second-hand bookshop in the vicinity of Charing Cross.

In the sputtering gas light of the dingy little shop Cullen started glancing half curiously, half indifferently at the faded, worn titles of a comglomeration of musty tomes that stood backs-upward on a scarred, stained Elizabethan draw-table. Suddenly seizing and opening a dusty, somewhat dilapidated volume of crown octavo dimensions, he uttered an exclamation. His indifference had suddenly vanished.

The volume that had excited his eager attention was Homer's *Iliad*, done in Spanish verse by Jose Gomez y Hermosilla. At the bottom of the title page appeared the name of a Madrid publisher and the dating 1825.

Cullen promptly decided that he must have the book. And since the book needed rebinding, and had obviously no particular collector's value, he experienced no difficulty in purchasing it for a mere pittance: a shilling or so.

8

Emerging from the shop with the Spanish Homer, the Bryants started strolling westward. Although the rain was increasing from a drizzle into a mild downpour, neither father nor daughter seemed inclined to call a cab. Indeed, the old man's experience of the few minutes just past had so thoroughly aroused his enthusiasm that he appeared oblivious of the rain. And as they passed from the narrow confines of Cockspur Street into the fashionable precincts of Pall Mall, Julia forgot to be ashamed of the shabby blue umbrella that Cullen held over them—that disgraceful old umbrella that he had persisted in carrying through unnumbered years.

"You know," Cullen was saying, as they plodded cheerfully past half the elite clubs of the British metropolis, "Homer takes my memory back almost sixty years." And he went on to speak of a far-off winter when, under the tutelage of Parson Moses Hallock at Plainfield, he had first read the *Iliad* in the original. And then he spoke of a still more remote time: those rainy afternoons at Cummington when he and Julia's Uncle Austin, armed with wooden swords and shields, had played Achilles and Agamemnon in the old barn.

Julia was delighted. Not since the Sunday of Appomattox, more than a year before her mother's death, had her father shown such verve, such enthusiasm.

She ventured to ask Cullen whether he had ever considered the possibility of a new English translation of the *Iliad*—a verse translation. A lengthy project such as that, it occurred to her, would be a godsend to her parent. She remembered having heard that in the years immediately following the tragic death of Frances Longfellow, Professor Longfellow had devoted himself to a metrical translation of Dante's *Divina Commedia*.

Yes, replied Cullen, he had thought of such a thing. To tell the truth, he had thought of it even before the death of Julia's mother. In fact, he had brought to Europe a pocket *Iliad* in the original—had intended to read a little in it every day. But somehow, till he had found this Spanish thing this morning, he had given no further thought to Homer.

9

In the autumn, at Cedarmere, the project got under way. Before putting a word of translation on paper, Cullen had read and re-read the *Iliad* from beginning to end, a task which, with the aid of his old college Greek grammar and lexicon, he had found not too arduous. Only rarely did he feel obliged to consult the literal English prose translation in the Bohn Library, and still more rarely did he bother to look at the freer English verse translations of Pope and Cowper respectively. A little more frequently, perhaps, did he dip into the Spanish version of Gomez y Hermosilla or the German version of Johann Heinrich Voss; and this he did not so much for instruction as from curiosity or from a desire to vary his Greek reading with the reading of modern languages. The Voss *Iliad*, it seemed to him, was more faithful to the original, if less graceful, than the Gomez y Hermosilla.

And meanwhile he discussed the matter informally with relatives and associates and friends: Julia or some Roslyn neighbor, at home; Parke Godwin or John Bigelow, at the *Evening Post* office; Henry Longfellow or Professor E. T. Thayer, of Harvard College—these last two by correspondence. Would there be a widespread demand for a new English metrical translation of the *Iliad*? If so, how should it differ from Pope's *Iliad* or from Cowper's? Should it be rhymed or unrhymed, and what metre should be employed? Should the characters bear their original Greek names or the more familiar Roman names?

10

About the wide appeal of a readable American translation of the *Iliad*, Cullen Bryant was not long left in doubt. A chance conversation with a Roslyn neighbor, a college-bred New York lawyer but a man of no pretensions to classical erudition, left the old man's mind free from the slightest doubt.

"Why, my dear Mr. Bryant," declared the lawyer unhesitatingly, "of course the public would like it. All of us who ever attended college—or, for that matter, academy—have been exposed to the ancient classics. And heaven pity the educated man who has formed no lasting love for those old Greek and Roman legends! Now, mind you, most of us don't keep up our Greek and Latin reading as you've done. As for me—and I know I'm typical—I haven't tried to read a page of Greek in thirty years. But that's all the more reason why I'd welcome an easy, painless way of renewing acquaintance with the *Iliad*. Yes, sir, I'd love the excitement of the Siege of Troy—love it more than I ever did when old Parson Griggs made me study it as a chore. No fooling with confounded declensions and conjugations this time! No thumbing a tiresome old lexicon—and sometimes forgetting the tarnal word before I could even get back to the passage! Why, Mr. Bryant,

[171]

what a splendid idea your translation is! What a delightful way of renewing acquaintance with an old familiar friend!"

And, of course, the lawyer-neighbor was right. In a day when every academy and high-school pupil studied Latin, and many studied Greek, the *Iliad* was as well known and well liked among educated people as—let us say—*Macbeth* or *Ivanhoe* or *David Copperfield*. Yes, indeed! A meritorious new American *Iliad* would sell almost as well as a meritorious new American novel, especially if that *Iliad* happened to come from a pen as distinguished as that of William Cullen Bryant.

11

In the matter of versification, Bryant appears to have followed his own counsel. Without even experimenting, he knew that Pope's rocking-horse couplets would not do. No, it was not a question of the bother of rhyme-hunting. It was the fact that Pope's sing-song rhymes were utterly alien to the whole epic spirit—more alien, even, than the fussy little Twickenham bard's pompous euphemisms and circumlocutions. No wonder Bentley had said, "A pretty poem, Mr. Pope; but you must not call it Homer." In Bryant's *Iliad* there would be no rhymes, couplet or otherwise.

But what about metre? Walking through his Cedarmere grounds one sunny afternoon, Cullen pondered over a statement that he had read the night before in Professor Matthew Arnold's "On Translating Homer." Arnold was insistent that the proper Homeric measure in English, as in Greek, was the classical dactylic hexameter. Well, reflected Cullen modestly, a professor-practitioner of poetry with an Oxford M.A. should be an incomparably more erudite scholar than a New York journalist whose formal education had ended after one year at a small New England college. Moreover, Voss had used the dactylic hexameter in German—with admirable results. But as Cullen tried framing a couple of long dactylic lines in English, he shook his head vigorously. No! Arnold and Voss to the contrary notwithstanding, the old metre was all wrong. For ancient Greek and Latin, indubitably, it was the heroic measure. But English is a different kind of language; English has too many monosyllabic words, too few connective particles. In English, as Surrey and Marlowe and Shakespeare and Milton discovered long ago, the heroic measure is the iambic pentameter.

[172]

"The big difference is," soliloquized Cullen, "that Greek verse scans by vowel quantities; English verse, by accentuation. Now who ever heard of an English poem in unrhymed dactylic hexameter? Let me think. Oh, yes, of course. There *is* Henry Longfellow's *Evangeline*. But"—and Cullen chuckled at the thought— "I'm sure Henry himself would never call his pretty-pretty Acadian romance an epic."

No, long before Cullen ended his stroll he had become convinced that there was only one suitable versification for an English epic, whether original or translated from a foreign tongue: the noble versification of Milton's *Paradise Lost*, the unrhymed iambic pentameter. Yes, Bryant's *Iliad* would be in blank verse.

12

The next morning, at breakfast, the old gentleman suddenly asked Julia whether she remembered who Hera was.

Julia frowned a frown of mental concentration. Hera? The named sounded vaguely familiar, vaguely classical, vaguely reminiscent of something that she had heard at boarding-school years ago; but she could not begin to identify it. Before she could reply to her father's question, even with a shake of the head, the old gentleman exclaimed triumphantly, "I knew it. I was sure you wouldn't remember."

Julia's response was an embarrassed, apologetic smile.

"No, no, my girl," said Cullen good-naturedly, "I'm not scolding you for your ignorance. I was merely trying to settle a question that's been plaguing my mind. And it's settled right now. Of course you remember who Juno was?"

"Oh, yes," answered Julia unhesitatingly; "Juno was the wife and sister of Jupiter."

"Exactly," agreed Cullen. "Now here's the point. In an English version of a Greek poem, should the characters bear Greek or Roman names? Well, I suppose Professor Arnold would insist that it would be outrageously unscholarly to give them Roman names, and maybe Thayer would agree with him. But I want readers who tackle my *Iliad* to enjoy it. And certainly, if they have to keep reaching for Bulfinch or the dictionary, they won't enjoy it. You've proved my point, Julia. Speak of Juno and Diana, and the mere English reader understands you at once. But speak

[173]

of Hera and Artemis, and he starts hunting his classical dictionary. Well, that settles it. All of the characters in my Homer, from
mighty Jupiter down to ugly, crippled little Vulcan, are going to
bear the familiar Roman names. No Zeus or Hephaestus for me."

13

But there still remained a few other little matters that needed
ironing out. On one of these matters Cullen unburdened himself
one evening to his son-in-law, Parke Godwin. Fan and the Godwin children being in Europe at the time, the lonely Godwin had
formed the habit of spending his week-ends at Cedarmere. On
that particular evening, while Bryant and Godwin were sitting in
the study, the younger man chanced to ask how the translation of
Homer was progressing.

The question was a timely one. "That's just exactly what I
wanted to tell you about," replied Cullen quickly. And he went
on to explain that for the past four or five evenings he had been
rereading William Cowper's translation. Frankly, he added, he
was very much disappointed with it. He had always said that
Cowper did a much better job than Pope, and he was as sure of
that as ever. Yes, surer. Cowper's diction, of course, was much
nearer to the Homeric simplicity. And Cowper caught the Homeric imagination and sensibility—two things that Pope and his
whole Queen Anne crowd missed entirely. But Homer had fire
and rapidity of narrative—and there was where Cowper failed
miserably.[15] Now slowness was just what Cullen Bryant himself
was going to have to guard against. Yes, goodness knew! if the
author of "John Gilpin's Ride" could not catch Homer's speed,
what in the world could one expect of the author of such unexcit-
ing tales as "Sella" and "The Little People of the Snow"?

Godwin was about to protest at his father-in-law's excessive
modesty. Cullen, however, was in no mood to listen to false flattery. He fully realized his serious limitations as a narrative poet.
"No," he said, more in soliloquy than to Godwin, "I'm no story-
teller—never have been. But," he added a moment later with more
enthusiasm, more confident conviction, "this time old Homer has
furnished me with the story—fire, speed, and all. And, by gracious!
I'm going to run along with Homer."

Yes, Bryant's Homer would have not only the Homeric simplicity and imagination and sensibility. It would have the Homeric fire and rapidity of narrative as well.

14

Before the first snow of winter had blanketed Long Island—indeed, before Thanksgiving—the actual metrical composition got under way. Cullen had planned to do the work methodically, all of it in the mornings, when he would be most alert and vigorous both physically and mentally. He even assigned himself an exact mathematical average of forty lines a day.

Very soon, however, he came to realize that even a translation is no mere journeyman's task—that it is best done by inspiration rather than by schedule. Seated resolutely at his desk he would repeat aloud the literal translation of a page or so of the original; and then—especially if the morning happened to be sunshiny—he would grow impatient. As in the old days of his original poems, he could think more clearly, more imaginatively, out of doors than within the confines of his study. And so, hastily donning hat and coat, he would set off at a brisk pace, sometimes across the fields of his own Cedarmere, sometimes along one of the less frequented public roads.

To more than a few of the farm people around Roslyn, the sturdy little old pedestrian—always strangely trim and citified in his well-fitting, well-tailored black or navy-blue broadcloth attire —became a familiar sight. His hoary beard and his long and equally hoary hair proclaimed him to be a patriarch; but his long, quick, vigorous footsteps, always made without the assistance of a cane, belied senility. If he chanced to meet some man or woman or child along the way, he spoke a friendly enough "good morning," always meeting the person's gaze squarely with his own frank, penetrating gray eyes; but never, on such occasions, did he show any disposition to stop and chat.

On one such day—a bright, bland late autumn day that was strangely, beautifully reminiscent of a certain day more than half a century earlier—a day when most of the trees were black and bare, but a day made lovely by blue sky and green pines and brown oaks—the opening lines of the *Iliad* came to him. Yes, as on that far-off "Waterfowl" day on the Cummington-Plainfield road, it was a time for the muse to sing. But this time Cullen was not headed toward a definite Plainfield; he was headed vaguely in the direction of Glen Cove, and within an hour or so he would retrace his steps. At any rate, long before he re-entered his own grounds he knew by heart the lines that he would write:

O Goddess! sing the wrath of Peleus' son,
Achilles, sing the deadly wrath that brought
Woes numberless upon the Greeks, and swept
To Hades many a valiant soul, and gave
Their limbs a prey to dogs and birds of air,—
For so had Jove appointed,—from the time
When the two chiefs, Atrides, king of men,
And great Achilles, parted first as foes.
Which of the gods put strife between the chiefs,
That they should thus contend? Latona's son
And Jove's. Incensed against the king, he bade
A deadly pestilence appear among
The army, and the men were perishing.
For Atreus' son with insult had received
Chryses the priest, who to the Grecian fleet
Came to redeem his daughter, offering
Uncounted ransom.[16]

15

During the ensuing months the translation proceeded steadily, but not without occasional doubts and discouragements. Once, after a peripatetic composition of some forty or fifty lines—a composition that had pleased him immensely—he discovered that he had omitted an entire passage of the original and would have to recompose at least a page.

And one dark, miserable January morning—a morning when wind and sleet and freezing slush kept him within the confines of his study—he momentarily despaired of the whole project. The pentameters simply would not come. The insistent rat-a-tat-tat of the sleet on the window panes, perversely beating a wrong rhythm, kept drowning them out. Even the Greek tropes and images refused stubbornly to be anything but Greek. As for the behavior of the gods and goddesses in that part of the narrative, it seemed particularly despicable that morning. After all, were not the deities of the *Iliad* the most detestable in the whole realm of Homeric folklore? And had not Cullen's old friend Dana warned him that if he was going to work on Homer at all, he had

[176]

better take the *Odyssey*—of which he had already translated and published one book years before?

Pushing aside his manuscript with a gesture of revulsion, he pulled a sheet of stationery from his desk drawer and began unburdening himself to his "literary" brother John in Illinois. Yes, he wrote, he was "half tempted" to give up the whole sorry business. True, Henry Longfellow had only recently written him a cordial letter of encouragement about the *Iliad*. But of all Cullen's circle of intimate friends, Henry was the one incorrigible optimist.

Julia, passing down the hall to give some directions to the cook, noticed that the study door was open. This was an unusual circumstance; for, almost invariably, when her father was at his literary labors he kept the door closed. She noticed also that the old gentleman, with back turned to desk, was holding his head in his two hands.

Entering the study, she put her hand on his shoulder and anxiously inquired whether he felt ill.

No, he answered a little gruffly; he was physically in the pink of condition. And then he went on to explain the whole difficulty. "Oh, how I wish," he concluded with a sigh, "that your mother were here! She would advise me. And her advice, as always, would be unerring."

"Yes," said Julia, quickly grasping the situation, "and you know what Mother would advise—would *insist* on."

Cullen nodded. The work, by all means, must proceed. But not any more this morning. Not any more today. Tomorrow, perhaps, the sun would be shining, and the footing on the Glen Cove pike might be not too bad. Yes, tomorrow would probably be a much better day in every respect; for the Long Island winter climate, if more fickle than that of the Berkshires, was likewise more genial. On Long Island a January squall did not presage eight or ten weeks of bitter weather. In a day or two, at most, a morning walk would be a pleasure once more; and then the pentameters and the images and the deities would return to their good behavior.

16

A year later the translation was finished. A few days after New Year's, 1870, the completed manuscript was on its way to Boston, to the publishing house of Fields, Osgood & Co. Long before that, an extensive correspondence between Bryant and James T. Fields had resulted in the acceptance of the work for publication. Now for Cullen there remained only such chores as the reading of galley proofs and page proofs—chores that the old *Post* man enjoyed rather than shunned.

Bryant's *Iliad,* published in the spring of 1870, was quite the popular success that he had tried to make it. What though the British critics greeted it with a cold indifference, "a frigid want of interest?" American critics, great and small, praised it lavishly. College and academy professors referred to it in most glowing terms. Small-town weeklies, as well as metropolitan dailies and urbane magazines, enthusiastically urged the public to read it. Typical of this widespread approval was the following excerpt from the June, 1870, issue of *Harper's Magazine:*

> There have, indeed, been no lack of previous translations, from the jingling and curiously un-Homeric lines of Pope, to the plain, bald prose of Buckley. . . . But of all which we have seen, . . . there is none to equal this work of our own poet. Nor can we conceive a medium more fitting for the rendition of the legends of the greatest of all bards than the blank verse of the author of Thanatopsis, the rhythm, natural grace, and stately dignity of whose lines are all his own.[17]

Indeed, the one complaint made by the *Harper's* reviewer was that the elegant printing, binding, paper, and gilt-edging of the book had placed it beyond the means of the average book-buyer.

Yes, the critics and the teachers urged the public to read Bryant's *Iliad.* And, despite its luxurious format, the public did read it. In 1882 Godwin could truthfully write: "It sold largely from the beginning; and still, twelve years from the time of its first appearance, it is a source of considerable emolument to its publishers and the heirs of the author."[18] As Professor Bradley saw the matter, "Bryant's success, at home at least, was enormous. . . . He had put Homer into an idiom that could be understood by a simple and practical people."[19]

17

Bryant's success with the *Iliad* prompted him to begin a comparable version of the *Odyssey.* Years earlier—indeed, long before he had even conceived the *Iliad* project—he had conducted the experiment of doing a single book of the *Odyssey* in English blank verse. That book was the fifth, and he had made it one of his *Thirty Poems* of 1864.

Now, at the ripe age of seventy-six, he might well have chosen to rest from literary labors, even the relatively unexacting labors of a translator. For without this work he was far from idle. What with overseeing his acres at Cedarmere, making an occasional public address, advising Godwin on the affairs of the *Evening Post* and even writing an editorial now and then, he was far from rusting unburnished in the chimney-corner.

But he had found the task of translating the *Iliad* pleasant, and not too strenuous. On the *Iliad* he had averaged not far from the forty lines a day that he had set as his goal, and he had done virtually all of the work in the mornings, when he was freshest in mind and body. On the new project he would work still more leisurely, not worrying as to whether or not he would live to finish the job. Yes, it would be wholly desirable to start the *Odyssey;* for, as he wrote to his brother John in Illinois, the *Odyssey* would give him an excellent excuse for declining less agreeable tasks that might be urged upon him.[20] Magazine editors still importuned him to send them original lyrics—importunings which were always in vain. Committees, by the score, begged him to attend banquets and make public addresses. And spry, alert, vigorous old Cullen Bryant was too active and, at the same time, too sensitive to decline these invitations on the ground of advanced age. The *Odyssey* would be a much better excuse for him to keep the noiseless tenor of his way.

The *Odyssey* was completed—and, all things considered, in an amazingly short time. On December 7, 1871, Bryant mailed to his publishers the manuscript of the twenty-fourth and concluding book. A few months later the work came off the press. The publishers of Bryant's *Odyssey* were J. R. Osgood & Co., successors to Fields, Osgood & Co.

It is doubtful that Bryant's *Odyssey* is in any way inferior to his excellent *Iliad*. Like the latter work, it neither adds nor subtracts. It is literally as faithful a translation as the exigencies of metre would permit, and, like Bryant's *Iliad,* it reproduces the Homeric spirit in every way. If it met with less public response than the *Iliad,* that is only another way of saying that the story of the wanderings of Ulysses has always been less popular than the saga of the Trojan War.

18

With regard to Bryant's Homeric translations, it is noteworthy that both of them were designed to be "popular" in the best sense. When Cullen explored the question of probable public demand for a new Homer done in English verse, he was not thinking in terms of royalties. Long before his days as a translator, he had become as wealthy a man as he ever desired to be. His object in trying to produce an English Homer of wide appeal was Utilitarian with a capital *U;* that is, Utilitarian in the Millsian philosophical sense rather than utilitarian in a venal sense. In short, he wished to make a translation that would give the greatest pleasure to the greatest number of readers. Hence his determination to reproduce all of the fire and narrative rapidity of the original. Hence, also, his decision to use the familiar Roman proper names in preference to the unfamiliar Greek.

As a matter of fact, William Cullen Bryant strove to be "popular" in every field of writing that he entered: editorials and original verse as well as translations. In his attitude toward the reading public he was quite as free from intellectual aloofness and snobbery as were Dickens and Longfellow and Whittier. John Quincy Adams's haughty dictum that "literature by its nature would always be aristocratic" was utterly alien to the Bryant point of view.

If Bryant did not succeed in appealing to stable-boys as well as statesmen—if he did not succeed in writing romances or ballads or idyls with the wide popular appeal of a Longfellow or a Whittier—his failures were due to talents of limited range rather than to lack of broad human sympathies. For all his genuine scholarliness, all his rich storehouse of reading, he never went out of his way to use an abstruse or a pedantic allusion. Never, for instance, did he resort to the Emersonian trick of alluding to a very familiar figure like Sir Francis Bacon by a very unfamiliar name like Verulam. And never did he display the undemocratic democracy of a Walt Whitman, who, while (sincerely) professing a love for the common man, wrote verse in a style that the com-

mon man found neither coherent nor comprehensible. To put
the matter tersely, William Cullen Bryant was as democratic in
his literary intents and purposes as he was in his political philosophy.

CHAPTER XI

Old Man Eloquent

1

On a mild, sunshiny afternoon in early November, 1874, a smallish, faultlessly attired old man might have been seen entering Central Park at the Scholars' Gate, at Fifty-ninth Street and Fifth Avenue.

Upon his large, well-shaped head, topping a fringe of long, curly locks, reposed a low black "billy-cock" or derby hat of the type that men of fashion had but recently started wearing for informal occasions. His neat, well-tailored broadcloth suit, black or perhaps very dark blue, consisted of a short, jacket-like sack coat, an unobtrusive, almost hidden vest, and baggy trousers from which the creases, vertical as well as horizontal, had been painstakingly obliterated by the tailor's iron. His rather small feet were encased in high-topped congress shoes whose dull cloth-and-rubber elastic sides contrasted sharply with the brilliant gloss of the highly polished leather. His plain, starched, immaculate white shirt and white turn-down collar were adorned by a small black bow cravat—which adornment, however, was largely concealed by his bushy beard. His hands were gloveless.

Pausing for a moment to admire the new Alexander von Humboldt bust, he dismissed with a disdainful sweep of the hand the proffered services of a Park phaeton. Then, as if eager to reach the view of the Pond, he proceeded rather briskly along the Mall. Although he walked firmly and without a cane, there was the faint suggestion of a limp in his gait. White-haired and white-bearded, he appeared to be about seventy years old. Actually he was eighty—eighty that very day.

To a passing stranger's cordial "How-d'ye-do, Mr. Bryant," the old man responded with a mildly startled look, a coldly courteous "Good afternoon," and a slightly accelerated pace. Why, he asked himself a little testily, must total strangers be always recognizing him and calling him by name? Only the winter before, when he had acquired this confounded limp by slipping and falling on the icy Broadway pavement, a total stranger had helped him to his feet and solicitously demanded, "Are you hurt, Mr. Bryant?" To a man as shy and retiring as Cullen Bryant, fame had its thorns as well as its roses.

On this gorgeous Indian Summer afternoon, however, annoyance passed as quickly as it came. When Cullen had last strolled in the Park, away back in May, the young leaves had been a tender green, and the early flowers beautifully frail and delicate. Nature, he had declared that day, had been "a young beauty, bare-armed, in short skirts, sandaled, unbonneted, and in the thinnest of morning dresses." Today, six months later, she was a comely matron in a festive afternoon gown of yellow and saffron and crimson. Yes, thanks to the mild New York October just past, the trees had not yet been denuded. By Thanksgiving the Park woods would be bare—too bare even to blush—but Thanksgiving was still a good three weeks away. On such a day as this, an hour in the Park was ample compensation for the tedious horse-car ride uptown and back.

Cullen was truly and justly proud of his Central Park. Yes, *his* Central Park; for years before the opening of this huge and lovely plot of verdure and recreation in 1856, his *Evening Post* editorials had taken the lead in demanding for the American metropolis a public park comparable to the Bois de Boulogne in Paris and Hyde Park in London. And, appropriately enough, he had served upon the first board of Park commissioners.

He was proud, too, of his city—the city that had been his home for almost half a century—the city for whose welfare he had wrought and written so much. He must have pondered a great deal upon the marvelous growth and development of the place.

When he had come to New York it had been an ambitious town of some 125,000 inhabitants; now it was a huge metropolis of well over a million (not counting Brooklyn), one of the four or five greatest cities in the world. And its development in elegance and conveniences had quite kept pace with its growth in population. Thanks in no small measure to Cullen Bryant's editorial urgings, the town now had comfortable horse-cars, excellent fire and police protection, fairly efficient street-cleaning, beautiful theaters and shops—among the latter, A. T. Stewart's great two-acre department store on Tenth Street, one of the mercantile wonders of the world.

As for office buildings, many of them were mounting skyward in an almost incredible manner. Within a few short years the widespread use of the "vertical railway" or hydraulic elevator had made the building of eight-story and even ten-story structures entirely feasible—a truly important consideration in a locality such as populous little Manhattan Island, where ground space was so increasingly precious. (But Cullen Bryant himself, much as he admired the ingenuity of the "vertical railway," still preferred climbing stairs, even nine flights of them!) As for New York hotels, were not such hostelries as the Fifth Avenue, the Park Avenue, the Astor House, and the Hoffman House already acknowledged to be "the most elaborately fitted in the world?" Where else, in either hemisphere, could one find seven stories of such luxury: such spacious public rooms and banquet halls and courtyards, such ornate galleries, such gorgeous carpets and draperies?

And then there were the town houses of the well-to-do. In half a century Cullen had seen the fashionable residential district creep steadily northward from the region of City Hall Park to that of Washington Square; from the latter region to that of Madison Square; from Madison Square, on up Fifth Avenue, into the Murray Hill district. Inevitably, within the next few years, it would reach to Central Park itself. And these new brownstone-fronted palaces, if no more trim or sightly than the red brick mansions of Philip Hone's heyday, were at least more pretentious and more substantial-looking. As for interior conveniences, the Argand gas lamps and the hot-air and hot-water furnaces were surely a far cry (and a welcome cry) from the dim candles and the cheery but ineffectual fireplaces of Bryant's first years in the

[184]

metropolis. In furniture and furnishings, too, the New Yorkers of the seventies considered themselves far in advance of their naive grandsires. What Fifth Avenue parlor of these later days was not resplendant with Eastlake and Marcotte cabinets and marble-topped tables, William Morris chairs and sofas, Rogers groups of statuary, alabaster tazzas, red plush albums, and pictures of fish and game and fruit—hand-painted by talented young ladies—on dainty chinaware?

If the New York of these guilded seventies was a town of fashionable houses, it was also a town of fashionable people—people who vied with the best-dressed citizens of London or even Paris. And old Cullen Bryant, like the young Cullen Bryant of fifty years earlier, was a devotee of fashion—at any rate, of fashion that did not degenerate into vulgar ostentation. At eighty as at thirty, he wore the correct hats and coats and trousers and accessories, and he always wore them trimly. Perhaps in these later days he sighed a little wistfully over the passing of bright colors in men's wear, especially the passing of plum-colored coats and (not-too-flamboyant) floral waistcoats. But, after all, were there not compensations in these changes that staid old Father Time had wrought? Did not these somber later-Victorian masculine blacks and grays enhance, by their very contrast, the brilliant blues and greens and maroons of the ladies' gowns? Had ever the ladies, especially the young ones, looked more winsome than in these days when the nineteenth century was nearing the three-quarter mark? Dresses and hair so becomingly plain in front, and so becomingly ruffled and curled behind! Dainty little narrow-brimmed, high-crowned hats, perched so captivatingly high on pretty heads! Yes, to tell the truth, the aged New York editor had as keen eyes for beautiful young women as the youthful Bridge-water law student had had. In a letter which he had written when well past seventy, he had grown positively lyrical in praise of the outward charms of a Miss Helen Waterston, lovely young grand-daughter of old Josiah Quincy. She was, declared the septuagenarian Bryant rhapsodically, "uncommonly beautiful in person. . . . Wherever she went, it is easy to see she was followed by looks of admiration." [1] And New York had hundreds of girls as beautiful as Helen Waterston!

In all seriousness, however, Cullen realized that the greatness of a great city is not measured solely in terms of imposing public buildings, princely mansions, fashionable gentlemen, and lovely ladies. There are nobler, more spiritual values. If New York had risen to true eminence in the nation and in the world, she owed much of that eminence to her outstanding men of vision and of conscience: civic-minded officials such as Andrew H. Green and Jackson Schultz, philanthropists such as Peter Cooper and Jonathan Sturges and Abiel Low and (the elder) Theodore Roosevelt, clergymen such as Henry Bellows and Stephen Tyng, reformers such as George William Curtis, statesmen such as John A. Dix and Samuel J. Tilden.

All too well, however, did Cullen Bryant realize that New York was still far from being an ideal metropolis. He and his *Evening Post* had contributed tremendously, incalculably, toward improving the town; but they had no more succeeded in creating a Utopia or a Zion on Manhattan Island than William Blake, three or four generations earlier, had succeeded in building a Jerusalem in England's green and pleasant land. Much, indeed, remained to be done. Thanks to political bosses of the stripe of Bill Tweed, municipal government was all too frequently inefficient and downright corrupt. Fortunately Tweed himself now languished in the Ludlow Street jail, preparatory to beginning a twelve-year term in the Ossining penitentiary. But the evil fruits of Tweed's public "services" would be all too manifest for years to come. The forty-odd million dollars that he had stolen from the city would be unrecovered. Tweed's "respectable" henchmen, such as suave, plausible ex-Mayor A. Oakley Hall, remained at large and safely out of the clutches of the law. Public indifference, despite occasional waves of reform, continued deplorably great.

There was too much ill-gotten wealth in the brownstone mansions of Fifth Avenue, too much poverty and squalor, vice and contagion, in the dingy hovels of the lower East Side. Tenements were overcrowded, insanitary, and inflammable. Too many men—and women and children—worked too many hours for too little pay in dismal sweat-shops. There were, as yet, no public museum of art, no metropolitan opera house, no central free library, no symphony orchestra, no zoological gardens, no smooth asphalt pavements, no adequate elevated railway system for rapid transit. For years, Bryant had tirelessly advocated all of these ameliorative projects, and he and his paper would continue to do so until every one of them became a functioning reality.

Some of these projects were already coming to fruition. For example, just five years earlier—in November, 1869—a group of New York art lovers had organized a museum committee; wealthy collectors, such as W. T. Blodgett, had generously donated paintings; the state legislature had been persuaded to appropriate half a million dollars for a museum building; and in another five years the spacious Metropolitan Museum of Art, at the east edge of Central Park, would open its doors to the public. An orchestra conducted by a talented violinist named Theodore Thomas was giving creditable concerts in Irving Hall and paving the way for a truly great symphonic organization. For some four years, elevated steam trains had been speeding up Ninth Avenue from the Battery to Thirtieth Street, and although a few carping old fogies (including horse-car interests) still complained of the noise and the dirt and the unsightliness of the "L," the vast majority of intelligent New Yorkers had long since come to accept it as the harbinger of a wonderful revolution in metropolitan rapid transit; in fact, there were already plans for a Sixth Avenue elevated line that would extend to the very gate of Central Park.

Did Cullen Bryant ever poetize the city? Yes, although he derived far more poetic inspiration from rural scenes than from urban—what bard in the nineteenth-century romantic tradition did not?— he nonetheless could write such lyrics as "The Crowded Street," "Spring in Town," and "Hymn of the City." And in the last-named piece he could declare:

> Not in the solitude
> Alone may man commune with Heaven, or see,
> Only in savage wood
> And sunny vale, the present Deity;
> Or only hear his voice
> Where the winds whisper and the waves rejoice.
> Even here do I behold
> They steps, Almighty!—here amidst the crowd
> Through the great city rolled,
> With everlasting murmur deep and loud—
> Choking the ways that wind
> 'Mongst the proud piles, the work of human kind.

Of all the American poets of that day, Walt Whitman was the only one to outdo Cullen Bryant in appreciation of the city.

Did Bryant feel any regrets at having deserted his native New England and migrated to New York? Did any of his more thoughtful admirers, Yankee or otherwise, feel such regrets? Suppose that in 1825 he had found an editorial opening in Boston instead of New York. In that event he would have become a leading citizen of the town which, though greatly outstripped by New York in commerce and industry and population, was to become the nineteenth-century literary and intellectual capital of America. As a member of the Transcendental Club and the Saturday Club he would have had frequent and intimate contact with such rare spirits as Emerson, Hawthorne, Longfellow, Whittier, Holmes, Thoreau, and Lowell. With some of these men he was on fairly intimate terms anyhow, but it was only at irregular and infrequent intervals that he ever met any of them face to face. In Boston he would have been a neighbor to all of them, and as the oldest in the group he would have been recognized as their dean, their patriarch. Perhaps in the mellow atmosphere of Beacon Hill and Harvard Square, with occasional pilgrimages to Concord and Amesbury, he might have become as transcendental a poet as Emerson, as versatile and prolific a poet as Longfellow or Whittier, as sententious a poet as Holmes or Lowell. But the fates decreed otherwise. The fates decreed that after his thirtieth year he should experience no real creative growth. As Professor Parrington declares, William Cullen Bryant "lived within himself, little swayed by modes of thought, slowly maturing the native fruit of his speculation." [2] And as Professor Foerster puts it, Bryant "never quite assimilated contemporary modes of thoughts." [3]

The difficulty was that New York, with all its greatness, could not provide him with the rich society of kindred creative spirits. From an inspirational standpoint, the Bread and Cheese Club and the Century Club were feeble, pallid substitutes for the Transcendental Club. The verse of Gotham's best-selling poet, Josiah Gilbert Holland, sounded pathetically thin and reedy beside the rich, full tones of a Longfellow or a Whittier. As a matter of fact, New York laid claim to no major poet but Bryant himself. True, Walt Whitman, perhaps the greatest of all nineteenth-century American poetic geniuses, belonged rightfully to New York; but it hardly occurred to Bryant or to any other discriminating and influential American of his day—save Emerson—that Whitman was a poet at all. As for other New York poets, there were Joseph Rodman Drake and Fitz-Greene Halleck, neither of whom was better than second-rate, and neither of whom had produced any verse after Bryant's first decade in New York. Drake, in fact, had died before Bryant left Great Barrington. Halleck had lived till 1867; but on receipt of a modest legacy in 1848 he had drifted back to his country home in Connecticut to spend his remaining days in unproductive leisure. Truly, as a poet in New York, William Cullen Bryant was a lonely spirit. Edmund Clarence Stedman and Thomas Bailey Aldrich, the foremost "younger" Gotham poets of the 1870's, were almost two generations Bryant's junior, and not until after Bryant's death did those facile rhymesters produce the best of their polished but conventional and undistinguished verse.

But if Bryant and New England and literature suffered as a result of Bryant's desertion of his native section, New York and journalism gained more than a little thereby. If ever a community needed the purifying breath of idealism, that community was nineteenth-century New York. And Bryant, with his New England conscience and vision, surely provided idealism. The New York of 1874, with all its evils and all its ugliness, was an incalculably better city because Yankee Bryant had chosen to become and to remain a Gotham Yankee. With nothing of the Pharisee about him, Cullen Bryant could yet remind his bustling, acquisitive fellow metropolitans, both by precept and by example, that man shall not live by bread alone. To quote Professor Parrington once more, this transplanted son of New England, with his Puritan heritage, contributed tremendously "to the idealism of a society rather too fond of material progress." [4]

3

As Cullen continued his stroll through the Park, his thoughts undoubtedly became less civic, more personal. This very morning of November 3 he had started working in his office; had been summoned home by a messenger; and had found awaiting him there a committee of prominent citizens, come to congratulate him upon his eightieth birthday. Benign-looking, bewhiskered old Jonathan Sturges, banker and railroad president, had been the committee's eloquent spokesman; and although the coffee and tea by which old Jonathan had gained his millions seemed indeed remote from the muses by which Cullen Bryant had gained his fame, no more fitting spokesman could possibly have been chosen. For Jonathan Sturges was far from being either a churl or a Philistine. Church warden, philanthropist, municipal reformer, patron of the arts, and sound Union (as well as sound money) man, he was a Christian gentleman after Bryant's own heart. Like Bryant, moreover, he was a Gotham Yankee: a New Yorker by adoption, but a New Englander by birth and rearing.

That morning when the merchant prince had presented his poet-editor friend with a scroll inscribed with the autographs of hundreds of well-wishers, the venerable poet-editor had been as embarrassed as a schoolboy—and almost as ill at ease. Modestly stammering a few words to the effect that he had "little to be proud of," but that he was proud of his friends, he had thanked the committee with more sincerity than eloquence. Although past-master in the field of prepared orations, Cullen Bryant was never very impressive as an extempore speaker. And this morning, despite the fact that he might reasonably have anticipated some such occasion, he had been taken completely by surprise.

4

Well, when one reached old age, birthdays had an ominous habit of rolling around with increasing celerity. It was precisely a decade, recalled Cullen soberly, since that most memorable birthday celebration of his life, the big dinner at the Century Club, at which George Bancroft had presided, Emerson had orated, and Holmes had read a most gracious little birthday poem such as only the incomparably charming Autocrat could have written. Cullen could still see the beautifully decorated dining-room, with its profusion of evergreens and autumn foliage and flowers, and its array of landscape paintings so thoughtfully presented by the artist club-members. He could still hear the strains of the birthday ode, composed by Bayard Taylor, set to music by Louis Long, and sung by "a band of choristers" who had stood in a balcony overlooking the banqueters. He could recall, too, his own banquet address, carefully prepared and memorized, a much more successful effort than his poor little speech of this morning. And then with a chuckle he remembered a little touch of frivolity. A waggish newspaper reporter, noticing the formidable array of bearded banqueters, had remarked that the only smooth chins at the speakers' table had been the respective chins of Emerson and Holmes and Julia Ward Howe. Yes, this was a bearded age— an age when almost the only bare-faced rascals beyond nonage were the actors and the Romish priests. Well, of course there were a few others: Sam Tilden and Charles Kingsley and Matthew Arnold. But what a ridiculous combination!

By no means, however, were all of the memories of that seventieth birthday dinner either amusing or happy. With a pang Cullen recalled that Fanny had been too poorly to accompany him to the banquet—his beloved Fanny, who had been laid in the Roslyn graveyard less than two years later. He recalled, too, that the most intimate of his old friends—Dana, Halleck, Longfellow, and Kate Sedgwick—had all been unable to come to the banquet—and that all except Longfellow, the baby of the lot, had been kept away by the infirmities of old age. And now all of them except Dana and Longfellow were gone—and Dana had reached the incredible age of eighty-seven. As for Cullen Bryant himself, on this mellow afternoon of his eightieth birthday, he was truly "gazing into the twilight." This evening after dinner he would don his bedroom slippers and read a chapter of *Don Quixote* in the original. And then he would go early to bed. Perhaps—although he still felt wonderfully hale and hearty—his innumerable days as a public figure were about over.

5

But, no! The importunate public would not let him keep to his fireside and his Cervantes. January found him boarding a train for Albany to pay a semi-official visit to an old friend, Samuel J. Tilden, newly installed occupant of the state Executive Mansion.

Through many years the friendship of Cullen Bryant and Sam Tilden had been both intimate and cordial. In fact, it went well back into the 1840's when the sandy-haired Tilden, a rising young lawyer and legislator some twenty years Bryant's junior, was supporting the Jacksonian wing of the Democratic party as aggressively as was Bryant himself. In common, Bryant and Tilden had unashamedly borne such sobriquets of radicalism as "Loco-foco" and "Barnburner." In common, in the campaign of

1848, they had bolted the "Hunker" Democratic nominee for President, Lewis Cass, to support the Free-Soil, honestly Jacksonian nominee, Martin Van Buren. In common, they had regarded the unequivocal Silas Wright as better presidential timber than the time-serving William L. Marcy.

After 1854 the paths of Cullen Bryant and Sam Tilden had somewhat diverged. Sam had never quite forgiven Cullen for having become a Republican, and Cullen had never quite forgiven Sam for having remained a Democrat. Moreover, the two men had discovered in each others' personalities certain traits that were uncongenial. Tilden did not care particularly for Bryant's poetry—or, indeed, for any poetry. Bryant, despite his occasional enjoyment of a bawdy anecdote, did not approve of Tilden's pet hobby: the collection of pornographic pictures and literature. And Bryant was alternately amused and irritated by Tilden's habit of subsiding into melodramatic whispers whenever Sam talked politics.

At the close of the Civil War, however, the two men's common zeal for municipal reform had brought them closer together than ever. Tilden's legislative measures and Bryant's incisive editorials, working in powerful unison, had struck the sledge-hammer blows that had smashed the Tweed Ring. And now that a grateful electorate had placed Sam Tilden in the Governor's chair, Sam insisted that his valued collaborator come to Albany and share a little of the glory.

In particular, the old poet-editor was to be put on display before the state legislature. Recalling Bryant's long and glowing record as Gotham's foremost occasional speaker—his layings of corner-stones; his dedications of monuments and statues and busts; his beautiful memorial tributes to such illustrious New Yorkers as Cole and Cooper and Irving and Halleck—Tilden was determined that citizens outside the metropolis should see and hear what charming manner of man was William Cullen Bryant.

At eighty, Bryant was a truly unique figure. Nestor of major poets, and Nestor of major editors, he was the one citizen of Gotham to whom every intelligent, respectable fellow citizen pointed with pride. Surely he had gone far since those law-office days in the village of Great Barrington. As Professor Boynton has pointed out, the venerable Bryant came to be regarded "with something approaching reverence," [5] if never quite with familiar affection. Recognized and revered wherever he was seen, whether on the street, or in the street-car, or on the rostrum, he seldom gave or received a cordial greeting; for, although his heart was warm and his impulse democratic, his manner with strangers was incorrigibly reserved—more, even, in his later years than in his earlier. Hawthorne's complaint that Bryant was "rather cold" and "not eminently an affectionate man" [6] in his manner was, unfortunately, well founded. Indeed, Lowell's rather bad pun about Bryant's "supreme iceolation" would probably apply more truly to the personality than to the poetry of William Cullen Bryant. And yet all New York realized fully that her most distinguished citizen was neither a snob nor a miser—that he was as kindly and sympathetic as he was shy and distant. Indeed, it was known far and wide that the old gentleman's gifts to charity, always made unostentatiously, had been both large and numerous. As for his oratorical gifts—well, "Old Man Eloquent" was what his fellow Gothamites called him. And now let the law makers from the Adirondack villages and from the Chautauqua County farms observe how well merited was that appellation.

The week of January, 1875, was "exceedingly cold"—too cold, declared the solicitous Julia, for an octogenarian to be roaming about the country. But when Cullen had grumblingly agreed to wear his caped ulster and his arctic galoshes, to pack his heaviest flannel nightshirt and nightcap in his carpetbag, to avoid drafts on the train, and to draw the buffalo robe well over him when he got into the sleigh at the Albany depot, she had reluctantly consented to let him go. How fussy Julia was! Much worse than either of the Fannys had ever been! What a pity she had never married! And yet—how could Cullen have done without her in those years since '66?

But if the weather was inclement, the Governor's Mansion, with its "ample dormitories" and its new-fangled furnace, was "very comfortable." As for the reception in the legislative chambers, it was warm indeed. Senator Robinson presented the guest of honor as "the most distinguished citizen of our State—I might say of our country—William Cullen Bryant." And the venerable guest of honor replied with one of the most felicitous occasional speeches of his career. Perhaps a twentieth-century audience would have found the flowery phrases quaint, if not a little pom-

[193]

BRYANT THE OCTOGENARIAN

pous and grandiloquent; but to these New York solons of 1875, here was "Old Man Eloquent" at his very best.

> I see before me [said Bryant in part] the representatives of our great, powerful, and populous State. I see men who come from our rich and beautiful valleys, from the grand and picturesque mountain regions of the north of the State, from the banks of our glorious rivers, from the borders of our immense lakes, from populous towns and pleasant villages; towns that are the seats of trade and industry,

cities noisy with the bustle of business and commerce, or resounding with the clash of looms, or the blows of ponderous hammers in our manufacturing establishments. . . . My wish is that this session may prove honorable to yourselves and useful to the community; that it may be closed with credit, and that it may be long remembered for the service it has done and the benefit it has conferred on the State to which you belong.[7]

6

Did any of those legislators recall Cullen Bryant's commencement address at Williams College some two or three years earlier? Most probably many of them did; for it had touched upon a subject which at that time was highly controversial, and it had received wide publicity in the press. Indeed, a few of those legislators—representatives from such near-Berkshire counties as Columbia and Rensselaer—might well have been present at that Williams commencement of '72 and made their contribution to the hearty applause. The controversial question was the evolutionary hypothesis as set forth by Charles Darwin.

In 1872, in American intellectual and religious circles, Darwinism was an especially lively and timely topic; for only the year before, a brilliant young Harvard man named John Fiske, addressing large audiences at his Alma Mater, had expounded and defended the Darwinian theory in a course of thirty-five lectures, in which he had awakened widespread interest not only in Darwin's *Origin of Species* and *Descent of Man,* but also in the writings of Darwin's most prominent British disciples, Herbert Spencer, John Tyndall, and William Henry Huxley. Young Fiske's lectures had thrown orthodox religionists into a state of panic; and many indignant clergymen, fulminating both in pulpit and in press, had vehemently denounced the lectures as "Harvard's raid on religion." Meanwhile, Darwinism had found other American champions—champions outside the Harvard circle— men such as Andrew D. White, President of the newly-founded Cornell University, and Edward L. Youmans, New York chemist and semi-popular lecturer on scientific subjects. It had also found learned American opponents: most notably, Noah Porter, President of Yale College, and Louis Agassiz, Swiss-American geologist.

Bryant did not like Darwinism, and in the address at Williams College he had taken the occasion to ridicule it with what Parke

Godwin called "witty comment." [8] In this connection, Bryant's attitude was not nearly so astonishing as might appear at first glance. In the first place, he was, as has been previously observed, a Unitarian of the right-wing variety; theologically he was much nearer to Longfellow than to Emerson; he could—and often did— listen with patience to the sermons of the orthodox Presbyterian minister at Roslyn. In the second place, it must be remembered that seventy years ago the opposition to Darwinism was by no means confined to orthodox Christians. Louis Agassiz, probably the most eminent and influential geologist of the day, and a man who was "totally out of sympathy with sects and creeds and the outer shell of Christianity," attacked Darwinism vigorously and repeatedly. It was not so much that Darwinism controverted special creation, as set forth in the Book of Genesis; it was rather that Darwinism—by implication, at least—refuted the theory of design in nature, a theory which was as dear to the hearts of free-thinking nineteenth-century theists as it had been dear to the hearts of eighteenth-century deists. Thomas Paine would not have liked Darwinism any better than Cullen Bryant did.

7

On a raw March morning in 1876, Cullen sat at his desk in the *Evening Post* office, pondering over a letter which he had just written and was about to seal. The missive, which was directed to General Joseph R. Hawley, President of the Centennial Commission, was a polite note of regret—regret that Bryant must decline the general's highly flattering request that he prepare an ode in honor of the great forthcoming exposition in Philadelphia. Old age, the missive protested with more than Cullen's usual frankness on that particular subject, is "another form of ill health, and implies a decline of both the bodily and mental faculties." In addition, there was Bryant's everlasting aversion to attempting "verses for particular public occasions." Finally, despite the fact that he was now in his eighty-second year, he was still engrossed in "certain tasks" which left him "no leisure" for the composition of an elaborate ode on such an important event. Nevertheless, as an unusual concession—in honor of a most unusual occasion— Bryant would consent to essay a very brief centennial hymn.

Yes, indeed; a most unusual occasion! For 1876 was America's *annus mirabilis;* and, for this year only, Philadelphia would be the city toward which all roads led. Was Gotham a little jealous of her Pennsylvania sister? Well, only a little. In general, Gotham had more than her share of prominence. As for the forthcoming exposition, every Gothamite realized that the only fitting place for celebrating in a big way the centenary of our national independence was the city in which that independence had first been proclaimed.

And what wonderful things there were to celebrate! what things undreamed-of by the founding fathers! To grow old in this marvelous nineteenth century, thought Cullen as he sealed the letter, was peculiarly fascinating; for not in all previous human history had the wheels of progress turned so rapidly as in the past generation or two. When Tennyson, a third of a century before, had sung of "the fairy tales of science," he and his readers had only begun to realize the true force of his words. Machinery Hall in Philadelphia would be teaming with new contrivances, some of which had been perfected within only the last year or two; and what would make their display the more appropriate was the fact that a surprisingly large proportion of them were the products of Yankee ingenuity. There was, for instance, that marvelous typewriting machine, destined to revolutionize both business correspondence and the transcription of newspaper "copy"; for about a year now, there had been one of those instruments in the office of the *Evening Post*. There was the still more marvelous "far-speaker" or *telephone*, by which one turned a little crank, rang a little bell, and proceeded to converse with someone furlongs or even miles away. In another year or two the *Evening Post*—and every other important metropolitan business concern— would be equipped with one of these devices. Within another decade, surely, messenger boys would have disappeared from the streets. There were models of great new locomotives and magnificent new railroad cars: replicas of the trains which, since '69, had enabled one to span the entire continent in speed and comfort.

On sober reflection, however, Cullen felt sure that the exhibits in Machinery Hall would interest him less than some of the others. Among these latter would be the displays of horticulture and the fine arts respectively. To see rare exotic plants under a glass roof might not be so good as to see them in God's first temples, but at any rate it would be a botanical education.

[197]

As for the art exhibit, that would bring to America the finest paintings that Europe had to offer—or, rather, the finest that she was willing to entrust to the hazards of a trans-oceanic voyage. And these, assuredly, would have a chastening effect upon every intelligent American visitor to the exposition. For they would forcibly remind discriminating Americans that however ingenious we Yankees might be in the field of mechanical inventions, we still lagged far behind the Old World in things esthetic. In this connection, many a New York visitor to the fair might comprehend for the first time that Tintoretto was not a Third Avenue fruit merchant, that Daubigny was not an Eighth Street restauranteur, that Van Dyck was not an aristocratic squire from up Peekskill way, and that Rosa Bonheur was not a ballet dancer at Tony Pastor's. More importantly, the art exhibit would remind ambitious young painters that America's unique opportunity in art still lay—and would always lie—in the faithful delineation of the American scene: native landscapes such as George Inness and Alexander Wyant and Homer Martin were doing in emulation of the great pioneers of the Hudson River School, Thomas Cole and Asher Brown Durand.

That evening at dinner Cullen broached the subject of the Centennial to Julia. Here was one epochal event, almost at Gotham's back door, that they must not miss. The ninety-mile trip in the railroad cars would be an easy one. They could go in May, soon after the opening, before the heat and humidity of a Philadelphia summer had a chance to get in its notoriously oppressive effect.

But Julia protested that her father wouldn't like the crowds. He didn't—any more. Above all, he hated being pointed out and lionized and interviewed. Why, Fairmount Park would not be big enough to hide him. Philadelphia reporters would hound him to no end. Schoolmistresses from Cincinnati and all points west would besiege him with their precious little autograph albums.

"I guess you're right, my girl," sighed her father reflectively. "Such, alas, is one of the penalties of fame!" And he smiled a melancholy little smile of disappointment.

Already, however, Julia had a happy inspiration. "Look, papa," she began, "why couldn't you arrange with General Hawley"—

"To visit the fair before the formal opening?" interrupted the old gentleman, eagerly snatching his daughter's question right out of her mouth.

Julia nodded brightly. To the devoted daughter, the father's enthusiasm was always contagious.

"By gracious!" exclaimed Cullen, emitting the strongest oath he ever used. "There's an idea!"

And it was so arranged. Thanks to the courtesy of General Hawley, Cullen and Julia Bryant visited the great fair a few days before the public began pouring in. They missed nothing— nothing but the annoyance of encountering the crowds.

8

Midsummer found Bryant engrossed in things political. Just four years earlier he himself had been seriously mentioned as a Presidential possibility. (The merest recollection brought to his countenance a faint blush of embarrassed annoyance.) That was the year—1872—when the very disappointing President Grant was up for re-election, and when the opposition had made the ghastly mistake of nominating the utterly preposterous Horace Greeley.

When Bryant had heard of Greeley's nomination he had been too thunder-struck for words. Greeley, · the mountebank, for President of the United States? Impossible! Why, the naming of P. T. Barnum would have been no more completely absurd than that. Greeley, with his white hat, flapping linen duster, and bulging cowhide boots! Greeley, with his baby face, stupid goggle-eyed stare, and farcical little fringe of whiskers! Greeley, with his shrill voice, profane tongue, and execrable manners! Greeley, with his fantastic social and economic schemes: Fourierism, anti-rent, vote-yourself-a-farm! Greeley, with his chameleonic politics, as variable as a weathercock—and not half so reliable!

Not until some days after the ticker had brought the incredible news could Bryant express himself coherently on the subject, and then he did so in a letter to a Unitarian clergyman friend in Chicago.

I should [he wrote], at any time beforehand, have said that the thing was utterly impossible—that it could not be done by men in their senses. But it is a fact that bodies of men as well as individuals sometimes lose their wits, and that the average reason of a large assembly is sometimes sheer insanity. It is certain that another candidate will be proposed to be supported by those who can neither support Grant nor Greeley.[9]

[199]

Certain that another candidate would be proposed? Well, most assuredly not Carl Schurz, the able leader of the Liberal Republican revolt against Grant; for Schurz, being a native of Germany, was ineligible to the presidency. And, just as certainly, not E. L. Godkin, whose brilliant editorials in the *Nation* had excoriated Grantism with devastating effect. No; for Godkin had been born in Ireland. Another candidate? Why, yes. Bryant's editorial friends—exclusive of the staff of the *Evening Post*—began declaring, in print and by word of mouth, that the one logical candidate would be New York's most distinguished citizen, William Cullen Bryant.

In a sense—in a very important sense—had not Bryant given the nation one of its choicest gifts: Abraham Lincoln? And had not Bryant guided Lincoln's steps aright during the most critical period in the history of the republic? Moreover, Bryant was as sane as he was liberal and idealistic. His low-tariff attitude would appeal to intelligent Democrats; his staunch Unionism, to intelligent Republicans; his anti-carpetbag-ism, to fair-minded independents; his anti-Tweed-ism, to decent citizens in and out of New York, irrespective of party affiliations. And, finally, Bryant was a gentleman of poise and dignity; a gentleman who would grace the highest of political offices; a gentleman who would command universal respect at home and abroad.

But the Bryant presidential boomlet "died a-borning." Bryant himself promptly killed it with a "card" in the *Evening Post*.

> Certain journals of this city [he wrote] have lately spoken of me as one ambitious of being nominated as a candidate for the Presidency of the United States. The idea is absurd enough, not only on account of my advanced age, but of my unfitness in various respects for the labor of so eminent a post. I do not, however, object to the discussion of my deficiencies on any other ground than that it is altogether superfluous, since it is impossible, if it were offered, that I should commit the folly of accepting it.[10]

Actually, except for the fact that he was then almost seventy-eight years of age, Bryant, in all probability, would not have made a bad President. Both in political knowledge and in intellectual vigor and integrity he was indubitably the superior of any President that we had between Lincoln and the first Roosevelt—not even excepting Hayes or Cleveland. But—and no one realized this more fully than Cullen Bryant himself—what an inept politician he would have made! What a wretched campaigner! Imagine the distant and dignified "Old Man Eloquent" swinging around the circle—hand-shaking, back-slapping, kissing babies! No, this eminent citizen who had once been town clerk, tithing-man, and justice of the peace in Great Barrington was not destined for a long or conspicuous political career. For office-seeking and for office-holding he had neither the taste nor the temperament.

9

As the presidential campaign of 1876 got under way, Bryant could think of several reasons for a feeling of intense satisfaction. In the first place, he himself was entirely removed from the presidential picture. In the second place, Grantism was at last on the way out; whatever replaced it was certain to be an improvement. In the third place, both major parties had properly celebrated this centennial year by nominating good men—men of much more statesmanlike qualities than either of the two leading presidential aspirants of 1872.

Rutherford B. Hayes, the new Republican nominee, had an enviable record both on the battle-field and in the political arena. As soldier his services for the cause of the Union had been so distinguished that during the course of the Civil War he had advanced from the rank of major to that of brevet major general. As two-term member of Congress and as three-term governor of his native state of Ohio he had given an equally gratifying account of himself in politics. His gubernatorial administration, indeed, had become nationally famous for its sound fiscal policies, its sponsorship of improved public education, and its complete freedom from all manner of political chicanery. Here at last was a candidate whom the more reputable elements in the Republican party could support without mental reservation. Should Hayes become President, the administration in Washington would be defiled by no egregious scandals such as had made the Grant regime a stench in the nostrils of all honest men. With Hayes at the helm, there would be no Whiskey Ring briberies involving the President's private secretary, no trading-post frauds leading to the very door of the War Department, no dealings in worthless mining stock by the Minister to the Court of St. James, no brazen public association of the President of the United States

[201]

with such pirates of high finance as Jay Gould and Jim Fiske. The President's official family would contain no such venal men as Orville E. Babcock, Secretary to the President; William W. Belknap, Secretary of War; and Robert C. Schenck, Minister to England. No high government officials would connive at defrauding the public treasury of millions of dollars. And if an honest cabinet minister, such as Benjamin H. Bristow, Secretary of the Treasury, should ferret out and expose large-scale corruption, his courageous public-spiritedness would not be rewarded by the contumely of an obstinately doltish chief executive. In brief, a Hayes administration, in happy contrast to the administration now drawing to an inglorious close, would be pure and of good report.

As for Hayes's Democratic opponent, Samuel J. Tilden, he was a most worthy foeman. Able lawyer, staunchly loyal Union man, forward-looking reformer, and proved executive, he was the most outstanding and upstanding candidate that his party had put forward in many and many a year. As member of the New York state legislature, and subsequently as Governor of New York, Tilden had won the everlasting admiration and gratitude of all lovers of good government by the courageous manner in which he had smashed both the Democratic "Tweed Ring" and the bi-partisan "Canal Ring." If Tilden should reach the White House, the country could rest assured that there would be no repetition of Grantism. A Tilden administration, like a Hayes administration, would be clean and able.

The new campaign found Cullen Bryant once more in a quandary. To choose between two such excellent candidates as Hayes and Tilden was as difficult as it had been to choose between two such objectionable candidates as Grant and Greeley. On the one hand, Bryant preferred the Civil War record, the sound-money tendencies, and the civil-service-reform promises of the Republicans. On the other hand, he had long been heartily sick of Grant inefficiency, Grant cabinet scandals, high tariffs, carpetbaggers, scalawags, and wavers of the bloody shirt—all of them bad eggs laid and hatched by the Republican party. Moreover, to complicate the situation, he was an old personal friend of Sam Tilden's; and when his esteemed *Evening Post* associate, John Bigelow, urged him to serve as a Tilden elector, he experienced great embarrassment and "deep pain" at feeling obliged to decline the honor.

[202]

How Bryant finally voted in that memorable election of 1876 will never be known. For that matter, who actually won the election will probably never be known. All that we know is that Hayes was finally seated, and that he turned out to be an eminently satisfactory President—except to the politicians, the spoils-men, and the radical Reconstructionists. Bryant never told how he voted. When asked, he merely smiled and reminded his questioner that the ballot is a secret affair. Writing to a Scottish friend on November 25, when the result of the election was still very much in doubt, he was equally non-committal.

> We have chosen a President [he wrote], and are trying to find out who it is. We shall be gainers at any rate. Let who will be awarded the Presidency, his administration is sure to be better than the present one. . . . Both parties profess to have the same ends in view; both have put up able and well-intentioned men for candidates. Tilden is the abler, and the more thoroughly a statesman, . . . but his party has suffered in character by the late rebellion.[11]

10

In that self-same year of 1876, Bryant wrote one of his most excellent as well as one of his most notable poems, "The Flood of Years." In this noble blank-verse essay, as in so many of his earlier poems, he reverts to a favorite theme: the power and permanence of inanimate nature in contrast to the frailty and transitoriness of human life. Yes, the never-ending Flood of Years rolls inexorably onward, engulfing individuals, cities, states, whole civilizations. It is no respecter of persons; for it may take the eloquent orator, the saintly preacher, the deft sculptor, the gifted painter, the inspired poet, the fond and fair young lovers, the youthful mother and her tiny babe, as well as the bent, white-haired old man of eighty winters. In the closing lines of this poem there is a new note—a note not often struck in a Bryant poem on the theme of man and nature. One day, declares the poet, this apparently never-ending Flood of Years will really spend itself. Its final act will not be destruction and separation, but the bringing together of old friends. On that day old sorrows will be forgotten, and wounded hearts that bled and broke will be healed forever. In "The Flood of Years," then, as in "October, 1866," the final stress is not upon human decay and death, but upon

[203]

human immortality. And here, as in the earlier poem, we find the New Testament conception of immortality, not the pantheistic. Did Cullen Bryant, as he advanced in years, suffer an increasing thanaphobia which led him into wishful thinking on the subject of personal immortality? That is a question which the commentator can answer no better than can the reader. To answer the question affirmatively, however, is to quarrel with Bryant's whole theological point of view. In this connection, it must be reiterated that William Cullen Bryant was a Unitarian of the right-wing persuasion.

11

Cullen Bryant's last earthly days were, in the main, happy ones. On his sixty-seventh birthday, November 3, 1861, he had ended one of his most intimately personal lyrics with this stanza:

Dreary are the years when the eye can look no longer
With delight on Nature, or hope on human kind;
Oh, may those that whiten my temples, as they pass me,
Leave the heart unfrozen, and spare the cheerful mind!

The years that whitened Bryant's temples and his "palmer-like beard" (as Hawthorne called it) did, indeed, deal kindly with the old poet-editor's heart and mind and body. Sound in health, clear in mind, and serene and benevolent in spirit, Cullen Bryant enjoyed life almost as much at eighty as he had enjoyed it at fifty or at thirty. Lifelong reserve and reticence, which had denied him the warm geniality of an Irving or a Longfellow, had limited the number of his intimate friends; but to no man had ever come friendships more firm, more enduring, than those that Bryant enjoyed with Dana and Verplanck and the Sedgwicks. As for his circle of admirers, it became indeed nation-wide. And even when the limelight, with its searching glare, palled upon him—as it was bound to pall upon so shy and modest a man—his complaints were more humorous than petulant in tone. Writing from New York to Mrs. L. M. S. Moulton, an old Roslyn neighbor, on March 2, 1878, he half plaintively, half playfully asks:

Is there a penny post, do you think, in the world to come? Do people there write for autographs to those who have gained a little notoriety? Do women there send letters asking for money? Do boys persecute literary men with requests for a course of reading? Are there offices in that

[204]

sphere which are coveted, and to obtain which men are pestered to write letters of recommendation? If anything of this kind takes place in the spirit world, it may, perhaps, be of a purgatorial nature, or, perhaps, be the fate of the incorrigible sinner.[12]

But if he did not like "fan mail" or autograph hunters, he did enjoy being a guest of honor and making what an old journalistic cliché would call "a few well chosen remarks." In this connection it is interesting to recall two gatherings that he attended in his eighty-fourth year. One of these was a German-American *kommers* at which he and Bayard Taylor were joint guests of honor. The other was a breakfast of the Clergymen's Club, a New York Episcopal organization.

The *kommers,* held on Monday evening, April 8, 1878, under the auspices of an organization known as the German Social Science Association, was evidently a hilarious affair; and evidently the aged but agile Cullen Bryant entered fully into the spirit of the occasion. Reporting the festivities to Mrs. Moulton, Bryant remarked enthusiastically that there were five hundred people at fifteen tables in an immense dining-hall; that the bill of fare consisted chiefly of beer and cigars; that the Arion singers in the gallery, topping the ascendant clouds of tobacco smoke, looked like Olympian gods; that there was much lusty singing and much lusty speaking, and that when the company became too boisterous, two officials armed with immensely long rapiers brought them to order with resounding thwacks upon the table; that they drank the health of the Nestor of American poets, whereupon the aforesaid Nestor arose and thanked them in German; and, finally, that the beer -was of so mild a brew that although many pots of it were tossed off, neither hosts nor guests got really tipsy. (Bryant says nothing about the quality of the cigars; for, of course, he did not sample any of them.) Apropos of this German-American affair, it should be remarked that sixty or seventy years ago, hyphenated Americanism did not have the sinister associations that it came to have a generation or two later. Even then, to be sure, Prussians were Prussians, and *Die Wacht am Rhein* was being sung with plenty of arrogance. But in an age when Carl Schurz and Leopold Damrosch were representative German-Americans, when Teutons still esteemed both ethics and

[205]

humanities, and when kaiser-stooges and Hitler-agents were as yet undreamed of, it was entirely possible for a decent, refined, cultivated American gentleman of Colonial stock to dine and sup with men of German race and speech and tradition.

The Episcopal clergyman's breakfast, held about three weeks later than the German-American *kommers,* brought Cullen Bryant into an atmosphere that he probably found more congenial, if less hilarious, than the Teutonic *bier-fest.* Bryant's background was, of course, much more English than German, and, if he did not quite like English social class distinctions, he did admire English cultural traditions and English political democracy. Moreover, despite his lack of enthusiasm for liturgical church services, he had doubtless come to feel more kinship with the Episcopalians than with any other religious group except his fellow Unitarians. Episcopalians, on the whole, were more tolerant, more liberal in their theology and ethics, more urbane, than Calvinists or Methodists or Baptists. Most of their clergy, for example, were cordially receptive to the higher criticism; were inclined to reject the harsh doctrine of eternal hell; and were unalterably opposed to fanatical, hysterical fulminations against such innocent pleasures as an occasional glass of wine or beer, an occasional waltz, an occasional rubber of whist, or an occasional good play or opera. Moreover, two of Cullen Bryant's dearest friends, Richard Henry Dana and Gulian Verplanck, had been lifelong Episcopalians. And, finally, like any other Unitarian, he was bound to prefer Anglican sedateness to evangelical "enthusiasm." "Whatever you do," he once cautioned his brother John, "don't commit the folly of marrying a woman whose religious notions are fanatical. Such a woman would be a plague to you." [13]

The event of that Clergymen's Club breakfast of May 1, 1878, which seems to have impressed Bryant most was his meeting another distinguished guest of honor, the Reverend Phillips Brooks, beloved rector of Trinity Church in Boston, "a man [observed Bryant] of gigantic size, towering head and shoulders above the tallest man at the board, and with a voice as soft and gentle as a zephyr." The thing that probably most impressed the majority of the other breakfasters was the eloquence of Old Man Eloquent, who recited and interpreted a number of Anglican devotional poems with a beauty and a dignity that were thoroughly in keeping with the spirit of both poems and occasion.

12

On the afternoon of May 29, 1878, a considerable crowd had gathered at the West Seventy-second Street entrance to Central Park. The occasion was the unveiling of a statue of Guiseppe Mazzini, the great Italian patriot and liberator. Deeply as the memory of Mazzini was revered by all liberty-loving citizens who had studied the European history of the middle years of the nineteenth century, it is safe to assume that most of the crowd had been attracted less by the identity of the statue than by the fact that the dedicatory address was to be delivered by Old Man Eloquent.

The aged poet-editor-orator was a little unwell that afternoon. For several days he had been suffering from a cold, and both his voice and his vitality were noticeably below par. Moreover, that very morning he had insisted upon going to the office of the *Evening Post* to read proof and attend to some correspondence. If Julia had been at home, he reflected a little grimly, he would have been kept in bed till noon, conserving his energies. But Julia happened to be down at Atlantic City recuperating from an illness of her own. And so he had rashly overtaxed himself—and on a day when he needed every ounce of his waning surplus strength.

The day of the dedication was sunny and exceedingly warm— more like mid-summer than like late spring. The speaker of the day, dressed more in keeping with the calendar and the formality of the occasion than with the rather unseasonable weather, wore a high silk hat, a long black frock coat, and striped gray trousers. And as the heavily-appareled old man, obviously oppressed by the heat, trudged wearily toward the small dais that had been erected beside the veiled statue, an audible murmur of compassion swept the crowd. A prosperous-looking middle-aged, side-whiskered, frock-coated gentleman who stood near the front of the assemblage appeared especially solicitous.

The gentleman turned to his wife, a lady in a voluminous and beruffled green satin gown. "I'm afraid," he whispered sadly, "that Mr. Bryant's failing fast. See how drawn and white he is. Why, he looks ages older than he did at the *kommers*. That night the old fellow was as boyish and chipper as could be—drank beer and joked with the best of us."

[207]

"It's asking too much," replied the beruffled lady in green indignantly. "Why couldn't they get a younger man for this dedication business? G. W. Curtis—or maybe Mayor Ely—or General Wilson himself? Anyhow, I don't know why Mr. Bryant's daughter let him do it. And upon my word! She isn't even here to look after him. As for that other Bryant girl—the married one—they say she's always gallivanting around Europe."

"You know," observed the side-whiskered gentleman, "he'll be eighty-four his next birthday."

"Oh, that horrid umbrella!" exclaimed the lady almost aloud. For at that moment General James Grant Wilson, the master of ceremonies, had raised Bryant's umbrella to protect him from the really torrid sun. Yes, it was the familiar old blue cotton umbrella, the shabby, beloved rain-stick that Cullen had carried at home and abroad for more years than he or anyone else could remember. And this afternoon, somehow, that faded umbrella appeared more in keeping with its owner than ever before.

"Hush, Mattie!" warned the side-whiskered gentleman. "They're about to begin."

As a matter of fact, they were beginning. During the first few moments of the oration, Old Man Eloquent spoke feebly and a little hoarsely. Nervous energy, however, soon lifted him to his wonted eloquence, and his peroration was surely as vibrant, as moving, as any he had ever delivered.

Image of the illustrious champion of civil and religious liberty, cast in enduring bronze to typify the imperishable renown of thy original! Remain for ages yet to come where we place thee, in this resort of millions; remain till the day shall dawn—far distant though it may be—when the rights and duties of human brotherhood shall be acknowledged by all of the races of mankind.[14]

13

Immediately following the ceremony, Bryant was inclined to return to his town house at 24 West Fifteenth Street. But General Wilson had other plans for the venerable and distinguished dedicator. Noticing that the oratorical effort had greatly wearied the old gentleman, he insisted that Bryant accompany him home for at least a brief rest before returning downtown. Reluctantly but graciously Bryant consented to walk with the general to the

Wilson residence, which stood only a few steps from that section of the Park.

At the very door of the Wilson house the aged man collapsed. Falling in such a manner as to strike his head upon a stone step, he was rendered unconscious. Carried by the general and a hastily summoned servant to a divan in the sitting-room, and revived by a glass of sherry, the injured old man complained of severe pains in the head, and begged to be taken home at once.

He had come to the Park in his own carriage; but for some unknown reason he had, upon arrival, dismissed his coachman with the announcement that he would return home by street-car. Consequently, General and Mrs. Wilson were all the more reluctant to let him be taken from the house—all the more eager to have him put to bed upstairs until medical aid could be summoned. But Cullen Bryant was a stubborn man. He wanted to get home—as speedily as possible. He wanted to make sure that he would be attended by no practitioner of what he called the outmoded allopathic school, but rather by his own trusted homeopathic physician, Dr. John F. Gray. Reluctantly and perturbedly, therefore, the general got his enfeebled but determined friend to and aboard a Madison Street horse-car and, of course, accompanied him on the journey. Despite the tender ministrations of the general—and of other passengers, most of whom certainly recognized the identity of the suffering old man—the long, slow ride downtown must have been a great tribulation.

When Cullen finally reached his own doorstep he did not quite know his whereabouts. The events of the past hour or so were equally obscure in his mind. Automatically, however, he pulled out his latch-key, unlocked his front door, and demanded to know whether General Wilson had come to see Miss Fairchild (Fanny's brother's daughter, who was acting as the Bryant housekeeper in the absence of Julia).

Miss Fairchild, quickly apprised of the misfortune that had befallen her uncle, sent a servant posthaste to summon Dr. Gray, the homeopathic physician who, twelve years earlier, had attended Fanny Bryant in her last illness. The malady being diagnosed as concussion of the brain, Dr. Gray called into consultation two specialists; but to no avail. The patient regained consciousness, rallied appreciably, and within the next few days even walked about the room and sat in his favorite chair. Meanwhile

[209]

he was cheered by the return of Julia from Atlantic City. Fanny Godwin, unfortunately, could not reach her father's side, for the Godwin family were in Europe.

On the eighth day after the accident, hemorrhage of the brain set in; and from that, of course, the old man never rallied. Lapsing into a coma, he peacefully breathed his last on the morning of June 12, exactly a fortnight after his last public appearance and fatal fall.

In "June," a lyric written early in his career—a much quoted lyric, by the way—Cullen Bryant had averred that it would be pleasant to be laid to rest

in flowery June,
When brooks send up a cheerful tune
And groves a joyous sound.

That melancholy pleasure he was destined to have.

14

In the dying hours of the year 1878—on the evening of December 30, to be exact—a capacity crowd gathered in the vast Academy of Music at Eleventh Street and Irving Place. Twenty-four to twenty-eight hours thereafter, a still greater crowd would be milling about the streets of that Greenwich Village region, listening to the chimes of Grace Church as they rang out the old year. The New Year's Eve crowd would be merry and motley; the Academy of Music crowd was staid and decidedly super-representative. Of the two thousand men and women who thronged the Academy of Music on that December evening, a very large proportion were outstanding citizens: leaders of bench, bar, pulpit, and press; celebrities in politics, letters, arts, sciences, commerce, and industry. Most of them were New Yorkers, but a few had come from afar. Of the latter the most notable, in position though hardly in personality, was mild-looking, square-bearded Rutherford Birchard Hayes, President of the United States, who had made a special trip from Washington for this occasion. In short, our nineteenth President had come to pay homage to a man born during the administration of our first President.

The occasion was, of course, a memorial meeting in tribute to the late William Cullen Bryant. The sponsor was the New York Historical Society, of which Bryant had long been a member, and under whose auspices he had delivered more memorial tributes than any other man—tributes to Cooper, Irving, Halleck, Verplanck, and many others.

The orator at the Bryant memorial meeting was, appropriately enough, another Gotham Yankee, George William Curtis, a native of Rhode Island, but long since an adopted son of New York. And there were other striking parallels between Bryant and Curtis. Both of them venerated nature, yet found their greatest work amid the turmoil of the metropolis. Both of them had traveled widely in the three continents of the Old World. Both of them were Puritan in heritage and conscience, yet liberal in theology and humanistic in taste and outlook. Both of them had acquired high culture through their own efforts rather than through formal education. Both of them were journalists of the first water—prolific, yet always substantial, never superficial. Both of them were indefatigable but sane reformers, at the same time despising fanaticism and sensationalism as much as they hated turpitude and apathy. Both of them were dignified, graceful, eloquent speakers. Of these parallels most of that huge Academy of Music crowd must have been fully cognizant as Curtis rose to deliver his address. True, the middle-aged, smooth-lipped, smooth-chinned George William Curtis, looking more like Matthew Arnold than like Saint Nicholas, did not bear much physical resemblance to the patriarchal, palmer-bearded Bryant who had been so familiar to those New Yorkers of the 1870's. Intellectually and spiritually, however, the kinship between those two most illustrious Gotham Yankees was indeed close. If Curtis had been a poet, or if Bryant had been a familiar essayist, the parallel would have been almost complete.

In that most notable of all memorial addresses on Bryant, Curtis said many obvious things. For instance, he praised Bryant as "the oldest of our poets, a scholar familiar with many languages and literatures," a lover and an apt interpreter of nature, a "serious, musing country boy" turned metropolitan editor and political leader, a public servant devoid of selfish ambition, "our Patriarch, our Mentor, our most conspicuous citizen." Less trite, less obvious, was Curtis when he declared, "We saw in his life the simple dignity which we associate with the old republics." In this connection, comparing Bryant with Lycurgus in Sparta and Cato in Rome, Curtis exclaimed, "How much greater was the man than the scholar [or poet or editor]! . . . his character was as fine as his genius!" [15]

Posterity is not likely to reverse that verdict. As Vernon Parrington said of William Cullen Bryant in 1927, "He may not have been a great poet, but he was a great American." [16]

TEXTUAL NOTES

CHAPTER I

1. William Aspenwall Bradley. *William Cullen Bryant* (English Men of Letters Series). New York, 1905. p. 1.
2. Parke Godwin. *A Biography of William Cullen Bryant*, 2 vols. New York, 1883. Vol. I, p. 58.
3. Bradley, *op. cit.*, p. 12.

CHAPTER II

1. Bradley, *op. cit.*, p. 18.
2. *Ibid.*, p. 22.
3. Godwin, *op. cit.*, I, 30.
4. *Ibid.*, I, 87.
5. *Ibid.*, I, 86.
6. *The Berkshire Hills* (American Guide Series, W.P.A. Project). New York, 1939, p. 30.
7. Bradley, *op. cit.*, p. 24.
8. *Berkshire Hills, op. cit.*, p. 31.
9. Bradley, *op. cit.*, p. 24.
10. *Ibid.*
11. *Berkshire Hills, op. cit.*, p. 33.
12. Betsey Gurney is not mentioned by any previous biographer of Bryant. In no sense, however, is she a fictitious character. Papers presented to the Geauga County (Ohio) Historical Museum by Betsey's granddaughter, Mrs. Bessie W. McMichael, of Buffalo, N. Y., reveal the following data regarding Betsey Gurney: (1) She lived at Cummington when she and Cullen Bryant were in their late teens. (2) She was considered the prettiest girl in the village. (3) Cullen was, for a time, infatuated with her. (4) She greatly admired Cullen—a fact which he seems never to have had the courage to ascertain. (5) A few years later she left Cummington, married a young man named Luther Snow, and migrated with him to the Western Reserve of Ohio. (6) In 1836, while on a trip West, Cullen Bryant made a special pilgrimage from Cleveland to the village of Chesterland, some twenty-five miles distant, to call on Betsey. (7) On learning that Betsey had died two years previously, Cullen "walked to the cemetery and tenderly placed flowers on her grave."
13. Godwin, *op cit.*, I, 94–95.
14. Vernon Parrington. *Main Currents of American Thought*, 2 vols. New York, 1927. Vol. II, p. 240.

CHAPTER III

1. Godwin, *op. cit.*, I, 69.
2. Tremaine McDowell (editor). *William Cullen Bryant* (American Writers Series). New York, 1935, p. 346.
3. *Op. cit.*, Vol. V (June, 1808), pp. 339–340.

4. Godwin, *op. cit.*, I, 73-74.
5. *Ibid.*, I, 149. See also John Bigelow. *William Cullen Bryant* (American Men of Letters Series). Boston and New York, 1890, p. 40.
6. Godwin, *op. cit.*, I, 150.
7. Frank Luther Mott. *A History of American Magazines, 1741-1850.* New York and London, 1930, p. 514.
8. Bradley, *op. cit.*, p. 53.

CHAPTER IV

1. Godwin, *op. cit.*, I, 105.
2. Evelina, anyhow, is what he calls her in at least one poem. See Godwin, *op. cit.*, I, 113.
3. Godwin, *op. cit.*, I, 119.
4. *Ibid.*, I, 124-125.
5. *Ibid.*, I, 128-130.
6. McDowell, *op. cit.*, p. 395.
7. Godwin, *op. cit.*, I, 145.
8. *Ibid.*, I, 203.
9. *Ibid.*, I, 148.

CHAPTER V

1. Godwin, *op. cit.*, I, 166-167.
2. McDowell, *op. cit.*, p. 395.
3. *Berkshire Hills, op. cit.*, p. 154.
4. Godwin, *op. cit.*, I, 169.
5. *Ibid.*
6. *Berkshire Hills, op. cit.*, p. 154.
7. Harry Hayden Clark. *Literary Criticism in the North American Review.* Madison, Wisconsin, 1940, pp. 308-309.
8. *Ibid.*, p. 313.
9. *Ibid.*, p. 315.
10. *Op. cit.*, April, 1825.
11. Bradley, *op. cit.*, pp. 70-71.
12. Godwin, *op. cit.*, I, 171-172.
13. *Ibid.*, I, 172-173.
14. Boston *Daily Advertiser,* Aug. 31, 1821.
15. Godwin, *op. cit.*, I, 175.
16. Clark, *op. cit.*, p. 316.
17. Godwin, *op. cit.*, I, 179-180.
18. McDowell, *op. cit.*, pp. 365-366.

CHAPTER VI

1. Godwin, *op. cit.*, I, 188.
2. *Ibid.*, I, 187.
3. *Ibid.*, I, 189.
4. *Ibid.*, I, 216.
5. *Ibid.*, I, 217-219.

6. Arthur D. Howden Smith. *John Jacob Astor, Landlord of New York.* New York, 1929, p. 98.
7. Van Wyck Brooks. *The World of Washington Irving.* Philadelphia, 1944, pp. 235–236.
8. Philip Hone. *Diary,* 2 vols. New York, 1889. Vol. I, p. 89.
9. Lawrence Barrett. *Edwin Forrest* (American Actor Series). Boston, 1881, p. 41.
10. Godwin, *op. cit.,* I, 238.
11. Allan Nevins. *The Evening Post.* New York, 1922, p. 123.
12. Godwin, *op. cit.,* I, 235.
13. Hone, *op. cit.,* I, 210.
14. New York *Evening Post,* June 13, 1836. See also McDowell, *op. cit.,* pp. 306–307.
15. W. E. Woodward. *A New American History.* New York, 1936, p. 410.
16. Nevins, *op. cit.,* p. 140.
17. William Leete Stone, born at New Paltz, New York, 1792, was about two years Bryant's senior.
18. Nevins, *op. cit.,* p. 139.

CHAPTER VII

1. Nevins, *op. cit.,* p. 92.
2. *Ibid.,* p. 91.
3. *Ibid.,* p. 136.
4. Godwin, *op. cit.,* I, 282.
5. "A Letter from Illinois." McDowell, *op. cit.,* p. 258.
6. Godwin, *op. cit.,* I, 285.
7. Nevins, *op. cit.,* p. 142.
8. Godwin, *op. cit.,* I, 284.
9. *Ibid.,* I, 285.
10. Van Wyck Brooks. *The Flowering of New England.* New York, 1936, p. 148.
11. Godwin, *op. cit.,* II, 119.

CHAPTER VIII

1. Godwin, *op. cit.,* I, 395.
2. John Forster. *A Life of Charles Dickens,* 3 vols. London, 1872–1874. New edition in 1 vol., edited and annotated by J. W. T. Ley. New York, 1928, p. 225.
3. Godwin, *op. cit.,* I, 397.
4. *Country Life,* Vol. VII, pp. 353–357 (Feb., 1905).
5. Godwin, *op. cit.,* I, 365.
6. *Ibid.,* II, 82.
7. Norman Foerster. *Nature in American Literature.* New York, 1923, p. 1.
8. Godwin, *op. cit.,* II, 58.
9. *Ibid.,* II, 74.

CHAPTER IX

1. Nevins, *op. cit.,* p. 352.

2. *Ibid.*
3. *Ibid.*, p. 348.
4. Godwin, *op. cit.*, I, 329.
5. New York *Evening Post*, Nov. 18, 1837. See also McDowell, *op. cit.*, p. 311.
6. Godwin, *op. cit.*, II, 56.
7. Nevins, *op. cit.*, pp. 261–262.
8. See Hesler photograph of Lincoln, taken in Springfield in 1860.
9. New York *Tribune*, Feb. 28, 1860.
10. *Ibid.*
11. Seymour Dunbar. *A History of Travel in America.* Indianapolis, 1915. New York, 1937, p. 1045.
12. Allan Nevins. *The Emergence of Modern America.* New York, 1927, p. 98.
13. Arthur Charles Cole. *The Irrepressible Conflict.* New York, 1934, p. 366.
14. Godwin, *op. cit.*, II, 179.
15. New York *Evening Post*, Sept. 15, 1862.
16. Nevins. *The Evening Post*, pp. 308–309.
17. For a terse and reliable account of the Draft Riots, see James Garfield Randall, *The Civil War and Reconstruction.* Boston and New York, 1937, pp. 413–416.

CHAPTER X

1. Nevins. *The Evening Post*, p. 434.
2. *Ibid.*, p. 396.
3. Godwin, *op. cit.*, II, 243.
4. *Ibid.*, I, 393.
5. *Ibid.*, II, 110.
6. *Ibid.*, II, 246.
7. *Ibid.*, II, 245.
8. *Ibid.*, II, 252–253.
9. *Ibid.*, II, 256.
10. *Ibid.*, II, 258.
11. *Ibid.*, II, 260.
12. *Ibid.*, 262–263.
13. *Ibid.*, II, 264.
14. See the *Living Age*, Vol. LXXX, p. 308 (Feb. 13, 1864).
15. Bradley, *op. cit.*, p. 186.
16. Bryant's *Iliad*, Book XXII, lines 379–388.
17. *Op. cit.*
18. Godwin, *op. cit.*, II, 287.
19. Bradley, *op. cit.*, p. 188.
20. Godwin, *op. cit.*, II, 296.

CHAPTER XI

1. Godwin, *op. cit.*, II, 117.
2. Parrington, *op. cit.*, II, 139.
3. Foerster, *op. cit.*, p. 16.
4. Parrington, *op. cit.*, II, 238.

5. Percy H. Boynton. *Literature and American Life*. Boston, 1936, p. 283.
6. Godwin, *op. cit.*, II, 113.
7. *Ibid.*, II, 359.
8. *Ibid.*, II, 299.
9. *Ibid.*, II, 323.
10. *Ibid.*, II, 323-324.
11. *Ibid.*, II, 379.
12. *Ibid.*, II, 391.
13. *Ibid.*, I, 281.
14. *Ibid.*, II, 403.
15. *Ibid.*, II, 418.
16. Parrington, *op. cit.*, II, 246.

BIBLIOGRAPHY

I. GENERAL

Atlantic Monthly, Vol. XIII (Feb., 1864)

Barrett, Lawrence. *Edwin Forrest* (American Actor Series). Boston, 1881

Barton, William E. *The Life of Abraham Lincoln*. 2 vols. Indianapolis, 1925

Berkshire Hills, The. (American Guide Series, W.P.A. Project). New York, 1939

Bigelow, John. *William Cullen Bryant* (American Men of Letters Series). Boston and New York, 1890

Boston *Daily Advertiser*, Aug. 31, 1821

Boston *Monthly Anthology*, Vol. V (June, 1808)

Boynton, Percy H. *Literature and American Life*. Boston, 1936

Bradley, William Aspenwall. *William Cullen Bryant* (English Men of Letters Series). New York, 1905

Brooks, Van Wyck. *The Flowering of New England*. New York, 1936

Brooks, Van Wyck. *The World of Washington Irving*. Philadelphia, 1944

Browne, Francis Fisher. *The Every-day Life of Abraham Lincoln*. Chicago, 1913

Capen, O. B. "Country Homes of Famous Americans." *Country Life*, Vol. VII (Feb., 1905)

Clark, Harry Hayden. *Literary Criticism in the North American Review, 1815-1835.* (Transactions of the Wisconsin Academy of Sciences, Arts and Letters, Vol. 32). Madison, Wis., 1940

Clark, Harry Hayden. *Major American Poets*. New York, Cincinnati, Chicago, 1936

Cole, Arthur Charles. *The Irrepressible Conflict*. (Vol. VII of Schlesinger-Fox series). New York, 1934

Dunbar, Seymour. *A History of Travel in America*. Indianapolis, 1915; New York, 1937

Fish, Carl Russell. *The Rise of the Common Man*. (Vol. VI of Schlesinger-Fox series). New York, 1927

Foerster, Norman. *Nature in American Literature*. New York, 1923

Forster, John. *A Life of Charles Dickens.* 3 vols. London, 1872-1874. New edition in 1 vol., edited and annotated by J. W. T. Ley. New York, 1928

Glicksberg, C. I. "William Cullen Bryant and Fanny Wright." *American Literature,* Vol. VI (Jan., 1935)

Godwin, Parke. *A Biography of William Cullen Bryant, with Extracts from His Private Correspondence.* (Published as Vols. I and II of *The Life and Writings of William Cullen Bryant).* 2 vols. New York, 1883

Harper's New Monthly Magazine, Vol. XLI (June, 1870)

Hone, Philip. *Diary.* 2 vols. New York, 1889

Jackman, Rilla Evelyn. *American Arts.* Chicago, 1928

Kirkland, Caroline Matilda Stansbury. *Little Journeys to the Homes of American Authors.* New York, 1896

Leonard, William Ellery. "Bryant." *Cambridge History of American Literature,* Vol. I. 3 vols. New York, 1917

Living Age, Vol. LXXX (Feb. 13, 1864)

McDowell, Tremaine (editor). *William Cullen Bryant* (American Writers Series). New York, 1935

McDowell, Tremaine. "Cullen Bryant at Williams College." *New England Quarterly,* Vol. I (Oct., 1928)

McDowell, Tremaine. "William Cullen Bryant and Yale." *New England Quarterly,* Vol. III (Oct., 1930)

Massachusetts. (American Guide Series, W.P.A. Project). Boston, 1937

Minnigerode, Meade. *The Fabulous Forties.* New York, 1924

Morison, S. E. *Oxford History of the United States.* 2 vols. London, 1927

Mott, Frank Luther. *A History of American Magazines, 1741–1850.*

Nevins, Allan. *The Emergence of Modern America.* (Vol. VIII of *A History of American Life,* edited by Arthur M. Schlesinger and Dixon Ryan Fox. 12 vols.). New York, 1927

Nevins, Allan. *The Evening Post.* New York, 1922

Nevins, Allan, and Commager, Henry Steele. *America: The Story of a Free People.* Boston, 1942

Nicolay, J. G., and Hay, John. *Abraham Lincoln: A History.* 10 vols. New York, 1890

Parrington, Vernon. *Main Currents of American Thought.* New York, 1927

Peckham, Harry Houston. *Josiah Gilbert Holland.* Philadelphia, 1940

Randall, James Garfield. *The Civil War and Reconstruction.* Boston and New York, 1937

Rider, Fremont. *Rider's New York City.* New York, 1924

Sandburg, Carl. *Abraham Lincoln: The Prairie Years.* 2 vols. New York, 1926

Sandburg, Carl. *Abraham Lincoln: The War Years.* 2 vols. New York, 1939

Schlesinger, Arthur M. *Political and Social History of the United States, 1829–1925.* New York, 1925

Schlesinger, Arthur M., Jr. *The Age of Jackson.* Boston, 1945

Smith, Arthur D. Howden. *John Jacob Astor, Landlord of New York.* New York, 1929

Van Doren, Carl. "The Growth of 'Thanatopsis.'" *Nation,* Vol. CI (Oct. 7, 1915)

Woodward, W. E. *A New American History.* New York, 1936

II. EDITIONS OF BRYANT'S WORKS

The Poetical Works of William Cullen Bryant (text supervised by the author). New York, 1876

The Poetical Works of William Cullen Bryant. (Published as Vols. III and IV of *The Life and Writings of William Cullen Bryant*). 2 vols. New York, 1883

The Poetical Works of William Cullen Bryant. (Roslyn Edition, containing R. H. Stoddard's "Memoir" and H. C. Sturges's "Chronologies"). New York, 1903

William Cullen Bryant. (American Writers Series. An abridged but exceptionally well annotated edition, containing a careful selection of Bryant's best known poems, as well as twelve uncollected pieces of prose, four uncollected poems, and seven unpublished poems. Listed above under McDowell). New York, 1935

Prose Writings of William Cullen Bryant. (Published as Vols. V and VI of *The Life and Writings of William Cullen Bryant*). 2 vols. New York, 1883

III. BIBLIOGRAPHICAL NOTES

Bryant's *Evening Post* editorials have never been collected or fully identified. Clark, McDowell, and Nevins (listed above) give valuable data on the identifiable Bryant editorials.

For comprehensive Bryant bibliographies, the reader is referred to McDowell's *William Cullen Bryant,* pp. lxxiii-lxxxii, and to Clark's *Major American Poets,* pp. 788–792. C. M. Pang's Bryant bibliography *(Cambridge History of American Literature,* I, 517–521), formerly considered definitive, lists no works published since 1911.

BRYANT CHRONOLOGY

1794   Born, Cummington, Mass., Nov. 3.

1808   Published "The Embargo."

1810–11   Attended Williams College.

1811   Wrote "Thanatopsis."

1811–14   Studied Law, Worthington and Bridgewater, Mass.

1815   Admitted to the bar; started practice of law, Plainfield, Mass.

1816   Removed to Great Barrington, Mass., continuing practice of law.

1817   Published "Thanatopsis" in *North American Review* (Sept. issue).

1821   Married Frances Fairchild. Read "The Ages" before Phi Beta Kappa chapter at Harvard College. Published *Poems* in Boston.

1825   Abandoned practice of law. Removed to New York to do editorial work.

1826   Joint editor of the *United States Review.* Delivered *Lectures on Poetry* before Athenaeum Society.

1827   Became assistant editor of the New York *Evening Post.*

1829   Succeeded William Coleman as editor-in-chief of the *Evening Post.*

Changed the *Evening Post* from a Federalist to a Jacksonian Democratic newspaper.

1832 Published *Poems* in New York; (under sponsorship of Washington Irving) in London. Visited Illinois.

1834–36 In Europe. Met Longfellow at Heidelberg.

1836 Editorially defended a group of striking New York journeyman tailors.

1837 Although not at that time a confirmed Abolitionist, paid eloquent editorial memorial tribute to Elijah P. Lovejoy, a martyr to the causes of Abolition and freedom of the press.

1842 Took prominent part in welcoming Charles Dickens to New York. Published *The Fountain and Other Poems.*

1843 Established country residence at "Cedarmere," Roslyn, Long Island.

1844 Published *The White-Footed Deer and Other Poems.*

1845 In Europe.

1849 In Europe.

1850 Published *Letters of a Traveller.*

1852–53 In Europe and the Near East. Grew his famous beard.

1854 Became affiliated with the newly organized Republican party.

1857–58 In Europe. Baptized in Naples by an American Unitarian clergyman.

1859 Published *Letters of a Traveller* (second series).

1860 Editorially championed the nomination and election of Abraham Lincoln to the presidency. Introduced Lincoln to New York audience at Cooper Union, Feb. 27.

1862 Editorially deplored Lincoln's lack of aggressiveness in prosecuting the war and lack of zeal for the cause of Abolition. Went to Washington to remonstrate with Lincoln.

1863 Unqualifiedly denounced the New York draft riots—in opposition to certain other prominent New York editors.

1864 Published *Thirty Poems.* Was tendered seventieth-birthday dinner at the Century Club, New York.

1865 Paid gracious memorial tributes to Lincoln, both in verse and in prose.

1866 Death of Mrs. Bryant.

1866–67 In Europe with daughter Julia.

1869 Published *Letters from the East.*

1870 Published metrical translation of Homer's *Iliad.*

1871 Published metrical translation of Homer's *Odyssey.*

1872 Mentioned as a presidential possibility; repudiated such mention. Reluctantly supported President Grant for re-election (as a lesser evil than the opposition candidate, Horace Greeley).

1878 Unveiled statue of Mazzini, Central Park, New York, May 29. Was fatally injured when he collapsed and fell a few minutes after the exercises. Died, New York, June 12.

INDEX

[223]

[227]

Van Buren, Martin, 91, 108, 140, 192
Van Dyck, Sir Anthony, 198
Vernon, France, 110
Verplanck, Gulian C., 71, 76, 81, 89, 105, 123, 160, 204, 206, 211
Vicksburg, Mississippi, 117, 153
Virgil, 9, 10, 12
Voss, Johann Heinrich, 171, 172

Waltham, Massachusetts, 68
Washington, D. C., 1, 25, 36, 41, 44, 45, 47, 68, 91, 100–101, 129, 142, 148, 149, 150–151, 161
Washington, George, 1, 25, 41
Waterston, Helen, 185
Waterston, Rev. R. C., 114, 128
Webster, Daniel, 115
Weed, Thurlow, 142–143
Wheeling, West Virginia, 102
White, Andrew D., 195
White, Henry Kirke, 34
White-Footed Deer, The, and Other Poems, 133
Whitman, Walt, 156, 180, 188–189

Whittier, John Greenleaf, 64, 138, 180, 188
William and Mary College, 15
Williams College, 12–21, 25, 29, 46, 63, 65, 195
Williamstown, Massachusetts, 12, 13, 15, 20, 32, 39, 45, 71
Willis, N. P., 23, 87, 127
Wilmington, Delaware, 149
Wilson, James Grant, 208–209
Wilson, John, 109
Woodhull, Jacob, 86
Woodward, W. E., 94
Wordsworth, William, 34, 35, 39, 57, 58, 59, 71, 113, 132
Worthington, Massachusetts, 38–39, 43, 45, 46, 56
Wright, Fanny, 93–94
Wright, Silas, 192
Wyant, Alexander, 129, 198

Yale College, 10, 12, 13, 15, 18, 19, 20, 21, 22, 23, 24, 29, 38, 46, 65
"Yellow Violet, The," 70–71
Youmans, Edward L., 195